研讨会开幕式

天津职业技术师范大学校长刘欣教授致辞

百余名中外专家、学者与会

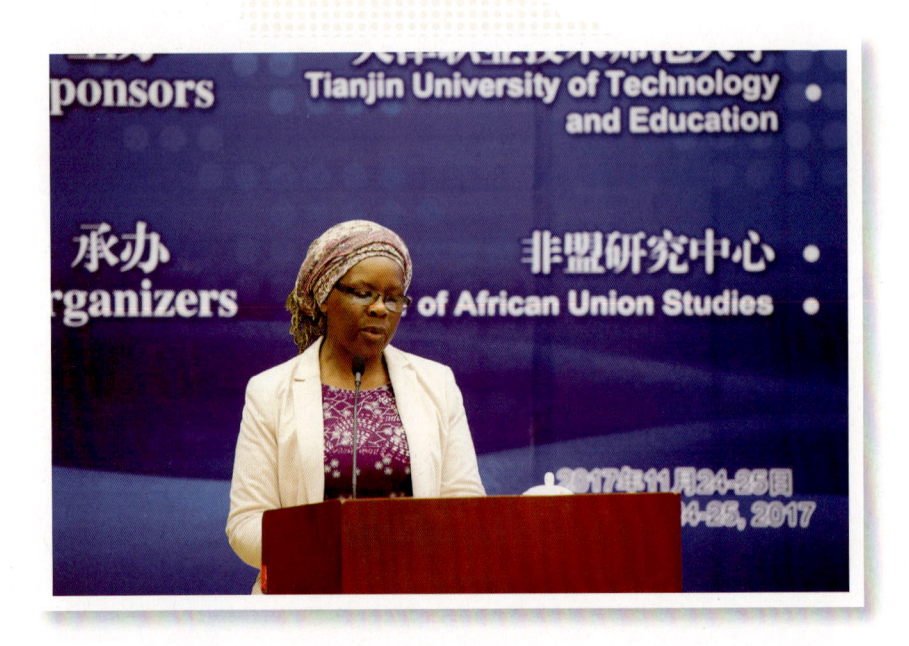

非盟委员会人力资源与科技司Beatrice Njenga主任致辞

与会专家、学者听取会议主旨发言

与会专家、学者相互交流和探讨

与会专家、学者相互交流和探讨

中非教育交流与产能合作
International Symposium on China-Africa Educati

参会代表合影留念

CHALLENGES AND PROSPECT OF CHINA-AFRICA EDUCATIONAL EXCHANGE AND INDUSTRIAL CAPACITY COOPERATION:
Selected Papers of the International Symposium of China-Africa Educational Exchange and Industrial Capacity Cooperation

中非教育交流与产能合作的现状和前景
"中非教育交流与产能合作国际研讨会"论文集

主 编：潘 良 甘振军
副主编：翟风杰 王玉华 李炜婷

上海社会科学院出版社
SHANGHAI ACADEMY OF SOCIAL SCIENCES PRESS

序

2017年11月24—25日,由天津职业技术师范大学和非盟委员会联合主办的"中非教育交流与产能合作国际研讨会"在天津召开。这次会议是主办方根据当前中非关系发展的需求而举办的国际学术研讨活动,也是中国与非洲学者学术交流日益活跃与深化的具体体现。会议的主题是中非教育发展与合作的现状和前景,提交的论文涵盖面广。来自埃塞俄比亚、南非、尼日利亚等国的非洲学者与中国各高校和科研单位的学者就中非教育合作、中非产能合作以及教育交流与产能合作的交接等方面进行了广泛研讨,既有中国学者的细致分析,也有非洲学者结合实地体验的深入探讨。

中非合作是建立在什么基础之上?为什么发展得如此迅速?客观地看,中国与非洲距离遥远,语言习俗不同,政治体制相异,不具备西方国家在长期殖民统治时期建立的历史联系。然而,中非合作存在自己的独特优势,我将其概括为十大优势。

第一,中非关系历史悠久。史料记载,东非海岸是海上丝路的重要抵达地。埃塞俄比亚、索马里、肯尼亚、坦桑尼亚、莫桑比克、马达加斯加等国的一些地名出现在中国古代的游记、正史和野史之中。在"一带一路"倡议的带动下,历史和现实的交汇正在显现。

第二,双方文化价值观诸多相似,非洲与中国价值观相同点甚多,这是南南合作的重要基础之一。

第三,双方历史遭遇相似。非洲与中国均是古老文明的发源地。在古代,两种文明相互辉映。非洲和中国共同经历了奴隶贸易和"猪仔"贸易的厄运,非洲和中国均成为列强的殖民地或半殖民地,再次遭受了政治压迫、经济剥削和种族欺凌。20世纪开始的民族解放运动使非洲各国和中国重新恢复了在世界舞台上的地位。目前,中国与非洲各国都在为自己的政治自主、经济自强和人民福利而努力。这种历史的相似性无疑为非洲成为海上丝绸之路的友好伙伴提供了有利条件。

第四,中非关系平等互利。双方的关系在早期是平等通商,在近代是友好同情,在现代是帮扶支持,在当代是合作双赢。双方平等相处成为南南合作的典范。长期形成的平等互利的理念和实践是合作的重要基础。

第五,非洲人对中国的感情友好真诚。尽管西方媒体把持着话语权,对中国在非洲的所作所为或造谣惑众,或一叶障目,但非洲国家对中国的友好态度客观存在。这种友好感情无疑为产能合作的开展创造了民意基础。

第六,非洲国家领导人对"一带一路"期望迫切。在2015年约翰内斯堡中非峰会中,非洲领导人一致认为,中方"一带一路"倡议对非洲同样重要,非洲国家欢迎中方积极参与非洲铁路、公路、港口等基础设施和互联互通建设并向非洲转移优质产能。高层的期盼为合作提供了保证。

第七,非洲国家民众对基础设施建设充满好感。中非合作在基础设施建设方面表现突出。非洲民众的这种认识和愿望无疑为中非战略合作增添了有利条件。

第八,非洲工业化与产能合作相契合。非洲各国的工业化与中国提出的产能合作高度契合。非洲快速工业化与产能合作不仅互相契合,而且潜力巨大。

第九,非洲国家的华侨华人资源。中非合作既需要国际合作,也需要中华儿女共同参与。华侨华人中蕴藏着社会资本、专业知识、经济实力和跨国营商经验。他们在非洲培育的投资环境为产能合作提供了良好基础,其网络媒体为投资非洲提供了信息。

第十，中非合作已有成熟的运作机制。中非合作论坛从2000年设立以来，体现了其强大的生命力。论坛表现的互利双赢的成功实践及合作精神证明了这一南南合作机制的可持续性。每次论坛均有高官级后续会议及为部长级会议作准备的高官预备会，分别在部长级会议前一年及前数日各举行一次，非洲驻华使节与中方后续行动委员会秘书处每年至少举行两次会议。论坛每三年召开一次，论坛举办的地点分别在中国和非洲国家之间轮换。这种模式成为其他国家效法的榜样。韩国、南美洲国家、印度、土耳其、伊朗等国家在中非合作论坛创立后的几年内纷纷建立了类似论坛，东京非洲发展国际会议（TICAD）目前也在非洲国家的要求下遵循中非合作论坛的模式。这种机制可在"一带一路"的实施中复制。

当然，机遇与风险共存。中国企业投资非洲也存在着十大风险：战争风险、政治风险（包括领导人更替）、恐怖主义风险、社会风险（包括公共卫生危机）、金融风险（包括汇率风险）、法律风险、安全风险（包括抢劫和疾病）、公共风险（包括排华危机）、信誉风险和劳资纠纷风险。尽管有这些风险，但仍有1万家中国企业在非洲打拼，绝大多数企业充满信心，对非洲的经营前景看好。这正应了一句斯瓦希里谚语："勤劳者树荫下面有佳肴。"

随着"一带一路"倡议得到多方响应以及中非产能合作的逐步落实，非洲在世界经济与政治中的地位也日益提高。2018年第七届中非合作论坛将再次在中国举办，双方合作将会得到更大提升。天津职业技术师范大学长期以来致力于为非洲国家培养科技人才。非盟研究中心对中非关系特别是非洲联盟的研究也在步步跟进。我们相信，中非合作的明天更美好。

是为序。

北京大学教授、中国非洲史研究会会长　李安山

目　录

序 ⋯1

中非教育发展与合作的现状和前景 ⋯1
African Students in China：Research，Reality，and Reflection
　　　　　　　　　　　　　　　　　　　　　　Li Anshan⋯3
略论丝绸之路历史对当代中非教育交流与产能合作的启示　张　象⋯61
Development as an Intellectual Process：The Case of Africa
　　　　　　　　　　　　　　　　Ngaka Sehlare Makgetlaneng⋯67
关于中非职业教育合作及相关问题　　　　　　　　　王　南⋯95
儒家教育思想和中非教育交流与合作
　　　　　　　　周志发　魏　莎　温国硅　郝子怡⋯100
中国对非洲教育援助项目中的人类学角色　　　　　牛忠光⋯132
埃塞俄比亚留学生价值观实证研究
　　——基于天津职业技术师范大学的数据　王　慧　翟风杰⋯147

中非教育交流与产能合作的战略对接 ⋯159
中非产能合作：挑战与对策 姚桂梅⋯161
中非海洋产业合作的对策建议 张振克⋯171
中非产能合作的法制化途径分析 朱伟东⋯177
China-Africa Industrial Capacity Cooperation: Achievements, Challenges and the Way Forward
Kabiru Adamu kiyawa & Prof. Emeritus Dr. Barjoyai Baradai⋯187
"一带一路"倡议背景下江苏与非洲的产能合作与教育交流 甘振军⋯205
Challenges and Prospects of Industrialization and Educational Development in Africa: Lessons and Experiences from China
Gambo Babandi Gumel⋯220
中非国际产能合作背景下职业教育的交流与合作
——以中国与埃塞俄比亚为例 李炜婷⋯238
职业教育服务"一带一路"倡议：进展、问题与对策 王 静⋯251

中非教育发展与
合作的现状和前景

African Students in China: Research, Reality, and Reflection*

Li Anshan

Abstract: With the fast development of China-Africa relations, the African community in China becomes an impressive phenomenon and an attraction for international academia. Various African diasporic groups exist in China such as traders, students, artists, professionals, etc., with students forming the second largest group. Although there have been debates about whether international students can be considered as immigrants, the opinion that they are largely prevails in the scholarly literature. Studying African students in the context of China-Africa relations, the article is divided into five parts. The first provides a survey on the research on the topic, followed by an overview of the history of African students in China. The third part is an analysis of China's policy towards African students. Why do the African students want to come to China? What

---

* This Article has been published in *African Studies Quarterly*, Vol. 17, Issue 4, February 2018, pp. 5 - 44.

attracts them? What are their purposes? The fourth part will discuss the favorable conditions for their coming to China and their motivations. The last part will describe their contribution to both the African and Chinese societies. I will argue that by their initiative the African students' existence in China and their interaction with the Chinese people has brought various new things to China and made a great contribution to Africa as a whole.

Keywords: African Students; China; Research; Reality; Reflection

Author: Professor and Director, Institute of Afro-Asian Studies and Center for African Studies, School of International Studies, Peking University

Research, Debates, and Views

The international community currently shows great interest in China-Africa relations. Different issues, contradictory views and various debates have been presented for some time.① Related to this issue, the African diaspora has also become a fashionable topic among academia. It is presumed that the African community appeared in China in recent years, yet there is a long history of diaspora and contact between China and Africa.② Owing to the fast growth of the bilateral trade volume, increasing from USD 10.8 billion in 2000 to more than USD 220 billion in 2014, it is undeniable that the African community has boomed in China during this period.

Since China-Africa trade occupies a very important component in the bilateral relations, traders thus by far constitute the largest group within the African community in China. So far the studies have generally focused on African trading communities in China or their economic activities in

---

① Li 2014.
② Li Anshan 2015a, 2015b.

Guangzhou, the commodity hub of China, and Yiwu, China's biggest commodity center.[①] Some have studied their business transactions and deals in Hong Kong and Macau.[②] Other researches include the living conditions, social practices, or religious activities of the African diaspora, and barriers between Africans and Chinese, management of the African diaspora by Chinese authorities, or the reaction of Chinese citizens.[③] African entrepreneurs are also described for how they have transmitted their conceptions of China into their own countries, thus explaining the impact of Chinese development in a global context.[④] More recently the research focus has gradually moved beyond Guangdong Province and its commercial hub Guangzhou.[⑤]

African students form the second largest group of African diaspora in China. Yet far fewer scholars have been involved in the study of this topic. The earliest work was done by a Ghanaian student, who had personal experiences in studying in China in the early 1960s. After their

---

① For African trading communities see Bertoncello and Bredeloup 2006, 2007a, 2007b, 2009; Bredeloup and Pliez 2009; Bodomo 2007, 2012; Ditgen 2010; Cissé 2013. For their economic activities in Guangzhou see Bodomo 2007, 2010; Lyons, et al. 2008, 2012, 2013; Li et al. 2008, 2009a, 2009b, 2012; Li and Du 2012a, 2012b; Bodomo and Ma 2010; Diederich 2010; Müller 2011; Haugen 2012; Bredeloup 2012. For Yiwu see Le Bail 2009; Bertoncello, Bredeloup and Pliez 2009; Osnos 2009; Pliez 2010; Bodomo and Ma 2010, 2012; Ma 2012.
② For Hong Kong, see Bodomo 2007, 2009, 2012; Ho 2012; Mathews 2011; Mathews and Yang 2012. For Macau, see Morais 2009; Bodomo 2012; Bodomo and Silva 2012.
③ Regarding living conditions, social practices, and religious activities see Li et al. 2008, 2009a, 2009b, 2011; Li and Du 2012a, 2012b; Bertoncello and Bredeloup 2009; Li et al. 2008; Bodomo 2009, 2010; Xu 2009; Yang 2011; Müller 2011; Haugen, 2013b. For barriers, etc., see Bredeloup 2007; Li and Du, 2009; Xu 2009; Osnos 2009; Morais 2009; Bodomo, 2010; Haugen, 2012.
④ Marfaing and Thiel 2014; Cissé 2013.
⑤ Bodomo 2016.

independence, fourteen African countries sent their students to China until the end of 1966 when China closed all universities because of the Cultural Revolution. Immanuel Hevi was among the group. He wrote the first book about African students in China, complaining about racism and other unpleasant phenomena. He listed six causes of African student dissatisfactions: undesirable political indoctrination, language difficulty, poor educational standards, inadequate social life, outright hostility, and racial discrimination.① Although he indicated that many African students returned back home in 1961 – 1962, there was disagreement about his statements.② While the book raised attention from the West, the study of the subject then almost stopped since all the African students returned back to their countries due to the Cultural Revolution. Until recently, scholars studying African students in China reviewed the historical context or explained the social background of China at the time.③

China resumed educational cooperation with Africa in 1973, and railway technology trainees arrived in China from Tanzania and Zambia in connection with Chinese funding of the Tanzania-Zambia Railway (TAZARA). There are several works on, TAZARA including documents, records, and the African trainees.④ As for the first systematic survey of African students in China, Gillespie's work is one of the few books that put African student experiences in the context of South-South relations, emphasizing the knowledge transfer of China's educational exchange programs for Africa.⑤

---

① Hevi 1963.
② Larkin 1971.
③ Liu 2013; Cheng 2014.
④ Zhang 1999; Monson 2009; Liu and Monson 2011.
⑤ Gillespie 2001.

There were several studies on the conflicts between African students and Chinese students in the 1980s with a criticism of Chinese racism. [1]

With the establishment of the Forum on China-Africa Cooperation (FOCAC), beginning with the first summit in 2000, the number of African students greatly increased (see Table 2 below). In terms of the study of African students currently in China, there is a greater interest among Chinese scholars (or African scholars in China) than those outside China. The first study on the issue in China was by the Center for African Studies at Peking University. It was a general survey with a series data based on the archives of the Ministry of Education, focusing on African students in China. [2] Current research about African students are generally focused on four subjects, namely cultural adaptation, China-Africa cooperation, educational management, and professional teaching such as language, mathematics, engineering, and so forth. Using key words "African overseas students" as an entry, forty-seven articles are found in the Chinese Journals Network (2003 – 2014) containing journal articles and MA dissertations. Among them, five are on cultural adaptation, six on educational management, and fourteen on teaching the Chinese language, with the rest on China-Africa relations. Reports and memoirs have also provided information about the experiences of African students in China. [3] There is an important study regarding the evolution and effect of China's policy towards African students, in which the author argues that the scholarship policy has contributed a great deal towards the success of China's international

---

[1] Seidelman 1989; Sautman 1994; Sulliven 1994; Li and Liu 2013.
[2] China Africa Education Cooperation Group, 2005, hereafter CAECG.
[3] Li and Li 2006; Li 2013; China Africa Project 2013.

educational cooperation, especially with African students.[①]

Psychology is often applied in cross-culture studies, and two works are worth mentioning. One is an article based on an SASS (Study Abroad Stress Survey) of Africans and western students in China that was carried out in 2003 with two hundred forms sent out to foreign students at colleges in three cities in China. The thirty questionnaires were divided into four categories, e. g. , interpersonal, individual, academic, and environment. One hundred and fifty-six valid forms were returned from eight-two Africans (forty-six males, thirty-six females) and seventy-four westerners (thirty-two males, forty-two females). Its purpose was to evaluate gender differences (male/female) and cultural differences (Africa/West) in the perception of stress. No group differences existed in the subtotal perception of the four stressors. Group variations existed only in their sub-divisional areas of stress. Cross-cultural orientation was suggested for foreign students. The study indicates that academic and interpersonal sources of stress were the most common and daily hassles defined as high pressure and challenges among both males and females.[②] Another psychological study was an MA thesis based on an investigation of 181 feedbacks out of 210 forms, a rather high ratio for an investigation. The author was an African student, and the aim of the study was to examine cultural shock and adaptation among African students in China. It found that cultural shock is common for African students in China, and the best remedy is to increase social contact with local people. It also found that although all African students experienced cultural shock, the

---

① Liu 2017.
② Hashim, et al. 2003; Hashim and Yang 2003.

extent is different according to the grade and gender, e. g. , more serious for undergrads than graduates, female than male. [1] Other studies are either on cultural adaptation, cultural differences and their impact, or different concepts of time and family. [2]

As for the role in China-Africa educational cooperation, Ketema et al. suggested that Chinese universities played an important role in bilateral cooperation, King used African students in China as an indicator of China's soft power, and Haugen analyzed China's policy for the enrolment of African students and its effect and outcome. [3] Others argued that China's educational assistance formed an essential part of China-Africa cooperation and offered substantial support to Africa. [4] Studies also discussed the management of African students or graduates in China, either in universities or society. [5] The fourth subject always involves teachers who are doing language teaching and probing better ways to teach the Chinese language to Africans. [6] African students themselves wrote about their experiences in China and emphasized African agency in their behavior in Chinese society. [7]

There are criticisms regarding the teaching methods and suggestions for improvement and different views on the effect of China's educational policy towards African students. One view holds that African scholarship holders

---

[1] Disima 2004.
[2] See Yi and Xiong 2013 and Gong 2014 for cultural adaptation, Long and Xiong 2014 regarding cultural differences and their impact, and Ye Shuai 2011 on different concepts of time and family.
[3] Ketema et al. 2009; King 2012; Haugen 2013a.
[4] Li 2006; Li and Luo 2013; Xu 2007; He 2007; Lou and Xu 2012.
[5] Cheng 2012; Zheng 2012, 2013a, 2013b; An et al. 2014.
[6] Song 2011; Lin and Ren 2010.
[7] Amoah 2012; Lokongo 2012.

are generally satisfied with their experiences in China, which thus promotes a positive view of the potential for strengthening China-Africa friendship with African countries through educational programs. [1] Although there are shortcomings and room for improvement, China's policy is rather successful in promoting China-Africa relations, building African capacity and bettering China's image. [2] Haugen, on the other hand, asserts that China fails to reach its policy objectives because of African students' disappointment with the quality of the education they receive, "Disappointment with the educational experience obstructs the promotion of Chinese values, thus obliterating the soft power potential of Sino-African educational exchanges."[3]

Similar features characterize the above-mentioned studies, e. g. , cross-cultural theory with questionnaires as methodology and concrete suggestions as the outcome. They involve the collection of direct data drawn from life experiences. Researchers sometimes are African students themselves. The shortcoming of such studies is that they are usually based on a case study of African students in a place (or a university) or from a country, and thus limitations are inevitable. How to apply theories in case studies is another issue. Bilateral migration provides both an opportunity and a challenge. There are similarities between Chinese culture and African culture, and mutual learning is always beneficial to both, especially through people-to-people contact. [4] Yet, we still lack a solid study on the topic.

---

[1] Dong and Chapman 2008.
[2] Li and Liu 2013; Niu 2016; Liu 2017.
[3] Haugen 2013a, p. 331.
[4] Li 2014.

History, Reality and Trends

The history of African students in China began in 1956, when four Egyptian students arrived. If we compare the figure with 61,594 African students in China in 2016, the trend is dramatic. The history of African students in China can be divided into four periods. The first started from 1956 to 1966 when the Cultural Revolution closed all the universities. The second is mainly about the trainees for Tanzania-Zambia Railway. The third runs from the 1970s to 1995. The fourth started from 1996 and got a promotion in 2000, the year of China-Africa Cooperation (FOCAC), and it lasts till the present.[①]

The period 1956 – 1966 forms the first contact of African students with China. In 1953, the Chinese youth delegation had broad contact with delegates from Egypt, Algeria, Tunisia, Morocco, Madagascar, and French West Africa during the International Conference of Defense of Youth Rights, held in Geneva, and students of both sides established links at the early stage. Even before the establishment of China-Egypt diplomatic relations on May 30, 1956, the two countries signed the agreement of cultural cooperation on April 15, 1956.[②] The program of Egypt-China educational cooperation started the exchange of scholars and students from both countries. Four Egyptian students came to China in 1956, three were under the academic supervision of the famous artist Prof. Li Keran to learn the skill of Chinese painting. They became well-known artists in Egypt after

---

[①] Li 2006; He 2007; Liu 2017.
[②] Jiang and Guo 2001, p. 524.

their studies in the China Central Academy of Fine Arts. ①

In 1957, eleven African students from Cameroon, Kenya, Uganda, and Malawi (all not yet independent countries) came to study in China. During the 1950s, twenty-four African students came under the scholarship of Chinese government. Many African countries won their independence in the 1960s and China started educational cooperation with them. African students or technicians arrived under various agreements or programs at Chinese universities for advanced study. In the 1960s, China sent various cultural delegations to Africa, learning different types of African dance while African countries sent young people to China for further study. In 1960, the number of African students in China increased to ninety-five. When the Cultural Revolution occurred in 1966, there were 164 students from fourteen African countries. The African students had to go back home since all the universities were closed during that time. ②

Among the young African students was a Ghanaian, Immanuel Hevi, who wrote a book complaining about racism and other unpleasant experiences in China. ③ His negative statements about the country immediately brought about applause from the West. What is more, he was from Ghana where President Nkrumah was strongly pro-socialist. Most importantly, the West was looking for something negative about China, and Hevi's book came out at just the right time. Hevi's complaint was somewhat understandable for several reasons. The first is the economic disaster in the early 1960s. Although African students, like all foreign students in China, enjoyed some

---

① Li 2006; Jiang and Guo 2001, p. 530.
② China Africa Education Cooperation Group 2005, pp. 14–17.
③ Hevi 1963.

privileges and a higher living standard than the ordinary Chinese citizen, yet China could not further improve the conditions as the early 1960s witnessed the worst economic period in China after the founding of the People's Republic of China. The second were the social conditions in the period. China's dogmatism, social taboos, and regulations set up a kind of "segregation" between African students and ordinary Chinese, especially African males and Chinese females. Thirdly, to make things worse, the pervasive politics created a vacuum for social interaction that made life less interesting for foreign students, including Africans.[1] However, this was also a period in which young African students saw China with their own eyes and had their first personal contact with Chinese people.

The 1970s was characterized by the notion of brotherly friendship because many of the African students were connected with TAZARA. During the 1960s and 1970s, two important events greatly improved contact between China and Africa: the dispatch of Chinese medical teams and the building of the Tanzania Zambia Railway (TAZARA). After China sent its first medical team to Algeria in 1963, Chinese medical teams were dispatched to forty-seven African countries.[2] Supported by the Chinese government, TAZARA was built specifically to break the transportation blockage by the white racial regimes of southern Africa. TAZARA not only made a great contribution to the transportation of minerals from Zambia to the port of Dar es Saalam, thus helping the landlocked countries at the time, but it also improved the livelihood of the local people. Moreover, the process of building TAZARA provided an opportunity for mutual contact,

---

[1] Cheng 2014.
[2] Li 2011.

since more than sixty thousand Chinese engineers, technicians, and workers joined the workforce in Africa, which enabled Africans to better understand China and the Chinese people. [1] In order to help Tanzania and Zambia run TAZARA, China agreed to train engineers for the two countries starting in June 1972. Thus the railway technology trainees came to China, followed by other African students who enrolled in Chinese universities in 1973.

This large group was trained for the future TAZARA project in various specialties. They started training courses at institutions such as Beifang Jiaotong University and the North University of Transportation. The two hundred would-be engineers from Tanzania and Zambia took different basic courses of public transportation, then trained in different special fields, such as transportation, Locomotive specialty, vehicle major, communication major, signal specialty, railway engineering specialty, and financial professional. Among this group, 179 finally graduated in September 1975. In 1973, China resumed the enrolment of international students. There were thirty-seven formal African students, followed by sixty-one in 1974. However, there was a great increase of African students in 1975, reaching 113, probably because Chairman Mao Zedong met with Zambian President Kaunda in 1974 when Mao put forward the "Theory of Three Worlds." In 1976, African students increased to 144. By the end of 1976, China had 355 students from twenty-one African countries, and the number with Chinese scholarships increased as well. [2] After their return home, they played an important role in the transportation and other fields in their own countries. [3]

---

[1] Monson 2009.
[2] CAECG 2005.
[3] Liu and Monson 2011.

The years 1978 to 1995 form the third period, and it indicates increasing contacts. Since the opening-up, China resumed normal educational cooperation with African countries. However, the economic situation in China was not good enough and the international students were rather limited. In 1978, China enrolled 1236 new international students with 95 percent enjoying Chinese Government Scholarships (CGS). Among them, 121 were African students, about 10 percent of the total.[①] Together with nearly three hundred African students enrolled during 1976–1977, there were more than four hundred African students in China, accounting for one quarter of foreign students then. However, only thirty Africans received CGS in 1979, forty-three in 1980, and eighty in 1981.[②]

The statistics indicate that African student numbers went on increasing in the 1980s except 1989 when the number dropped to 249 from 325 of the previous year. The number kept fluctuated between two and three hundred in the following years, never surpassing three hundred. The situation might be explained by the clashes between African and Chinese students around the 1980s, especially with the clash at Hehai University in Nanjing in 1988.

Table 1 African Students in China (1976–1995)

Year	Scholarship	Self-financed	Total
1976	144	0	144
1977	142	0	142
1978	121	0	121
1979	30	0	30

continued

---

① Chen and Xie 2010.
② China Africa Education Cooperation Group 2005.

Year	Scholarship	Self-financed	Total
1980	43	0	43
1981	80	0	80
1982	154	0	154
1983	230	0	230
1984	247	0	247
1985	314	0	314
1986	297	0	297
1987	306	0	306
1988	325	0	325
1989	249	2	251
1990	252	6	258
1991	272	15	287
1992	267	20	287
1993	225	58	283
1994	220	246	466
1995	256	721	977
Total	4,174	1,068	5,242

With more African students, problems occurred, and racial tensions broke out during the 1980s. For many Chinese, it was the first time they saw foreigners and they could not help pointing to foreign students, especially African students. This became a very complicated issue, which was due to various factors such as African student complaints about economic or living conditions, political divergence between the US and Middle East, different social values, Chinese prejudice towards Africans, etc.[1]

Complaints and grievances resulted in conflict and even demonstrations. Clashes between African and Chinese students occurred in Tianjin, Nanjing, Beijing, Shanghai, and other cities during the 1980s. African students

---

[1] Li and Liu 2013.

voiced their grievances by taking different forms, such as demonstrations inside or outside of campus, boycott of classes, hunger strikes, petitions. Occasionally, Chinese students took part in the demonstrations, which resulted in clashes. The incidents were described as "national racism" by some scholars.[①] Analyzing from today's perspective, differences of social systems, values, and culture might be the major cause. For a people with a rather traditional character, the Chinese were not used to the close relations between males and females in public, while African students took a more open attitude about the issue. Therefore, the trigger of conflicts was usually the close contact between African male students and Chinese girls, which was disliked by ordinary Chinese. Of course, China was undergoing a dramatic social transformation at the time. With six students in a room, the Chinese students were not happy with the better treatment of foreign students who lived in a room with only two. In addition, foreign students enjoyed stipends and better conditions in other aspects on campus. Therefore, it was natural for the Chinese students and ordinary citizens to complain about the special treatment of foreign students. Combined with other inequalities or social dissatisfaction, this complaint gave vent to grievances, which led to the conflicts.

Table 2 African Students in China (1996 - 2011)

Year	Scholarship	Self-financed	Total
1996	922	118	1,040
1997	991	224	1,215

continued

---

① Sautman 1994; Sulliven 1994.

Year	Scholarship	Self-financed	Total
1998	1,128	267	1,395
1999	1,136	248	1,384
2000	1,154	234	1,388
2001	1,224	302	1,526
2002	1,256	390	1,646
2003	1,244	549	1,793
2004	1,317	869	2,186
2005	1,367	1,390	2,757
2006	1,861	1,876	3,737
2007	2,733	3,182	5,915
2008	3,735	5,064	8,799
2009	4,824	7,609	12,433
2010	5,710	10,693	16,403
2011	6,316	14,428	20,744
2012	6,717	20,335	27,052
2013	7,305	26,054	33,359
2014	7,821	33,856	41,677
2015	8,470	41,322	49,792
Total	67,231	169,010	236,241

Source: *China Education Yearbook*, 2003–2015; *Brief Statistics of Foreign Students Studying in China*, 2012–2015, Department of International Cooperation and Exchanges, Ministry of Education of China.

One phenomenon was impressive, i. e. , self-financed students from Africa who were increasing during the first half of the 1990s. In 1990, there were six, then fifteen in 1991. The number increased to thirty and then to fifty-eight in 1993. The figure jumped to 246 in 1994 and 721 in 1995. More and more African youth wanted to go to China for further study, and the low fees and easy access to visas might explain the situation. After 1996, the history of African students in China entered a period of rapid development.

The significance of 1996 was because in May that year President Jiang Zemin visited six African countries—Kenya, Ethiopia, Egypt, Mali, Namibia, and

Zimbabwe. This was the first time a Chinese Head of State visited the sub-Saharan Africa. During the visit, Jiang put forward five proposals for China and Africa to build a long-time stable and all-round cooperation for the 21st century based on the principles of sincere friendship, equality, solidarity and cooperation, common development, and the future. The visit and policy brought about a great increase of CGS for African students, which leaped from 256 in 1995 to 922 in 1996. With 118 self-financed students that year, African students for the first time surpassed one thousand in China.[1]

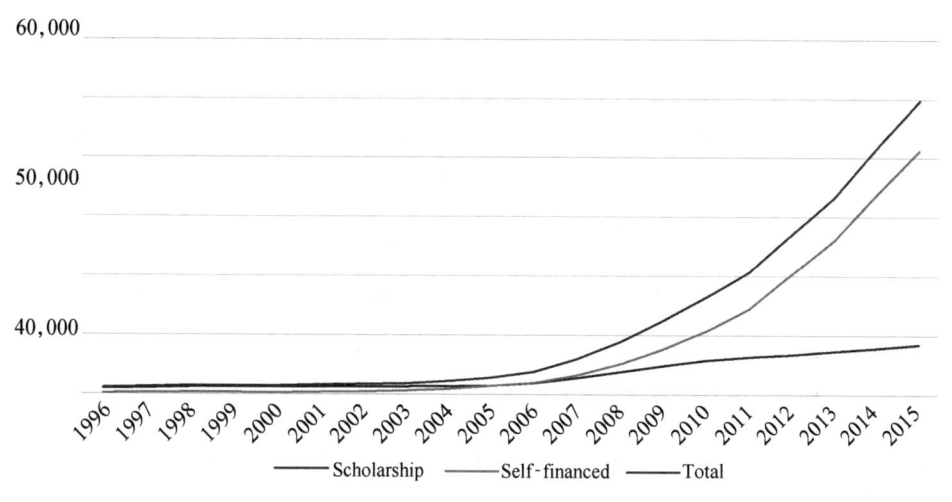

Figure 1 African Students in China (1996–2015)

After the Forum on China-Africa Cooperation (FOCAC) in 2000, promoting China-Africa educational cooperation became an important issue. By the end of 2002, there were 1,600 Africans among the 85,800 foreign students.[2] In 2009, foreign students in China surpassed 230,000, and

---

[1] China Africa Education Cooperation Group 2005, p. 16.
[2] China Education Yearbook 2003, p. 343.

African students numbered 12,436.[1] The figures indicate that the increase of African students was closely linked to that of international students. During 1996 – 2011, there were 84,361 African students in China, with 36,918 holding CGS while 47,443 were self-funded.

The year 2005 was a turning point when self-funded students (1,390) from Africa outnumbered scholarship students (1,367) from Africa. This change may have been due to the success of the scholarship programs and the Chinese Education Exhibitions in Egypt and South Africa since 2003. However, this trend was also in sync with the situation of international students as a whole. In 2005, there were 133,869 self-funded students from 175 countries studying in China, about 94.88 percent of the total international students, a growth rate of 28.56 percent from 2004. In 2009, of the 238,184 foreign students at 610 Chinese universities and scientific research institutions, 219,939 were self-funded.[2] The dramatic increase may be explained by Beijing Olympic Games. In 2011, the self-funded African students reached 14,428, doubling the number of African CGS holders (6,316). In 2015, there were 8,470 African CGS holders while self-financed students numbered 41,322. Most African students in China, no matter whether CGS holders or self-financed, are pursuing degrees and the degree-seeking students increased rapidly. In 2014, 84 percent African students in China set earning a degree as their goal, while only 16 percent chose non-degree courses.

The impressive trend of African students has three characteristics. First, the increase is rapid, along with the general increase of international

---

[1] China Education Yearbook 2010, p. 440.
[2] China Education Yearbook 2009, p. 440.

students. Second, the number of self-financed African students increased faster than the CGS holders. Third, the overwhelming majority of African Students are pursuing degrees.

Policy Implementation and Effect

While China received foreign students as early as the 1950s, yet in the 1950s – 1970s, its policy for international education cooperation was mainly ideologically oriented, i. e., to unite African countries in the struggle against the capitalist camp headed by US in the first stage, then against the two hegemonies, the US and the USSR in the second stage.

After the opening-up, China started to emerge into the international arena of educational cooperation. As a newcomer, the Chinese government has learned from its international partners, made its policy towards international students and carried it out step by step. There is no specific law regarding any group of international students such as US students or African students, yet the policy is the product of international relations. No doubt, China's policy of international educational cooperation is closely linked with or even decided by its strategy. Since China's international education policy has gradually formulated after the opening-up, the article's focus is on the policy since the 1980s.

As early as 1978, the State Council endorsed a document to request that Chinese be more friendly to foreign students, that foreign students be allowed to go shopping publicly and be allowed to marry Chinese.[1] The

---

[1] Ministry of Education, Ministry of Foreign Affairs, Ministry of Public Security, "Request for Instruction of better administration of social management of foreign students," April 29, 1978. See also Liu, 2017.

1980s witnessed the establishment of primary rules, regulations, and policy in the management of foreign students. In 1985, the State Council approved the "Measures of Administration of Foreign Students" issued by State Education Commission, Ministry of Foreign Affairs, Ministry of Culture, Ministry of Public Security and Ministry of Finance. The government realized that "the enrolment and training of foreign students is a strategic work in our diplomacy" and required ministries and different levels to carry out the instruction. The document has eight chapters with forty-three clauses, covering general principles, enrolment and status management, teaching, professional practice/field work, various types of management, such as ideological work and political activities, livelihood and social, and organization leadership. [1]

It seems that the Chinese government regarded foreign students as an element of the Chinese society and the management was dogmatic and strict. Its policy covered a broad range of topics including courses, Chinese language teaching, teaching materials, physical training, etc. As an important document, it governed the management of international students for many years. On July 21, 1999 the Ministry of Education issued a document for the administration of the enrolment of foreign students by primary and secondary schools. [2] In 2000, " Provisions on the

---

[1] State Council Document No. 121[1985]. Circular of State Council's endorsement of "Methods of Management of Foreign Students" issued by State Education Commission, Ministry of Foreign Affairs, Ministry of Culture, Ministry of Public Security and Ministry of Finance. October 14, 1985. http://www.chinalawedu.com/news/1200/22598/22615/22822/2006/3/he999524311118360023570-0.htm.

[2] Decree No. 4 [1999] "Provisional Measures of the Ministry of Education for the Administration on Enrolment of Foreign Students by Primary and Secondary Schools." July 21, 1999. http://www.pkulaw.cn/fulltext_form.aspx? Gid=23504.

Administration of Foreign Students in Universities" was issued by the government, which had eight chapters with fifty clauses. The provisions contain two added chapters on "Scholarship" and "Entry-Exit and Residence Procedures," which made implementation more applicable. These regulations were more systematic than the previous one. [1]

In March 2017 three ministries issued a new document regarding the enrolment and training of international students, which went into practice on July 1, 2017. Its purpose is to standardize the enrolment, advising, and management of international students, provide them better services, and promote foreign exchange and cooperation in China's education, thus raising the level of internationalization. It covers four levels: pre-school, primary school, middle school, and university. Although the specific work is the responsibility of the local government, the educational administration under the State Council takes charge of the management of international students, including making the general policy for their enrolment and development and guiding and coordinating the concrete work of the local government, while ministries of foreign affairs and public security are in charge of the management accordingly. Since this document covers all education institutions, the previous ones of the same type issued in 1999 and 2000 were annulled. [2]

---

[1] Decree No. 9 [2000] "Provisions on the Administration of Foreign Students in Universities" issued by Ministry of Education, Ministry of Foreign Affairs and Ministry of Public Security. January 31, 2000. http://www.moe.edu.cn/s78/A20/gjs_left/moe_861/tnull_8647.html.

[2] Decree No. 42 [2017] "Measures of the Administration of Enrolment and training of International Students by the Educational Institution," issued by Ministry of Education, Ministry of Foreign Affairs and Ministry of Public Security. March 20, 2017. http://www.gov.cn/xinwen/2017-06/02/content_5199249.htm.

Although the related legal regulations and rules cover all foreign students, there are specific measures regarding African students, especially when some special events or unusual things occurred. For example, during the troublesome days in the early 1980s, racial discriminations occurred in Shanghai. Some Chinese called the African students names, and there were clashes here and there. In one case, the Minister of Education had to call a meeting with the leader of African diplomatic corps and fifteen African ambassadors in February 1983 to explain the problems between Shanghai residents and African students. The African ambassadors warned that the Chinese government should teach policemen as well as residents since African students were often harassed by the policemen, either being stopped by them without reason or getting a scolding, which was a nuisance for African students. If the situation persisted, Africa-China friendly relations would be damaged. Therefore, different local governmental departments also promulgated various documents regarding specific issues related to African students.[①]

During the mid-1990s, after their graduation in China, some African students did not go back to their home countries. Instead, they took jobs in a third country other than China and their homeland. This phenomenon did not fit with the original intention of the Chinese government to help capacity building for African countries. In 1996, the Ministry of Education of China issued a document that requested the institution of management to hand African graduates a return-ticket directly to the embassy of the student's country in Beijing at the end of the academic year in order to facilitate the

---

① Li and Liu 2013. For specific cases, see Liu 2017, pp. 167-171.

students returning directly home. This has become routine now. A recent report commented on this: "Due to Chinese visa rules, most international students cannot stay in China after their education is complete. This prevents brain-drain and means that China is educating a generation of African students who — unlike their counterparts in France, the US or UK — are more likely to return home and bring their new education and skills with them."[1]

In 2005, when Chinese President Hu Jingtao participated in the High-Level Meeting on Financing for Development at the Sixtieth Session of the United Nations, he promised that over the next three years, China would increase its assistance to developing countries, African countries in particular: "China will train 30,000 personnel of various professions from the developing countries within the next three years so as to help them speed up their human resources development."[2] Since the CGS is closely related to China's international strategy, it is also a reflection of the focus of China's policy.

As we see from the statistics, before 2005 the number of African students who received CGS was always smaller than that of European students. Yet the situation started to change since 2006, a year after Hu Jintao's declaration. Although in 2006 African students and European students accounted for equal proportions, the actual number of African CGS holders (1,861) surpassed that of Europeans (1,858) for the first time. From 2007 onward, the number of African students with CGS began to increase substantially.

There were continuous policy promotions. During the China-African Summit (as well the Third FOCAC) in 2006 in Beijing, the CGS specifically

---

[1] The Conversation 2017.
[2] Hu 2005.

for African students was increased from two thousand to four thousand annually. In the Fourth FOCAC in 2009, the CGS again increased to 5,500 every year. The number reached 5,710 in 2010.① In 2012, the Fifth FOCAC announced the scholarships would reach twenty thousand for next three years. That is why the CGS for African students increased rapidly. In 2011, the number was 6,316. Bu 2015, African CGS holders reached 8,470.②

In order to implement the policy, different strategies were planned by the agents, universities, municipalities, various departments, and even individuals.③ Regarding CGS, there was no evaluation system until 1997, when the State Education Commission issued the "Provisional Measures of Annual Review of Scholarship of Foreign Students." The measures made it clear for the first time that students had to undergo review according to certain standards with either "pass" or "no-pass" results.④ Within three years, 7,118 CGS holders took the review exam; 7,008 passed and 110 did not (1.55 percent). In 2000, two documents were issued by the Ministry of Education regarding the CGS annual review system and method.⑤ With more accurate standards and more autonomy for the institutions entitled to enroll foreign students, the receiving universities now had the real authority to carry out their own review of foreign students. In the same year, 2,342

---

① Li Anshan et al. 2012, pp. 58 – 60.
② China Education Yearbook 2010 – 2016.
③ Li and Liu 2013.
④ "Provisional Measures of Annual Review of Scholarship of Foreign Students," issued by the State Commission of Education, March 28, 1997. http://www.bjfao.gov.cn/affair/oversea/wglxsfg/23801.htm.
⑤ Education (Jiaowailai) No. 29 [2000] "Notice of the Ministry of education on the implementation of the annual review system of the Chinese Government Scholarship," April 26, 2000. http://www.moe.edu.cn/s78/A20/gjs_left/moe_850/tnull_1183.html.

CGS holders at eighty-one universities underwent the review; 2,314 (98.8 percent) passed, 28 did not. Among the unqualified students, seventeen were Asian, seven European, two African, and two American.[①] As for the universities that have the authority to offer CGS, there are strict qualifications. Usually only those universities that have high-level education, qualified professors who can offer courses in foreign languages, and adequate educational facilities can enroll international students. In 2015, only the 279 designated Chinese universities under the CGS-Chinese University Program were entitled to accept individual scholarship applications.[②]

The Chinese government wanted to get actively engaged in international educational cooperation. Therefore, different ministries, provinces, municipalities, and companies started to offer various types of scholarship. Owing to the complicated scholarship system and space, we describe one example, that of Shanghai Government Scholarship.

Table 3 Shanghai Government Scholarship — Class A
(Unit/time: RMB¥/Annual)

Supporting Categories	Field of Study	Tuition	Accommodation	Stipend	Medical Insurance	Total
Undergraduate students	I	20,000	8,400	30,000	800	59,200
	II	23,000	8,400	30,000	800	62,200
	III	27,000	8,400	30,000	800	66,200
Master's students	I	25,000	8,400	36,000	800	70,200
	II	29,000	8,400	36,000	800	74,200
	III	34,000	8,400	36,000	800	79,200

continued

---

① China Education Yearbook 2002.
② China Scholarship Council, "Chinese Government Scholarship Application," August 12, 2015, http://en.csc.edu.cn/laihua/newsdetailen.aspx?cid=66andid=3074.

Supporting Categories	Field of Study	Tuition	Accommodation	Stipend	Medical Insurance	Total
Doctoral students	I	33,000	12,000	42,000	800	87,800
	II	38,000	12,000	42,000	800	92,800
	III	45,000	12,000	42,000	800	99,800

Source: "Shanghai Government Scholarship — Class A," China Scholarship Council Date: 2016-03-28 http://www.csc.edu.cn/Laihua/scholarshipdetailen.aspx?cid=105andid=1293.

Note: (1) Full scholarship covers tuition waiver, accommodation, stipend, and comprehensive medical insurance; (2) Field of Study I includes Philosophy, Economics, Legal Studies, Education, Literature, History, and Management; Field of Study II includes Science, Engineering, and Agriculture; Field of Study III includes Fine Arts and Medicine.

At the end of the 1990s, a general framework for international student education was in place in China, which was compatible with Chinese culture and China's own educational system. Since then, China has kept improving its international educational cooperation in an effort to make itself one of the most popular destinations for foreign students. In the meantime, as economic globalization accelerates, international demand increases greatly for those young talents who can speak Chinese or have a solid knowledge about China. As a result, the number of China's international students continues to grow rapidly. In 2016, they increased to 442,773, 45,138 more than 2015 (a growth rate is 11.35 percent). African students increased 11,802 to reach 61,594, which was a growth rate is 23.7 percent.[1] International education in China gets more popular every year.

Western countries have long dominated African development theory and practice. Since gaining independence, few African countries have developed

---

[1] Ministry of Education, "Statistics of Foreign students in China in 2016," http://www.moe.edu.cn/jyb_xwfb/xw_fbh/moe_2069/xwfbh_2017n/xwfb_170301/170301_sjtj/201703/t20170301_297677.html.

successfully under western guidance, and many have gotten into difficult situations.[1] In recent years, the world economy has been volatile, and major changes have taken place in the international balance of power. On the one hand, the US financial crisis and the debt crisis in Europe landed the western economies in trouble; on the other hand, emerging economies have become the driving force of the world economy. Thus "Look East" becomes a tendency of some African countries.[2] Asia's experience with poverty alleviation and development becomes a model for Africans who want to find a way for their own countries out of poverty, and China offers an alternative development model for African governments. Nigerian historian Femi Akomolafe explained it this way: "Now to the lessons Africa can learn from the world's new economic giant: The first and most profound is that: It is possible! Whichever way we throw it around, China's economic performance is nothing short of a miracle. It shows what a people with confidence, determination and vision can achieve."[3]

The Chinese experience is that to pursue the development of its own economy, a country can only rely on the concerted efforts and determination of its own people. Never in the history of mankind did a nation depend entirely for its own economy on foreigners.[4] One of the ways for the African

---

[1] According to Johns Hopkins University Professor of Development Studies Deborah Brautigam (Brautigam 2009, p. 308), "Where the West regularly changes its development advice, programs, and approach in Africa ... China does not claim it knows what Africa must do to develop. China has argued that it was wrong to impose political and economic conditionality in exchange for aid, and that countries should be free to find their own pathway out of poverty. Mainstream economists in the West today are also questioning the value of many of the conditions imposed on aid over the past few decades."
[2] ACET 2009.
[3] Akomolafe 2006, p. 49.
[4] Li 2013a.

governments to learn from China is to send their young people to China for further study. In 2005, the Rwanda government signed an agreement with the Ministry of Education to train their undergraduates, with Rwanda government scholarships. That same year, the Tanzania government also signed an agreement with the China Scholarship Council and agreed to train Tanzanian students in China's universities with Tanzanian scholarships. ①

Reasons, Motivations, and Purpose

Why do more and more Africans come to China for further study? There are various reasons, such as the favorable conditions provided by China, various motivations of young people and pragmatic purposes for personal development. ② To know more about China and to learn more advanced technology from China are the main reasons that young Africans go to China for further studies.

The West has dominated the African media, and there are various untrue stories or even rumors about China. A typical one is the 1991 *New York Times* article "China Used Prisoner Labor in Africa" by Roberta Cohen, former Deputy Assistant Secretary of State for Human Rights in the Carter Administration. ③ There was no source or explanation for what she

---

① China Education Yearbook 2006.
② Liu 2017.
③ Cohen (1991) wrote that "I learned of the case of a Chinese construction company building a road in Benin using prison labour. 70 to 75 percent of the construction workers were known to be prisoners … The company was the Jiangsu Construction Company … The company was able to underbid all its competitors by a wide margin because its labor costs were so cheap." There was no source and no explanation. Since she is a former US top official, the rumor of "China's prison labor" spread all over the world (Yan and Sautman, 2012, 2017).

wrote, but since she was a former top US official, the rumor of "China's prison labor" spread around the world.[①] BBC's irresponsible report "Angola's Chinese-Built Ghost Town" is another example.[②] The residential area soon sold out after it opened to the public for sale.[③] Africans used to know very little about China, and most of the young Africans come to China in order to see China with their own eyes. China's economic development and strong economy are the true attractions to young Africans. The Beijing Olympic Games in 2008 showcased China as never before to Africans and they were surprised to find an impressive China as shown on TV.[④] The event served as a stimulus to attract African youth who want to know more about China's growth and its experience of development with modern technologies. They want to understand why China can be Africa's largest trading partner for consecutive years and is now the second largest economy in the world. It is China's growing presence in Africa, the commodities, television shows, Confucius Institutes, and Chinese people working in Africa that have aroused growing interest among African students. Maxwell Zeken is a 16-year-old Liberian who lives in rural Nimba County. Asked

---

① Yan and Sautman 2012, 2017.
② Redvers 2012.
③ Situated in a spot about 30km outside Angola's capital, Luanda, Nova Cidade de Kilamba is a newly-built mixed residential project of 750 eight-storey apartment buildings for half-million people with a dozen schools and more than 100 retail units, all sold out soon after its finish. To report an unfinished residential project as "no residents" and the area as "ghost town" before it opens for sale is really a biased view, if not a malicious slander. I visited the area in February 2016 and it was prosperous. At a China-Africa Media Cooperation seminar held at Remin University on April 26, 2017, I exchanged ideas with Venancio Rodrigue, a reporter of Angola, who verified that BBC's report is a twisted story.
④ Several African students told me about their deep impression when they saw a different China in TV during the Olympic Games in 2008.

where he dreams of studying, he says: "I want to study engineering in China and come back to Liberia to build our roads and our cities. They say you must visit the Great Wall of China. I regret that my country didn't build something like that."[1]

China's readiness for educational cooperation has surely promoted the boom of African students coming to China. In recent years, the Chinese government has worked hard to strengthen its relations with African countries and has adopted several measures to encourage African students to become familiar with China, such as the Confucius Institutes, learning Chinese, and scholarships to provide favorable conditions to attract African students.[2] By 2017, there were forty-eight Confucius Institutes and twenty-seven Confucius Classrooms located in thirty-three African countries, which provide various levels of Chinese language learning (see Appendix for a listing of the Institutes and Classrooms).

Many African students learned Chinese before applying for a Chinese scholarship or for enrolment at a Chinese university.[3] For example, Dr. Belhadj Imen first won the top prize in a Chinese Bridge Competition in Tunisia, and the Chinese government then offered her a scholarship to study in the Department of Chinese Language and Literature at Peking University. Since Peking University is the top university in China, many international students have to learn Chinese before applying there for enrolment or a scholarship. It is the same case with other Chinese universities entitled to enroll international students. At the Shanghai Institute of Technology,

---

[1] Pilling 2017.
[2] Liu 2008.
[3] Niu 2016.

about 130 African students are majoring in civil engineering and architecture. In their first year, they master Chinese and take a language proficiency test. This is a normal way for international students including Africans pursuing their degrees in China. Christian King, a student in philosophy and international trade at Renmin University, told Panview: "I started studying Chinese back home in Zimbabwe and it was very difficult at first. The tones and characters were challenging, but after several years in China I am almost fluent. I love and enjoy Chinese now."[1]

Scholarships also promote African students going to China. With Africa's importance in China's international strategy, the scholarships become more and more inclined toward African students. As for CGS holders, Asian students are always at the top. It is natural both for the geopolitical reasons and the many overseas Chinese in Asian countries neighboring China. Europe, although with fewer CGS recipient countries than Africa, had been long time at the second place. Yet the situation has changed since 2006 when Africa moved into second place in terms of CGS awardees.

Table 4 Comparison of CGS Holders between Africa and Europe (2003 – 2010)

Year	Total Scholarship	Africa	Percent (%)	Europe	Percent (%)
2003	6,153	1,244	20.2	1,442	23.4
2004	6,715	1,317	19.6	1,880	23.5
2005	7,218	1,367	18.8	1,761	24.4
2006	8,484	1,861	21.9	1,858	21.9

continued

---

[1] "Africans learning Chinese can boost cooperation channels," March 23, 2015, CCTV. com. http://english.cntv.cn/2016/03/23/ARTIvEEYI0kItdGxV6F2JBK0160323.shtml.

Year	Total Scholarship	Africa	Percent (%)	Europe	Percent (%)
2007	10,151	2,733	26.9	2,107	20.8
2008	13,516	3,735	27.6	2,628	19.4
2009	18,245	4,824	26.44	3,022	16.56
2010	22,390	5,710	25.5	3,283	14.66

As the Table 4 shows, the percentage of CGS for Africa and Europe was about the same in 2006, but by 2007 the number of Africans had risen to 2,733, 2007, outnumbering Europeans by 626. The CGS holders of Africa increased every year. Today, students from fifty-one African countries are eligible for Chinese government scholarships (for Europe, the number is thirty-nine). In 2010, there were 22,390 beneficiaries, with 11,197 were offered to Asia (50.01 percent), 5,710 to Africa (25.5 percent), 3,283 to Europe (14.66 percent), 1,761 to America (7.87 percent), and 439 to Oceania (1.96 percent).[①] Clearly Africans have become the second most important in terms of CGS holders.

Besides the CGS, there are other types of scholarships offered to international students, such as provincial scholarships, ministerial scholarships, university scholarships, and various scholarships with specific purposes provided by companies, charity organizations, etc. CGS covers the waiver of various expenses, including tuition, teaching material fees, research and survey fees, dissertation guidance fees, one-off resettlement fees, on-campus accommodation, medical insurance, a round-trip international airfare each year for home visits, and one-time round-trip international airfare for all students. In addition, international students

---

① China Education Yearbook 2011.

receive their stipends monthly. With the country's continued economic development, the value of the scholarship has raised many times over the past years.[①] More and more African students enjoy CGS or other scholarships.

Self-funded African students, however, have greatly surpassed the Chinese scholarship holders since 2005. In 2015, among 49,792 African students in China, only 8,470 were CGS holders while 41,322 were self-funded. I once met a Zambian student in the Shangdi region in north Beijing where I live. He told me that he came to learn Chinese in a small language school in Wudaocao, an area well known among foreign students. That surprised me because he looked very young and had come to China alone. He was living in a residential area far away from the city center, and he showed his determination to study Chinese language.

There are different motivations underlying Africans deciding to study in China. For instance, some like the reputation of Chinese universities and others want to pursue specific fields.[②] China's experience of development with advanced technologies has inspired young Africans. Chinese companies are building roads, bridges, hospitals, schools, dams, oil refineries, and modern railways in Africa. What is more, Huawei, a networking and telecommunications equipment and services multinational company, has been successful in African IT industry and China is cooperating with Nigeria in the field of satellites. The localization of Chinese companies has attracted talented youngsters in different countries. I have met various African

---

① "China's government scholarship for international students raised," http://old.moe.gov.cn//publicfiles/business/htmlfiles/moe/s5147/201501/183255.html.
② King 2013; Tsui 2016.

students who were in master's programs, such as Serge Mundele at Beijing University of Science and Technology and Oodo Stephen Ogidi, a Nigerian student who worked as a post-doctoral fellow in electrical engineering at Dalian University of Technology. African students are also engaged in the social sciences, such as Erfiki Hicham, a Moroccan student who received his PhD. from the School of International Studies at Peking University. The aforementioned Tunisian scholar Imen Belhadj earned her M. A. in Chinese language and literature and Ph. D. in international politics and then undertook post-doctoral studies in Arab studies, all at Peking University.

All these phenomena make China an ideal country for young students to pursue further studies. In recent years, more African students are engaged in professional studies.[①] According to a survey of two thousand samples in 2014, 84 percent of African students had as their goal earning a degree: 41.61 percent applied for medical science as their major, 21.56 percent chose engineering related subjects, while 13.94 percent chose business and management. In all, 98.33 percent applied for admission to the Top Five majors.[②] A student from the Republic of Congo came to China in 2007. He once told me that after he saw several telecommunications products in the market that were "made in China" he decided to go to China. With a dream of becoming the minister of telecommunications in his country, he is now a graduate student in telecommunications at the Beijing University of Posts and Telecommunications.

Obviously there are other practical reasons, among them the fact that

---

[①] Bodomo 2011, p. 29.
[②] "EOL and CUCAS jointly published 2014 Report of International Students in China," http://www.eol.cn/html/lhlx/content.html. Accessed June 25, 2017.

tuition and fees are lower and it is easier to get student visas than for western countries. Moreover, if one has learned Chinese and has an understanding of Chinese culture, it is easier to find a good job at a leading Chinese companies such as Huawei and ZTE (also a telecommunications multinational) back in their own country. To be sure, the Chinese know very little about Africa, and there is surely widespread ignorance regarding the African skin color. However, the friendliness and warm feelings of the Chinese people may also encourage young Africans to study in China. ①

Role, Contributions, and Agency

Since African students are becoming a big group in China, what role do they play? What contributions do they make to both China and Africa, or to bilateral relations? Human history is a history of (im)migration. Although international students are not always considered immigrants or members of a diaspora, their linkage with a diaspora is obvious. The first reason for considering them as such is their role as a bridge. As the second largest group within African community in China, they constantly function as a bridge between African culture and Chinese culture. As soon as they enter China and begin their social life on campus, they engage in cultural exchange

---

① Regarding whether there is racism in China, views are different. A Ghanaian student talked about her experience in China, saying, "Others often ask me if I found Chinese to be racist, and whether their treatment of me as a spectacle — taking pictures, touching my hair, rubbing my skin, staring at me — does not indicate a racist attitude. I respond that I find them curious. Many of the experiences I had were borne of ignorance, not racism. Despite always being identified as 'black' and 'African', I never felt discriminated against or antagonized, but rather treated with warmth and friendliness. Because I spoke Mandarin, I could often understand what people said about me, and they were rarely disparaging or maligning." (Baitie 2013).

and play a role as a bridge between different cultures through conversation with their fellow students, contact with the authorities and ordinary Chinese, courses and debates, social interaction, etc.

In a new situation, young Africans in common with other humans always face new challenges and have to experience cultural shock — more serious for undergraduates than graduates, females than males.[1] Cultural exchange or adaptation thus becomes important, since it can occur in daily life, the learning process, and social contact, and it brings about better relations with the host community.[2] Cultural adaptation becomes an active response to new conditions, a process of mutual learning. I personally have supervised many African graduates, including three Ph. D. recipients from Tunisia, Morocco, and the Democratic Republic of Congo. They told me various stories about their experiences involving ignorance and biased views on the one hand and on the other friendliness with warm feelings.

African students become the bridge between Africa and China. Moses is a Nigerian student majoring in Chinese language teaching. He came to China in 2013 and has a typical Chinese name "Wu Wengzhong." Having learned Chinese in Nigeria from his childhood, he became addicted to Chinese culture during his stay in China. He has learned various kinds of Chinese arts and performances, including some superior arts such as *Xiangsheng* (Chinese cross-talk or comic dialogue) and lion dance, and has attended various performances and art shows. With his profound interest in Chinese language and culture, Moses participated in the "Hebei Provincial Foreign Scholars' Chinese Talents' Show" in November 2014. He showed his *Kung*

---

[1] Disma 2004.
[2] Hashim, et al. 2003.

Fu skills, recited Chinese classic poems, and performed self-composed Chinese cross-talk with his foreign partner. Thanks to his excellent performance and skill, he won "Best Creative Award," "Best Eloquence Award," and the "Silver Award of Recitation of Classic Poem." He also received the "Best All-Around King" for his talent show presentation of Chinese culture. Owing to his capability in Mandarin and understanding of Chinese culture, his Chinese friends called him "China-hand."[①]

Tuition from African students has no doubt contributed to China's economy. Besides, their cultural knowledge about their home countries has contributed to multi-culturalism in China. Significant cultural exchanges are ongoing between African and Chinese students. Africans are learning the Chinese language, culture, and work ethic.[②] At the same time they are transmitting African culture, values, and skills.[③] Chinese students also learn about African culture on different occasions. There are various African culture clubs in Chinese cities, such as African dance, African music, and African drumming, which are the result of African students' contribution.[④] For example, Francis Tchiégué, a Cameroonian student, came to China for further study many years ago, having already received his Ph. D. in Cameroon. In China, he was attracted by the similarity between Cameroonian culture and Chinese culture and thus started to learn Chinese art, cultural skills, and cross-talk. He introduced African culture to the Chinese through various activities, and he even made a Chinese traditional

---

① Yang, et al. 2016.
② King 2013.
③ Amoah 2013.
④ Shikwati 2012.

costume from Cameroonian cloth. Francis was named "Envoy of Art Exchange between China and Africa." He is now trying his best to introduce African films to China. ①

There is an annual International Cultural Festival in Peking University, and African students set up booths to proudly introduce their own culture to the Chinese audience. ② My student Antoine Lokongo played the drum in the festival, and many Chinese students tried to learn this skill. In order to introduce African culture to ordinary Chinese, the Center for African Studies at Peking University and the *Half-Monthly Talks* co-run a special column entitled "Entry into African Culture." So far fifteen articles on different topics about African culture have been published, covering African world heritage, languages, films, the role of chiefs, Léopold Sédar Senghor, Nobel Prize winner Wole Soyinka, Ibn Battuta, Ibn Khaldun, the civilization of Ethiopia, etc.; some of them were written by African students. ③

Chinese students in London serve as a bridge between Chinese culture and British culture and between Chinese diaspora in Britain and British society. ④ African students play the same role. They not only serve as a bridge between African culture and Chinese culture but also a bridge between the African community in China and Chinese who are interested in

---

① "Cameroonian Tchiégué's life in China," http://tv.cntv.cn/video/C10616/3ce5c25b1bfc476095406544b5971b8a.
② "African student's speech at International Festival in Peking University", October 29, 2013. http://www.fmprc.gov.cn/zflt/chn/zxxx/t1094003.htm.
③ Shikwati 2012; Li 2015.
④ Wu Bing 2015, 2016.

China-Africa bilateral relations.① Thanks to the effort of African students, Chinese have begun to get familiar with African values, ideas, dance, drumming, pictures, sculpture, etc. A good example is my former student Wang Hanjie who wrote her B. A. thesis on "The History and Spread of Djembe Drum in China." When asked why she chose this topic, she told me with a smile that she was a member of the Djembe Club at Peking University.② In Wuhan, an important metropolitan city in middle China where advertisements projecting western brands and tastes are very popular, in an interview with some local women about their tastes for African cultural products in China they found it *hen ku* (very cool). "Their choice showed that they were avant-garde, cosmopolitan and even modern in their fashion tastes and preferences. This African cultural influence in Wuhan has been facilitated in no small measure by the annual Wuhan University Autumn International Cultural Festival."③ In other universities in Beijing, such as Minzu University of China, there is even a specific African Culture Day.

Although some African students choose to move to a third country after they finish their university studies in China, many decide to return home after graduation and make important contribution to their own countries.④ In addition to their participation in different fields of work, some of them were put in important positions and assumed high posts in theirs government. As of 2005, for example, eight former recipients of Chinese government scholarships were holding ministerial positions or above in their

---

① Bredeloup 2014.
② Wang 2013.
③ Amoah 2012, p. 108.
④ Bodomo 2011; Li and Liu 2013.

respective home countries, eight were serving as ambassadors or consuls to China, six were working as secretaries to their countries' presidents or prime ministers, three were secretary-generals of Associations for Friendship with China, not to mention many experts and elites in other fields.① Taking Peking University as example, its former student Mulatu Teshome Wirtu became Speaker of the Parliament in Ethiopia and now is the President. After her education, Lucy Njeri Manegene worked for the Ministry of Foreign Affairs in Kenya. Rakotoarivony R. J. Manitra went back to Madagascar after her M. A. studies and now serves in the Madagascar Embassy in China. Mapulumo Lisebo Mosisili returned to Lesotho after being awarded an M. A. and is now Principal Secretary of the Labor Department in Lesotho.②

Another important aspect of African student experiences in China is that they develop Pan-African connections on their campuses. When answering the BBC's question of why he came to China, Mikka Kabugo, a Ugandan in the African Students Association of Peking University, said he started to learn about China through a traditional Chinese medical doctor in Uganda. When he came to China, he found that Beijing was a global village where he could exchange ideas about African affairs with fellow African students from other countries. Such exchanges among African students helped broaden their global perspective. With fellow students in the same association, they examine African issues from a Pan-African perspective and

---

① China Africa Education Cooperation Group 2005, pp. 20 – 21.
② Lisebo Kikine to Li Anshan, Tue, 12 Feb 2013 00: 18: 24 +0800 (CST) (Li, 2013b).

think about how they can help their home continent.[1] What is more, through classes, debates, and various seminars held jointly by the African Students Association and the Center for African Studies at Peking University, they have learned a great deal about world affairs and the African situation, problems, and solutions.

Following their fellow students at Peking University, the Tsinghua University African students also formed an African Students Association on African Day, May 25, 2017, with members from twenty-seven African countries. During the opening ceremony, African students discussed various issues such as the thoughts of Presidents Julius Kambarage Nyerere and Nkrumah, heard a presentation by Dr. Chabalala, a student from the School of Public Health at Tsinghua University, about the continent's contribution to knowledge development shared, and listened to Professor Tang Xiaoyang from the School of International Relations and Carnegie-Tsinghua Center talk about the structural change of China-Africa relations. Professor John Akokpari, Center for African Studies at Peking University, led a discussion about opportunities for African students in the diaspora to become change makers in the development of their own countries. There are other African student associations as well, such as the General Union of African Students in China (GUASC) and the General Union of African Students in Tianjin (GUAST).[2]

Although most international students are not normally classified as immigrants, Bodomo correctly pointed out that the process of trading

---

[1] BBC World Service Newsday, "Why are African students flocking to Chinese universities?" http://www.bbc.co.uk/programmes/p0577s49? ocid=socialflow_facebook.

[2] King 2013.

between Africa and China began with Africans who studied in China and remained there engage in business, and some ended up in trade with China.① African students are often the first to carry out business between their home country and China. Although they have little capital to begin with, yet a solid social and linguistic background is to their advantage. Gradually they became major trade intermediaries between Africa and China, thus contributing to the economic activities between both sides. Dr. Abdul, a veterinary official for the Niger Government, is a good example. He received a Niger-China Friendship Scholarship from the Chinese government. After finishing his degree, he decided to change his profession by opening a new occupation that was unfamiliar for him but more profitable. Since 2000, Dr. Abdul has established himself in Guangzhou to export medicine and related veterinary products to Africa and Europe, obtaining these products directly from factories in north China with which he is familiar due to his training in China. After this success, he resumed his connections with the Niger government. Now fluent in Mandarin, Dr. Abdul serves as honorary consul for Niger and is responsible for conveying the demands of Nigerian students with scholarships at Chinese universities to any Nigerian minister who visits Guangzhou. He describes his role as turning "brain drain" to "brain gain." According to Bredeloup, this type of situation has resulted from two facts: the opportunities created by China's rapid economic development and the change of or even devaluation of the position of civil servants in Africa. There are quite a few examples like Abdul, including Patrick from the Democratic Republic of Congo, Aziz from

---

① Bodomo 2013; Haugen 2013.

Mali, etc.① As indicated in other studies, some of the self-funded African students and even CGS holders in Guangdong and Zhejiang entered trading activities for the first time in their life and became settled businessmen while studying in China.② Now, many African students like Dr. Abdul now serve as a business and cultural bridge between Africa and China.

It is generally assumed that China has made every move in developing China-Africa relations while the African agency in shaping and influencing deepening relations with China is either paralyzed or non-existent. It is interesting that an African student researched African agency in the making of Africa-China relations. Adu Amoah, a former Ghanaian government official, later became a student in China and married a Chinese woman. As president of the Wuhan University African Students' Representative Committee, he used his own observations and experiences to indicate how African students can be the master of their own lives in China. He described a lively African migrant community emerging in Wuhan, "which may potentially add to the makings of an African diaspora in contemporary China" and that "this migrant African population is constituted fundamentally by students," "comprising a dynamic fashion of those pursuing their course of study and those who stay on after graduation." Taking Wuhan as an example, Amoah describes how the African presence in China influenced the reality of Chinese society in the form of fashion, inter-marriage, the exchange of language learning (Africans can explain their own worldview and experience in Mandarin while teach English to Chinese

---

① Bredeloup 2014.
② Bodomo 2012; Amoah 2013; Haugen 2013.

students), and through the management of African enterprises such as nightclubs run by Africans. "This is necessary to dispel the interpretation of Africa 'under the sign of crisis' ... in popular and academic discourses in general and specifically, the patronising idea of Africa as a clueless, pliant and suppliant partner in Africa-China relations."[1]

African students have not only immensely improved cooperation between Africa and China and contributed a great deal to cultural exchange, but they also have promoted the internationalization of China's universities.[2] For African students, there are definitely cultural shocks, homesickness, issues of social adaptation, psychological stress and frustrations, and difficulties and problem in daily life. Moreover, there are misunderstandings and prejudice from Chinese students and other international students as well as language barriers in the educational process. The English proficiency of Chinese teachers is not always good enough, which makes the learning process for African students more difficult.[3] In the future, there is thus much room for improvement.

Conclusion

In terms of the subject of this article, international educational cooperation involves three parties: China, African countries, and African students. At this juncture we can ask certain questions to the Chinese government, African countries, and African students.

---

[1] Amoah 2012, p. 110.
[2] Liu 2017.
[3] Hashim et al. 2003.

Regarding the Chinese dimension, it is important that Africa is not a totality but a continent of fifty-four countries, which have different conditions and needs.[①] African students are not a totality but different individuals. Besides scholarships, does the Chinese government provide adequate living conditions for African students with their different religions, lifestyles, and cuisine in a society that is unfamiliar to them? Are Chinese teachers sufficiently qualified in their skills for transmitting their knowledge to African students? Are there good measures for African students to introduce their own culture to the Chinese society? Is there sufficient opportunity for African students to exchange ideas and experiences with their Chinese counterparts? China certainly needs to better address these and other issues.

As for the African countries, they must remember that the African students returning home are those who love their own countries and want to contribute the knowledge learned in China to their homelands. Do African governments offer a good opportunity for African students to work at home after their graduation in China? Do they show enough concern and care for their academic studies and life in China and create better conditions to facilitate their studies and daily living requirements? Do the embassies provide suitable channels of communication with their students in China, look after their interests, and respond effectively to their reasonable demands?[②] Better conditions should be prepared for those who would like to return home for service on behalf of their own countries.

[①] Apithy 2013.
[②] I supervised several Ph. D. students from Africa. Some of them came across difficulties in finding a decent job after return. An absurd case is that one of them was even asked to translate his dissertation, which was written in Chinese, into French in order to prove his academic capability.

For African students in China, we should remind them that they are studying with great dreams for themselves, great expectations from their countries, and great hopes from their families. Do they make good use of their scholarships or give their best efforts by studying hard to meet the challenges ahead and thus be fully prepared for their futures? Do they take every opportunity to introduce African culture or the culture of their own countries to ordinary Chinese or to fellow students from other countries? Do they learn from having had good experiences or from the lessons of development of other countries and thus make good provision for the opportunity to use them when they want to realize their dream upon their return home?

The June 28, 2017 report "China tops US and UK as destination for Anglophone African students" that appeared in *The Conversation* underscores the need for China, African countries, and African students to address vigorously questions such as those posed above. "According to the UNESCO Institute for Statistics," the report stated, "the US and UK host around 40,000 African students a year. China surpassed this number in 2014, making it the second most popular destination for African students studying abroad, after France which hosts just over 95,000 students."[①] More and more African youth have come to study in China in recent decades, and their number is constantly increasing. They serve as carriers of African culture, mediators of bilateral trade and business, transmitters of social organizations and ways of life, and as a bridge between Africa and China. "It's still too early to tell how these new dynamics might be shaping geopolitics on the continent."[②] African students are definitely creating a new

---

① The Conversation 2017.
② Ibid.

world. To integrate into a host society does not mean giving up one's own culture. To build a linkage between two cultures and transform from an "enclave" to a "bridge" remains a difficult task but one that is worth trying and is workable.

Postscript

On November 11, 2017 the first "Amanbo Cup" of Employment/Innovation Competition for African Students was held in Shenzhen. Jointly organized by the Center for African Studies of Peking University, the China-Africa International Business School of Zhejiang Normal University, and the Center for China-Africa Sustainable Development, the competition was sponsored by Shenzhen Right Net Tech Co. Ltd. and was aimed at training and development young African talent for innovation and entrepreneurship.[①] The six finalists were selected from more than two hundred submitted African student projects. Those of contestants from five universities involved health care (1st Award), biological pharmacy and ecological farms (2nd Award), and water resources protection, recycling economy, and preschool education (3rd Award). The competition is significant in three aspects. It was the first time for an African student entrepreneurship competition in China, and it will definitely play an important role in the future of China-Africa cooperation. Secondly, it was initiated by and under the sponsorship of a private enterprise and presided over from the beginning to the end by civil organizations. Thirdly, it was

---

① http://www.chinafrica.cn/chinese/focus/201711/t20171114_800109951.html.

the first joint efforts university-institution effort to promote China-Africa cooperation with a focus on the development of young African talent.

Coincidentally, on November 15th, the African Students' Job Fair was held in Beijing with the theme of "The Belt and Road Initiative and Prospects of African Youth Employment" and organized by the Chinese People's Association for Friendship with Foreign Countries (CPAFFC) and the University of International Business and Economics. This was a recruitment effort of Chinese companies specifically for African students. A total of sixty-six state-owned, local, and private Chinese enterprises provided nearly five hundred job opportunities on the African continent. African youth both in China and Africa showed a great interest in the fair, with nearly four hundred attending the job fair in person and about one thousand young Africans from fifty-two African countries submitted their resumes online in advance.[①] With the opportunity for Chinese enterprises to enter Africa under the special opportunity of capacity cooperation, the road for China-African cooperation will become broader and broader.

Appendix

Confucius Institutes and Confucius Classrooms in African Countries(-Feb. 2017)		
Country	Confucius Institutes	Confucius Classrooms
Angola	Agostinho Neto University	
Benin	University of Abomey-Calavi	1

continued

---

① http://ge.cri.cn/20171116/c5c7ee5f-147e-a879-c315-8114acae8e4c.html.

Confucius Institutes and Confucius Classrooms in African Countries(-Feb. 2017)

Country	Confucius Institutes	Confucius Classrooms
Botswana	University of Botswana	
Burundi	University of Burundi	
Cameroon	University of Yaounde II	1
Cape Verde	University of Cape Verde	
Comoros		University of Comoros
The Republic of Congo	Marien Ngouabi University	
Côte d'Ivoire	University of Felix Houphouette Boigny	
Egypt	Cairo University, Suez Canal University	3 at the Nile Television of Egypt
Equatorial Guinea	National University of Equatorial Guinea	
Eritrea	National Board for Higher Education of Eritrea	
Ethiopia	Confucius Institute at TVET Institute of Ethiopia, Addis Ababa University	Mekelle University, Hawassa University (in total 5)
Ghana	University of Ghana, University of Cape Coast	
Kenya	University of Nairobi, Kenyatta University, Moi University	2 at CRI in Nairobi
Lesotho		Machabeng College International School
Liberia	University of Liberia	
Madagascar	Antananarivo University, University of Toamasina	1
Malawi	University of Malawi	
Mali		Lycee Askia Mohamed
Mauritius	University of Mauritius	
Morocco	University of Mohammed of V-Agdal University Hassan II	
Mozambique	Eduardo Mondlane University	
Namibia	University of Namibia	

continued

Confucius Institutes and Confucius Classrooms in African Countries(-Feb. 2017)		
Country	Confucius Institutes	Confucius Classrooms
Nigeria	University of Lagos, Nnambi Azikiwe University	1
Rwanda	College of Education, University of Rwanda	1
Senegal	Cheikh Anta Diop University, Dakar	
Seychelles	University of Seychelles	
Sierra Leone	University of Sierra Leone	
South Africa	University of Stellenbosch, University of Cape Town, Rhodes University, Durban University of Technology, University of Johannesburg	The Cape Academy of Mathematics, Science and Technology, Westerford High School, Chinese Culture and International Exchange Center (in total 5)
Sudan	University of Khartoum	
Tanzania	University of Dodoma, University of Dar es Salaam	Zanzibar Journalism and Mass Media College of Tanzania
Togo	University of Lome	
Tunisia		CRI in Sfax
Uganda	Makerere University	
Zambia	University of Zambia	2
Zimbabwe	University of Zimbabw	
Total	48 Confucius Institute	27 Confucius Classrooms

References

African Center for Economic Transformation (ACET). *Looking East: A Guide to Engaging China for Africa's Policy-Makers*, Vol. II, 2009. *Key Dimensions of Chinese Engagements in African* Countries. http://acetforafrica.org/site/wp-content/uploads/2009/05/lookingeastv2.pdf.

"African Communities in China Hail Xi's Visit." *China Daily*, March 24, 2013. "African Community Needs More Attention." *China Daily*, November 2, 2009. "Africans Create

Community in Guangzhou." *China Daily*, October 14, 2013. African Union. "Report of the Meeting of Experts from the Members of the States on the Definition of African Diaspora." April 11 – 12, 2005. Addis Ababa, Ethiopia.

Akomolafe, Femi. "No One is Laughing at the Asians Anymore." *New African*, Vol. 452 (June), 2006, pp. 48 – 50.

Amoah, Lloyd G. Adu. "Africa in China: Affirming African Agency in Africa-China Relations at the People to People Level." In James Shikwati (ed.), *China-Africa Partnership: The Quest for a Win-Win Relationship* (Nairobi: Inter Region Economic Network), 2012, pp. 104 – 115.

An Ran, et al. "African Students' Educational Needs And The Recruitment Style." *High Education Exploration*, Vol. 5, 2007, pp. 110 – 113.

Apithy, Sedozan. "The Policy Of Sino-African Educational Cooperation: What Does Africa Expect for Sino-African Educational Cooperation?" *Annual Review of African Studies in China 2012* (Beijing: Social Sciences Academic Press), 2013, pp. 326 – 329.

Baitie, Zahra. "On Being African in China." *The Atlantic*. August 28, 2013. (also https://www.theatlantic.com/china/archive/2013/08/on-being-african-in-china/279136/).

Bertoncello, Brigite and Sylvie Bredeloup. "La migration chinoise en Afrique: accélérateur du développement ou 'sanglot de l'homme noir'." *Afrique Contemporaine*, Vol. 218, 2006, pp. 199 – 224.

————. "De Hong Kong à Guangzhou, de nouveaux 'comptoirs' africains s'organisent." *Perspectives chinoises*, Vol. 98, No. 1, 2007a, pp. 98 – 110.

————. "The Emergence of New African 'Trading Posts' in Hong Kong and Guangzhou." *China Perspectives*, Vol. 1, 2007b, pp. 94 – 105.

————. "Chine-Afrique ou la valse des entrepreneurs-migrants." *Revue européenne des migrations internationales*, Vol. 25, No. 1, 2009, pp. 45 – 70.

Bertoncello, Brigite, Sylvie Bredeloup, and Olivier Pliez. "Hong Kong, Guangzhou, Yiwu: de nouveaux comptoirs africains en Chine." *Critique internationale*, Vol. 44, 2009, pp. 105 – 121.

Bodomo, Adams. "An Emerging African-Chinese Community in Hong Kong: The Case of Tsim Sha Tsui's Chungking Mansions." In Kwesi Kwaa Prah (ed.), *Afro-Chinese Relations: Past, Present and Future* (Cape Town: Centre for Advanced Studies in African Societies), 2007, pp. 367 – 389.

————. "Africa-China Relations in an Era of Globalization: The Role of African Trading Communities in China." *West Asia and Africa*, Vol. 8, 2009a, pp. 62 – 67.

————. "Africa-China Relations: Symmetry, Soft Power, and South Africa." *The China Review: An Interdisciplinary Journal on Greater China*, Vol. 9, No. 2, 2009b, pp. 169 – 178.

————. "The African Presence in Contemporary China." *China Monitor*. January (University of Stellenbosch, South Africa), 2009c.

————. "The African Trading Community in Guangzhou: An Emerging Bridge for Africa-China Relations." *The China Quarterly*, Vol. 203, 2010, pp. 693 – 707.

————. "African Students in China: A Case Study of Newly Arrived Students on FOCAC Funds at Chongqing University." PPT Outline, University of Hong Kong, 2011.

————. *Africans in China: A Sociocultural Study and Its Implications on Africa-China*

Relations. New York: Cambria Press, 2012.

———. "African Diaspora Remittances are Better Than Foreign Aid Funds." *World Economics*, Vol. 14, No. 4, 2013, pp. 21-28.

———. "Africans in China: A Bibliographical Survey." In Li Anshan and Lin Fengmin (eds.), *Annual Review of African Studies in China 2013* (Beijing: Social Sciences Academic Press [China]), 2014, pp. 109-121.

———. *Africans in China: Guangdong and Beyond*. New York: Diasporic Africa Press, 2016.

A. Bodomo, and Grace Ma, "From Guangzhou to Yiwu: Emerging Facets of the African Diaspora in China," *International Journal of African Renaissance Studies*, Vol. 5, No. 2, 2010, pp. 283-289.

———. "We are what we eat: food in the process of community formation and identity shaping among African traders in Guangzhou and Yiwu." *African Diaspora*, Vol. 5, No. 1, 2012, pp. 1-26.

Bodomo, A. and Roberval Silva. "Language matters: the role of linguistic identity in the establishment of the lusophone African community in Macau." *African Studies*, Vol. 71, No. 1, 2012, pp. 71-90.

Bork, T., et al. "Global Change, National Development Goals, Urbanization and International Migration in China: African Migration to Guangzhou and Foshan." In F. Kraas, S. Aggarwal, M. Coy and G. Mertins (eds.), *Megacities: Our Global Urban Future* (London: Springer), 2011, pp. 140-142.

Brautigam, Deborah. *The Dragon's Gift: The Real Story of China in Africa*. New York: Oxford University Press, 2009.

Bredeloup, S. "African trading posts in Guangzhou: emergent or recurrent commercial form?" *African Diaspora*, Vol. 5, No. 1, 2012, pp. 27-50.

Bredeloup, Silvye. "West-African Students Turned Entrepreneurs in Asian Trading Posts: A new facet of Globalization." *Urban Anthropology* (Special Issue on African Global Migration), Vol. 43, No. 1/2/3, 2014, pp. 17-56.

Brief Statistics of Foreign Students Studying in China, 2012-2015, Department of International Cooperation and Exchanges, Ministry of Education of China.

Chen, Changgui and Xie Liangao. *Approaching Nationalization: Research on International Exchange and Cooperation of Education in China*. Guangzhou: Guangdong Educational Press, 2010.

Cheng Tao and Lu Miaogeng (eds.). *Chinese Ambassadors Telling African Stories*. Beijing: World Affairs Press, 2013.

Cheng, Yinghong. "An African student's impression of China of the 1960s." *Phoenix Weekly* 14, 2014. http://www.ifengweekly.com/detil.php?id=4901.

China Africa Education Cooperation Group. *China Africa Education Cooperation*. Beijing: Peking University Press, 2005.

China Africa Project. "Leading China scholar Li Anshan recalls his experiences teaching African students." 2013. http://www.chinaafricaproject.com/leading-china-scholar-li-anshan-recalls-his-experiences-teaching-african-students-translation/Accessed June 4, 2014.

China Education Yearbook, 2003-2015. Beijing: People's Education Press.

Cissé, Daouda. "South-South migration and trade: African traders in China." 2013. *Policy Briefing* Center for Chinese studies n° 4/2013.

Cohen, Roberta. " China Has Used Prison Labor in Africa." *New York Times*, May 11, 1991. *The Conversation*. "China tops US and UK as destination for anglophone African students" June 28, 2017. http://theconversation.com/china-tops-us-and-uk-as-destination-for-anglophone-afri can-students-78967. (With website of sources of Ministry of Education of China; Accessed: June 30, 2017).

Cui Kuai, et al. "Study on the trade pattern of African community in Guangzhou." *Economic Outlook the Bohai Sea*, Vol. 5, 2009, pp. 14 – 17.

Dang Fangli. "British media's coverage of immigrants and its enlightenment to Chinese media: Basing on the event of Africans' protest in Guangzhou." *Tangdu Journa*, Vol. 29, No. 5, 2013, pp. 82 – 86.

Diederich, Manon. "Manoeuvring through the spaces of everyday life. Transnational experiences of African women in Guangzhou, China." Dissertation, University of Cologne, 2010.

Disima. "Cultural adaptation of foreign students in China." M. A. thesis, Nanjing Normal University, 2004.

Dittgen, Romain. "L'Afrique en Chine: l'autre face des relations sino-africaines?" Economie, China Institute, 2010.

Giese, Karsten, and Laurence Marfaing (eds.). "Entrepreneurs africains et chinois: Les impacts sociaux d'une recontre particulière." Paris: Karthala, 2015.

Gillespie, Sandra. *South-South transfer: A study of Sino-African exchange*. New York: Routledge, 2001.

Gong Sujuan. "A study on African students in China and their cross-cultural adaptation." *Journal of Kaifeng Institute of Education*, Vol. 34, No. 2, 2014, pp. 127 – 130.

Han, H. "Individual Grassroots Multilingualism in Africa Town in Guangzhou: The Role of States in globalization." *International Multilingual Research Journal*, Vol. 7, No. 1, 2013, pp. 83 – 97.

Harris, Joseph E. (ed.). *Global Dimensions of the African Diaspora*. 2nd ed. Washington, DC: Howard University Press, 1993.

Hashim, Ismail Hussein, et al. "Cultural and gender differences in perceiving Stressors: A cross-cultural investigation of African and Western Students at Chinese Colleges." *Psychological Science*, Vol. 26, No. 5, 2003, pp. 795 – 799.

Hashim, I. H., and Z. L. Yang. "Cultural and gender differences in perceiving stressors: a cross-cultural investigation of African and Western students in Chinese colleges." *Stress and Health*, Vol. 19, No. 4, 2003, pp. 217 – 225.

Haugen, H. Ø. "Chinese exports to Africa: Competition, complementarity and cooperation between micro-level actors." *Forum for Development Studies*, Vol. 38, No. 2, 2011, pp. 157 – 176.

———. "Nigerians in China: A second state of immobility." *International Migration*, Vol. 50, No. 2, 2012, pp. 65 – 80.

———. "China's recruitment of African university students: policy efficacy and unintended outcomes." *Globalisation, Societies and Education*, Vol. 11, No. 3, 2013a, pp. 315 – 344.

————. "African Pentecostal Migrants in China: Marginalization and the Alternative Geography of a Mission Theology." *African Studies Review*, Vol. 56, No. 1, 2013b, pp. 81–102.

He Wenping. "A summary analysis of China-Africa educational exchanges and cooperation: development phases and challenges." *West Asia and Africa*, Vol. 3, 2007, pp. 13–18.

Hevi, Emmanuel. 1963. *An African Student in China*. London: Pall Mall Press. Hu, Jintao. "Written Statement by President Hu Jintao of China at the High-Level Meeting on Financing for Development at the 60th Session of the United Nations." September15, 2005. http://politics.people.com.cn/GB/1024/3696504.html. Accessed June 12, 2017.

Jiang, Chun, and Guo Yingde. *History of China-Arab Relations*. Beijing: Economic Daily Press, 2001.

Ketema, Meskela et al. "The Research on Educational Cooperation Between China an Africa: An African Perspective." *Studies in Foreign Education*, Vol. 36, No. 1, 2009, pp. 50–53.

King, Kenneth. *China's Aid and Soft Power in Africa The Case of Education and Training*. Suffolk: James Currey, 2013.

————. "China's cooperation in education and training with Kenya: A different model?" *International Journal of Educational Development*, Vol. 30, No. 5, 2010, pp. 488–496.

Larkin, Bruce D. *China and Africa 1949–1970: The Foreign Policy of People's Republic of China*. Berkeley: University of California Press, 1971.

Li, Anshan. "African Studies in China in the Twentieth Century: A Historiographical Survey." *African Studies Review*, Vol. 48, No. 1, 2005, pp. 59–87.

————. *Chinese Medical Cooperation in Africa: With Special Emphasis on the Medical Teams and Anti-Malaria Campaign*. Discussion Paper 52, Uppsala: Norkiska Afrikainstitutet, 2011.

————. "China and Africa: Cultural Similarity and Mutual Learning." In James Shikwati (ed.), *China-Africa Partnership The Quest for a Win-Win Relationship* (Nairobi: Inter Region Economic Network), 2012, pp. 93–97.

————. "African Countries Encouraged to 'Look East'." March 28, *Guangming Daily*, 2013a.

————. "My African students." In Cheng Tao and Lu Miaogeng, *Chinese Ambassadors Telling African Stories* (Beijing: World Affairs Press), 2013b, pp. 156–168.

————. "Changing Discourse on China-Africa Relations since the 1990s." *World Economy and Politics* Vol. 2, 2014, pp. 19–47.

————. "African Diaspora in China: Reality, research and reflection." *The Journal of Pan African Studies*, Vol. 7, No. 10, 2015a, pp. 10–43.

————. "Contact between China and Africa before Vasco da Gama: Archeology, Document and Historiography." *World History Studies*, Vol. 2, No. 1, 2015b, pp. 34–59.

————. "A Long-Time Neglected Subject: China-Africa People-to-People Contact." In Garth Shelton, Funeka Yazini April, and Li Anshan (eds.), *FOCAC 2015: A New Beginning of China-Africa Relations* (Pretoria: Africa Institute of South Africa), 2015c, pp. 446–475.

————. "African Studies in China in the 21st Century: A Historiographical Survey."

Brazilian Journal of African Studies, Vol. 1, No. 2, 2016, pp. 48 – 88.

Li Anshan, et al. *FOCAC Twelve Years Later: Achievements, Challenges and the Way Forward*. Uppsala: Nordic Africa Institute, 2012.

Li, Anshan and Liu Haifang. "The evolution of the Chinese policy of funding African students and an evaluation of the effectiveness." Draft report for UNDP, 2013.

―――. (eds.). *Annual Review of African Studies in China (2015)*. Beijing: Social Sciences Academic Press, 2017.

Li, Baoping. "On the Issues of China-Africa Educational Cooperation." 2006. http://www.docin.com/p-747065460.html. Accessed June 2, 2017.

Li Jiangtao and Li Xiang. "China is my second hometown: African students' life in Beijing." 2006. http://news.xinhuanet.com/world/2006 - 10/21/content_5232813.htm.

Li, Jun. "Ideologies, strategies and higher education development: a comparison of China's university partnerships with the Soviet Union and Africa over space and time." *Comparative Education*, Vol. 53, No. 2, 2017, pp. 245 – 264.

Li Zhigang, et al. "The African enclave of Guangzhou: A case study of Xiaobeilu." *ACTA Geographica Sinica*, Vol. 63, No. 2, 2008, pp. 207 – 218.

―――. "The local response of transnational social space under globalization in urban China: A case study of African enclave in Guangzhou." *Geographical Research*, Vol. 28, No. 4, 2009a., pp. 920 – 932.

―――. "An African enclave in China: The making of a new transnational urban space." *Eurasian Geography and Economics*, Vol. 50, No. 6, 2009b, pp. 699 – 719.

Li Zhigang, et al. "China's 'Chocolate City': An Ethnic Enclave in a Changing Landscape." *African Diaspora*, Vol. 5, 2012, pp. 51 – 72.

Li Zhigang and Du Feng. "Production of China's new social space in city under 'transnational entrepreneurialism' A case study on African economic zone in Guangzhou." *Urban Space Studies*, Vol. 36, No. 8, 2012a, pp. 25 – 31.

―――. "The transnational making of 'Chocolate City' in Guangzhou." *Renwen Dil.*, Vol. 27, No. 6, 2012b, pp. 1 – 6.

Liu, Haifang. "China-Africa Relations through the Prism of Culture — The Dynamics of China's Cultural Diplomacy with Africa." *Journal of Current Chinese Affairs (China aktuell)*, Vol. 3, 2008, pp. 9 – 44.

―――. "A study on the evolution and effect of China's scholarship policy towards African students." In Li Anshan and Liu Haifang (eds.), *Annual Review of African Studies in China 2015* (Beijing: Social Sciences Academic Press), 2017, pp. 141 – 192.

Liu, Haifang and Jamie Monson. "Railway Time: Technology Transfer and the Role of Chinese Experts in the History of TAZARA." In Ton Dietz, et al. (eds.), *African Engagements: Africa Negotiating an Emerging Multipolar World* (Leiden and Boston: Brill), 2011, pp. 226 – 251.

Lin Lunlun and Ren Mengya. "A socioliguistic study upon Chinese language learning concept of African overseas students." *Journal of Hanshan Normal University*, Vol. 31, No. 5, 2010, pp. 32 – 37.

Liu, P. H. "Petty annoyances? Revisiting John Emmanuel Hevi's *An African Student in China* after 50 years." *China An International Journal*, Vol. 11, No. 1, 2013, pp.

131 – 145.

Lokongo, Antoine Roger. "My Chinese connection." *CHINAFRICA* 50, 2012.

Long Xia and Xiong Lijun. "The influence of Sino-African cultural difference on the education of African students in China: Taking Angola students as the example." *Journal of Chongqing University of Education*, Vol. 27, No. 1, 2014, pp. 133 – 136.

Lou Shizhou and Xu Hui. "The development and transition of China-Africa educational cooperation in the new period." *Educational Research*, Vol. 10, 2012, pp. 28 – 33.

Lyons, M., et al. "The 'third tier' of globalization: African traders in Guangzhou." *City*, Vol. 12, No. 2, 2008, pp. 196 – 206.

———. "In the dragon's den: African traders in Guangzhou." *Journal of Ethnic and Migration Studies*, Vol. 38, No. 5, 2012, pp. 869 – 888.

———. "The China-Africa Value Chain: Can Africa's Small-Scale Entrepreneurs Engage Successfully in Global Trade?" *African Studies Review*, Vol. 56, No. 3, 2013, pp. 77 – 100.

Ma Enyu. "Walking into the Yiwu Muslim community." *China Religion*, Vol. 6, 2010, pp. 56 – 57.

———. "Yiwu mode and Sino-African relations." *Journal of Cambridge Studies*, Vol. 7, No. 3, 2012, pp. 93 – 108.

Marfaing, Laurence and Alena Thiel. "*Agents of Translation*: West African Entrepreneurs in China as Vectors of Social Change. Working Paper, No. 4, DFG Priority Program 1448, 2014. http://www. spp1448. de/fileadmin/media/galleries/SPP_Administration/Working_Pa per _Series/SPP1448_WP4_Marfaing-Thiel_final. pdf.

Marsh, Jenni. "Afro-Chinese marriages boom in Guangzhou: but will it be 'til death do us part'?" June 1, 2014. http://www. scmp. com/magazines/post-magazine/article/1521076/afro-chinese-marriages-boom-guangzhou-will-it-be-til-death. Accessed June 24, 2014.

Mathews, G. "Les traders africains a Kong Hong (Hong Kong) et en Chine", *Les Temps Modernes*, No. 657 (Janvier-mars, 2000), 2000, pp. 110 – 124.

Mathews, G. and Yang, Y. "How Africans pursue low-end globalization in Hong Kong and mainland China." *Journal of Current Chinese Affairs*, Vol. 41, No. 2, 2012, pp. 95 – 120.

Monson, J., *Africa's Freedom Railway: How a Chinese Development Project Changed Lives and Livelihoods in Tanzania*. Bloomington and Indianapolis: Indiana University Press, 2009.

Morais, I. "'China Wahala': The Tribulations of Nigerian 'Bushfallers' in a Chinese Territory." *Transtext(e)s Transculture: Journal of Global Cultural Studies*, Vol. 5, 2009, pp. 1 – 22.

Müller, A. and R. Wehrhahn. "Transnational business networks of African intermediaries in China: Practices of networking and the role of experiential knowledge." *DIE ERDE-Journal of the Geographical Society of Berlin*, Vol. 144, No. 1, 2013, pp. 82 – 97.

Müller, Angelo. "New Migration Processes in Contemporary China — The Constitution of African Trader Networks in Guangzhou." *Geographische Zeitschrif*, Vol. 99, No. 2, 2011, pp. 104 – 122.

Niu, Changsong. "A survey of African students' satisfaction of Chinese Government Scholarship." 2016. http://www. docin. com/p-1445264169. html. Accessed: June

25, 2017.
Osnos, Evan. "The Promised Land: Guangzhou's Canaan market and the rise of an African merchant class." *The New Yorker*, February 9 – 16, 2009, pp. 50 – 56.
Pilling, David. "Ports and roads mean China is 'winning in Africa.'" May 6, 2017. Construction Review Online. https://constructionreviewonline.com/2017/05/ports-and-roads-mean-china-is-winning-in-africa/.
Pinto, Jeanette. "The African native in diaspora." *African and Asian Studies*, Vol. 5, No. 3 – 4, 2006, pp. 383 – 397.
Pliez, O. "Toutes les routes de la soie mènent in Yiwu (Chine). Entrepreneurs et migrants musulmans dans un comptoir économique chinois." *Espace Géographique*, 2, 2010, pp. 132 – 145.
Redvers, Louise. "Angola's Chinese-Built ghost town". July 2, 2012. http://www.bbc.com/news/world-africa-18646243.
Rennie, N. "The lion and the dragon: African experiences in China." *Journal of African Media Studies*, Vol. 1, No. 3, 2009, pp. 379 – 414.
Sautman, Barry. "Anti-Black Racism in Post-Mao China." *The China Quarterly*, Vol. 138, 1994, pp. 413 – 437.
Seidelman, Raymond. "The Anti-African Protests: More Than Just Chinese Racism." *The Nation*, February 13, 1989.
Shelton, Garth, Funeka Yazini April, and Li Anshan (eds.). *FOCAC 2015: A New Beginning of China-Africa Relations*. Pretoria: Africa Institute of South Africa, 2015.
Shikwati, James (ed.). *China-Africa Partnership The quest for a win-win relationship* (Nairobi: Inter Region Economic Network), 2012, pp. 93 – 97.
Sulliven, M. J. "The 1988 – 1989 Nanjing Anti-African Protests: Racial Nationalism or National Racism?" *The China Quarterly*, Vol. 138, 1994, pp. 438 – 457.
Tsui, Chak-Pong Gordon. "African university students in China's Hong Kong: Motivations, aspirations, and further exchanges." In Adams Bodomo (ed.), *Africans in China: Guangdong and Beyond* (New York: Cambria Press), 2016, pp. 119 – 137.
Wang, Hanjie. "The spread and distribution of African drums in China." In Li Anshan and Liu Haifang (eds.), *Annual Review of African Studies in China (2012)* (Beijing: Social Sciences Academic Press), 2013, pp. 442 – 458.
Wang Luxin. "Educational exchange and cooperation between China and African countries." In Lu Ting-en and Ma Ruimin (eds.), *China and Africa* (Beijing: Peking University Press), 2000.
Wu, Bin. "Links between Chinese International students and overseas Chinese communities: An empirical study in Nottingham, UK." *Overseas Chinese History Studies*, Vol. 2, 2015, pp. 1 – 11.
———. "Local Engagement of Chinese international students in host societies: A perspective of diasporic Chinese community building." *The International Journal of Diasporic Chinese Studies*, Vol. 8, No. 2, 2016, pp. 13 – 30.
Xu Hui. "Sino-Africa educational cooperation under the FOCAC framework." *Educational Development Research*, Vol. 9, 2007, pp. 1 – 7.
Xu Tao. "An analysis on Africans social relations and interaction logics in Guangzhou." *Youth*

Research, Vol. 5, 2009a, pp. 71-86.

―――. "African's social support in Guangzhou: Weakening, fracture and reconstruction." *South China Population*, Vol. 24, No. 4, 2009b, pp. 34-44.

―――. "Re-analysis of the relations of social contact of African merchants in Guangzhou." *Journal of Zhejiang Normal University*, Vol. 4, 2011, pp. 10-15.

―――. "Analysis of characteristics of the behavior of African merchants in Guangzhou." *Journal of Zhejiang Normal University*, Vol. 4, 2012, pp. 55-63.

―――. *The Social Adaptations of African Merchants in China*. Hangzhou, China: Zhejiang People's Press, 2013.

Yang, Y. "African Traders in Guangzhou." In G. Mathews, G. L. Ribero and C. A. Vega (eds.), *Globalization from Below: The World's Other Economy*. London and New York: Routledge, 2013.

Yan, Hairong and Barry Sautman. "Chasing Ghosts: Rumours and Representations of the Export of Chinese Convict Labour to Developing Countries." *The China Quarterly*, Vol. 210, 2012, pp. 398-418.

―――. *China in Africa: Discourses and Reality*. Beijing: Social Sciences Academic Press, 2017.

Yang, Mengjie, et al. "China-hand's dream of mandarin." November 28, 2016. Chinanews, http://www.chinanews.com/sh/2016/11-28/8076600.shtml.

Ye Shuai. "A comparative analysis of the cross-cultural communication based on the Somali students and the Chinese students on time and family concepts." *Kexue Wenhui*, Vol. 11, 2011, pp. 30-31.

Yi Pei and Xiong Lijun. "An empirical study of intercultural adaptation of African students in China." *Journal of Shenyang University (Social Science)*, Vol. 15, No. 3, 2013, pp. 364-368.

Zeleza, Paul Tiyambe. "Rewriting the African Diaspora: Beyond the Black Atlantic." *African Affairs*, Vol. 104, No. 414, 2005, pp. 35-68.

―――. "The challenges of studying African diasporas." *African Sociological Review*, Vol. 12, No. 2, 2008, pp. 4-21.

Zhang, Tieshan. *Friendship Road: A Report on the Construction of Tanzania-Zambia Railway*, Beijing: China Economic and Foreign Trade Press, 1999.

Zheng Jianghua. "Research on safety management of African students on university campus." *Journal of Tianjin University of Technology and Education*, Vol. 22, No. 4, 2012, pp. 72-74.

Zheng Jianghua. "Construction of community management system for foreign students in universities." *Vocational and Technical Education*, Vol. 34, No. 23, 2013a, pp. 66-68.

Zheng Jianghua, "Exploration of compound applied talents training mode on African Students," *Journal of Tianjin University of Technology and Education*, Vol. 23, No. 4, 2013, pp. 64-70.

略论丝绸之路历史对当代中非
教育交流与产能合作的启示

张 象

> **内容摘要**：中非交往的历史是与丝绸之路的历史结合在一起的。今天我们探讨中非之间的教育与产能交流合作问题，不能忘掉此"初心"，要从其中吸取历史的经验与教训。本文旨在从丝绸之路的历史史实和故事中，谈一些与中非教育交流与产能合作有关的启示，供讨论参考。
> **关 键 词**：丝绸之路历史；中非教育交流；产能合作；启示
> **作者简介**：张象，南开大学历史学教授，中国非洲史研究会与中国非洲问题研究会顾问

天津职业技术师范大学和非洲联盟委员会联合举办了"中非教育交流与产能合作国际研讨会"。这在中国非洲学界还是第一次，在中非关系史上也是一次罕见的活动，具有历史意义。特别是这次会议的背景非同一般。非洲国家完成独立大业后，正在非洲联盟的倡议下实现非洲复兴梦，急需中非交流合作，研讨新机遇与新问题。从中方讲刚提出

了"一带一路"倡议,最近又在中共十九大提出构建人类命运共同体的方略。如何将新的外交理念,落实到中非关系的具体交流合作领域,更急需创新研究,所以这次会议也具有重要的现实意义。

探讨此课题需要多方面研究,历史的考察则是不可忽视的。习近平主席在访问非洲时多次谈到要重视历史传统。他明确指出:"一带一路"传承"古丝绸之路的精神",最近在中共十九大他又强调要"不忘初心"。中非交往的历史是与丝绸之路的历史结合在一起的。这是一条东西方国家包括中非在内的物质文明与精神文明交流的国际大道,创造着人类历史的进步,科技文化的交流是其中的内容之一。今天我们探讨中非之间的教育与产能交流合作问题,不能忘掉此"初心",要从其中吸取历史的经验与教训。

本人是研究历史的老学人,从 20 世纪 60 年代起就投入非洲史的教学研究,故在这里愿从丝绸之路的历史史实和故事中,谈一些与会议主旨有关的启示,供大家讨论参考。我认为有如下几点值得注意:

一、丝绸之路的起始史告诉我们,要进行中非之间的项目交流一定要把人民的愿望和需求的考查摆在首位

丝绸之路是东西方的文明交融之路。它最初是由沿线各地人民为追求美好的生活,通过一站传一站的间接交流方式而开创出来的。古代世界有四大文明中心,最西为非洲的埃及,最东为中国。无论是中国的丝绸,还是古埃及的玻璃都有很高的技术含量,丝绸是高级手工业制品,玻璃是硅酸盐化合物,制成宝石球等器物需要高工艺,拿出交流更是不易。但在上古时期,在东西两大文明中心之间的交流实现了。其动力是沿途人民的需求帮助。这种民间的间接交流从何时开始,至今尚难确定。但至迟在公元前 6 世纪由于波斯帝国修了东至埃及、西至大夏的"御道"。随后希腊亚历山大帝国打通了到印度河流域的通路。这种间接交流完全可能了。

今天西方国家各语种"丝"的发音,"Se"、"Silk"都来自汉语,这是民间交流的证明。公元前 2 世纪,汉武帝为了抵抗匈奴的侵扰,派张骞通西域,不幸被匈奴扣押了 10 多年,他是在人民的帮助下而逃脱的。由于他秉承了沿途人民求和平交流的丝路精神,成功地到达大夏,使丝路由民间转向官方交往。

今天我们开展中非的各项交流只有先调查研究清楚非洲人民的需求和其实际情况,再进行才有效。例如,中国发展模式与非洲的对接问题,必须先了解非洲人民的真实反应才行。如果片面强调"用中国视角研究和对待非洲"则是错误的。

我们对来华学习的非洲学生,要求他们多了解中国的情况,但绝不要求他们回国后照搬"中国模式",而是要鼓励他们与非洲的实际相结合,有所创新。

二、弘扬丝路精神是中非间各类项目合作的前提

习近平主席满怀深情地说:"古代丝绸之路是一条贸易之路,更是一条友谊之路。在中华民族同其他民族的友好交往中,逐步形成了以和平合作、开放包容、互学互鉴、互利共赢为特征的丝绸之路精神。"[①]此精神萌芽于丝路早期民间的间接交往时期,后被张骞、班超等使团采纳,形成古代中国政府的外交方略。古代世界分为南北对立两大部分,北部为游牧世界,南部为农耕世界,经常发生冲突。东方大国汉王朝受匈奴的侵扰,西方大国罗马(中国古称大秦)受日耳曼人的侵扰,罗马的方针是向南侵略北非、埃及以补偿。最后结果是罗马帝国崩溃。汉王朝弘扬了丝路精神,团结了西域诸国战胜了匈奴,使汉文化继续发扬。到了 7 世纪中古时期,世界分为三大部分,西部是信仰基督的文明区,东部是信奉儒学与佛学的文明区,中部为信奉伊斯兰的阿

---

① 《习近平谈治国理政》(第二卷),北京:外文出版社 2017 年版,第 50 页。

拉伯文明区。西方世界对阿拉伯世界采取敌对态度,视其为异端,多次发动"十字军东征",长达数百年之久。东方中国则不然,弘扬丝路精神与阿拉伯世界友好、合作、包容互惠,使丝绸之路大发展。唐朝以前虽有海路,但仍是以陆路为主。只有从唐朝起国家兴盛了,并与阿拉伯人合作相处,一同从事海洋活动,才有丝路的海陆路并举。宋元时期海上丝绸之路大发展。明初郑和七下西洋多次到达非洲,使海上丝路达到顶峰。这种交流促使了中国指南针、印刷术、火药三大发明的问世,领先于世界。

所以今天我们与非洲开展各项交流活动必须与"一带一路"倡议相结合。必须不忘丝路精神,要使国家富起来、强起来。科学文化才能领先世界。具体交流活动项目决不能脱离国家的总方针、总政策。这是历史经验告知我们的。

三、丝路经验还告诉我们,开展项目合作必须与发展经济相结合

从唐宋到明与清初,中国的科技在世界上是领先的。海上丝路的昌盛,是与经济的发达分不开的。这时期丝路交流物品,瓷器、茶叶取代了丝绸的地位。考古在东非沿海的基尔瓦、蒙巴萨、桑给巴尔、摩加迪萨等地都有大量的中国古瓷器和钱币被发现,说明这些地区与中国已有频繁的经贸交流。特别是这些瓷器、钱币还流传至相邻的内地,如津巴布韦、刚果(金)等地。史实说明从中国的泉州、广州到阿拉伯半岛的麦加、巴格达,再到东非沿海各地城邦,已形成一条繁荣的经济带。这时斯瓦希里文明的兴起,《基尔瓦编年史》等文献的出现,都证明这一情况是存在的。可以说将近千年世界的形势是先进的东方面对落后的西方。《马可·波罗游记》等著作都说明此情况。14世纪,中国地理学家绘制的非洲地图是倒三角形,很实际准确。而西方学者绘制的非洲地图是无边际的一片,只画一个国王手拿黄金,表示这里富有。西方对非洲和世界的了解远远落后于东方国家。

今天随着"一带一路"倡议的落实,许多中外合作项目涌现了,例如,扼阿拉伯海,中巴合作修建起瓜达尔港,扼亚丁湾中国兴建吉布提基地和通往亚的斯贝亚的铁路,东非重镇蒙巴萨至内罗毕的铁路已建成并向内地深入,坦桑尼亚新港正在扩建辅助坦赞铁路功能。可以说一条新型经济带在萌生,与古代的经济带相呼应。所以今天我们要不忘发展经济的革新理念,和建设现代化的经济体系。这是历史的重要启迪。

习近平主席在论及"不忘初心,继续前进"时指出:"今天,我们回顾历史,不是为了从成功中寻求慰藉……而是为了总结历史经验,把握历史规律,增强开始前进的勇气和力量。"[①]丝路历史也给我们诸多教训值得记取。

例如,交流项目的不断创新问题,就很值得我们深思。古丝路的发展动力是皇权。"天朝观念"、"大国思维"的作怪,只重视"朝贡",并不重视对"朝贡国"的研究。"三大发明"的外传我方从不禁止,但却不注重其再创新。马克思分析中国三大发明在西欧所起的作用,在中国没有出现,它们促进西方社会的改革,资本主义的兴起。"火药把骑士阶层炸得粉碎,指南针打开世界市场并建立了殖民地,而印刷术则变成新教工具,总的来说变成科学复兴的手段,变成对精神发展创造必要前提的最强大的杠杆。"[②]资本的原始积累使西方国家富起来了,西方殖民主义的掠夺剥削却使东方国家变成殖民地半殖民地,东方落后西方的态势出现了。约 500 年的苦难,折磨着数亿亚非地区人民。这一沉痛的历史教训要永远记着。在项目交流时,无论中方还是非洲方都要继续创新。

四、项目交流一定不忘坚持时代潮流的方向

15—16 世纪世界历史的时代潮流正在变化之中,世界朝着整体化方向

---

① 《习近平谈治国理政》(第二卷),第 32 页。
② 马克思:《机器、自然力和科学的应用》,北京:人民出版社 1978 年版,第 67 页。

发展，当时中国与亚非诸国的领导人并不认识到这一点。中国明、清政府，面对逆时代潮流的诸多事件，便实行"锁国"、"海禁"政策，郑和的壮举夭折了。东方将海上丝绸之路的主导权和基地，拱手让给西方殖民主义者。它们先是利用海上丝绸之航路线和交流商品开辟新航路，大发横财。进而贩卖鸦片，开来军舰。用火炮打开中国商贸大门，篡夺丝绸之路主导权，并改变其性质，导致丝绸之路的消失。这是最悲惨的历史教训。

用马克思主义总结历史的经验教训至关重要，中共十九大号召"不忘初心，牢记使命"。我们在回顾历史之后，要高举中国特色社会主义伟大旗帜，为全面建成小康社会和实现中华民族的伟大复兴，建成社会主义现代化的强国而不懈奋斗。同时要深入开展非洲研究，配合我国全方位外交布局，帮助非洲国家探索符合本国国情的可持续发展道路，尽快实现复兴梦。中国人民要与非洲人民一道，共建和平、民主、包容、互惠、安全、绿色的人类命运共同体，共创世界美好的未来。

Development as an Intellectual Process: The Case of Africa

Ngaka Sehlare Makgetlaneng

Abstract: This work deals with development in Africa. It maintains that development is an intellectual process characterised by the primacy of production of goods for the satisfaction of human needs and demands though their distribution. It maintains that African countries provide other countries, especially those outside the continent with employment, wealth and development opportunities by exporting to them their natural resources in raw form. Prices of these resources are relatively cheap while those of finished products they import from these countries are relatively expensive. These goods are made from products of African countries. The solution to this structural problem is for African countries to have requisite knowledge to be able to convert their natural resources into finished products so as to primarily satisfy their national needs and demands. Africa's mineral and agricultural resources are enormous and attractive for investment and catalysts of its development. Knowledge, skills and talents of its organic intellectuals committed to its development should be used best and most effectively as a proud continental asset in the advancement and achievement of development satisfying needs and demands of the majority of its people. Without this intellectual endeavour, the continent will not achieve its developmental objectives.

Keywords: Development; Intellectual Process; Africa

Author: Ngaka Sehlare Makgetlaneng, Rated researcher in African Affairs, Senior Researcher, Institute for African Renaissance Studies, College of Graduate Studies, University of South Africa, Pretoria, South Africa

Today the wealth of nations is built on knowledge and less on raw materials.

— Nahas Angula[1]

The Centrality of the People in Development

The African people as social agents for their development and of their countries and continent was confirmed, among others, by the International Conference on Popular Participation in the Recovery and Development in Africa, held in Arusha, Tanzania from 12 to 16 February 1990. The conference, a collaboration effort between African governments, the United Nations agencies and African non-governmental organizations, pointed out that the crisis engulfing Africa was not only an economic process, but also human, legal, political and social process. It was a process of unprecedented and unacceptable proportions manifested "not only in abysmal declines in economic indicators and trends", but also "more tragically and glaringly in

---

[1] Nahas Angula, "Enhancing Namibia's Potential for Growth," *The Namibian* (Windhoek), 25 October 2011, p. 7.

the suffering, hardship and impoverishment of the vast majority of African people."① Pointing out that "the political contest of socio-economic development has been characterized, in many instances, by an over-centralization of power and impediments to the effective participation of the overwhelming majority of the people in social, political and economic development," it concluded that:

As a result, the motivation of the majority of African people and their organizations to contribute their best to the development process, and to the betterment of their own well-being as well as their say in national development has been severely constrained and curtailed and their collective and individual creativity has been undervalued and underutilized. ②

The conference affirmed that the majority of the African people are indispensable to the achievement of the continent's sustainable development. The crisis engulfing the continent cannot be "resolved and the human and economic conditions improved without the full and effective contribution, creativity and popular enthusiasm of the vast majority of the people."③ Even "nations cannot be built without the popular support and full participation of the people." It concluded that the structural transformation of political

---

① International Conference on Popular Participation in the Recovery and Development Process in Africa, African Charter for Popular Participation in Development and Transformation, *Africa's Development Thinking Since Independence: A Reader*, Pretoria: Africa Institute of South Africa, 2002, p. 297.
② Ibid.
③ Ibid.

power relations is a prerequisite condition to the resolution of "Africa's perpetual economic crisis" and "socio-economic development" problems.[①] African countries have no choice except to recognize practically, "more than ever before", that their "greatest resource is their people and that it is through their active and full participation that Africa can surmount the difficulties that lie ahead."[②]

Unfortunately, some African political leaders working together with their external allies have superseded the masses of the African people as social agents of development of their countries and continent. They have also made the continent more vulnerable to external actors antagonistic to the achievement of its development. According to Claude Ake, the consequences of their programme of action is that what "prevails is development against the people — not of them or for them."[③] The obsession of some African leaders and their organic intellectuals with what they regard as the marginalisation of Africa by developed countries is not the problem. The point is that "the problem is not Africa's marginality to the rest of the world but the marginalisation of Africans to the development of Africa" by the majority of African leaders. The masses of "the people of Africa will have to empower themselves to repossess their own development."[④] According to Ake, development is "not economic growth."

---

① International Conference on Popular Participation in the Recovery and Development Process in Africa, African Charter for Popular Participation in Development and Transformation, *Africa's Development Thinking Since Independence: A Reader*, Pretoria: Africa Institute of South Africa, 2002, p. 297.
② Ibid.
③ Claude Ake, *Democracy and Development in Africa*, Washington, D. C: Brookings Institution Press, 1996, p. 118.
④ Ibid., pp. 122 – 123.

It is "the process by which the people create and recreate themselves and their life circumstances to realise higher levels of civilisation in accordance with their own choices and values." It is the process which the people "must do for themselves." If "people are the end of development, they are also necessarily its agent and its means."[①]

Fantu Cheru agrees with Ake when he points out that the "overwhelming consensus among the poor in Africa today is that development" since the achievement of political independence in their countries "has been an instrument of social control." For them, "development has always meant the progressive modernization of their poverty."[②] Given their continued misfortune or the "absence of freedom, the sacrifice of culture, the loss of solidarity and self-reliance," they have lost confidence that their political leaders will solve their problems or they have decided to be their own liberators:

> *As such, the struggle for emancipation from debt-bondage must not rest on the very bankers, finance ministers, and foreign governments responsible for building up the debt in the first place. The oppressed themselves must now seize this opportunity and make their own history. Otherwise, they will continue to pay dearly for the extravagant mistakes of the powerful.*[③]

---

① Claude Ake, *Democracy and Development in Africa*, Washington, D. C: Brookings Institution Press, 1996, p. 125.
② Fantu Cheru, *The Silent Revolution in Africa: Debt, Development and Democracy*, London: Zed Books, 1993, p. 20.
③ Ibid.

Development requires members of societies with qualities conducive for its achievement and sustenance. This means that its realisation requires people with exceptional intellectual qualities and leadership in the production, dissemination and utilisation of knowledge, skills and talents, training and extensive experience in education and training, and research. The masses of the people cannot achieve their development without African scholars serving as their organic intellectuals in playing a leading role using their knowledge and talents in leading and serving in institutions and organisations.

Development as an intellectual process

Development is an intellectual process in which resources are produced and distributed for their use by members of society for the satisfaction of their needs and demands. Central to this process is production not consumption in terms of importance. This means that creation is primary in relation to distribution or redistribution of resources. There is a primacy of creation over distribution or redistribution. Distribution or redistribution of goods is a secondary process depending on the creation of what should be consumed for the satisfaction of the human needs and demands. Human beings as actors are social agents for development refusing to be fields of action acted upon by structural enemies of progress for their interests antagonistic to theirs.

Development is an intellectual process in which the creation of a society's resources to ensure a better life of its citizens is a central issue. The best, most effective and efficient way to do justice to this cause is to place the people at the centre of development in terms of policy, debate and advocacy. The people are the "real wealth" of the nation whose development should be the task of creating and sustaining environment in which they enjoy creative, healthy, secure and long life. This view of the link between the people and development is "often forgotten in the immediate concern with the accumulation of commodities and financial wealth."[1]

Development is the process about the people enlarging their choices. It is "more than GNP growth, more than income and wealth and more about producing commodities and accumulating capital."[2] The most critical of these choices are to "live a long and healthy life, to be educated and to have access to resources needed for a decent standard of living. Additional choices include political freedom, guaranteed human rights and personal self-respect." This means that development as an intellectual process of creation should "at least create a conducive environment for people, individually and collectively, to develop their full potential and to have a reasonable chance of leading productive and creative lives in accord with their needs and interests."[3] Briefly, development is the process of "structuring a society's conditions of life to enable its citizens' lives to be better."[4]

The restructuring of the educational system and internal socio-political and economic relations is of vital importance in sustaining this comprehensive view of development not only as economic process, but also

---

[1] Mahbub ul Haq, quoted in Human Development Report 1990, *United Nations Development Programme*, New York: Oxford University Press, 1990, p. 9.
[2] Ibid., p. 1.
[3] Ibid.
[4] John McMurtry, *The Cancer Stage of Capitalism: From Crisis to Cure*, London: Pluto Press, 2013, p. 74.

as the totality of the social, political, economic, human resources development, cultural, religious and technological process achieved by the people in creating, expanding and sustaining their choices. This is of a particular political, economic and ideological relevance to the African continent where development, because of its low level, is often viewed in an economistic way or only in terms of its economic aspect.

Africa's human capital is of vital importance for the success of its development efforts. While its sectors of its economy such as mining and agriculture are popularly regarded as key drivers of its development, the indispensable role of its human capital should be recognised in theory and practice. Economic sectors derive their importance to development from human beings using their skills and determination. The role of Africans with requisite knowledge whose "main value" lies "in its ability to help us develop our potentials and live a more fulfilling and independent life"[1] is critical in providing Africa with means to successfully confront structural impediments to development. Their role can best be understood if we come to grips with the reality that the majority of African countries do "not yet have the necessary technologies, institutions and organizational skills to deal" with "adverse consequences" of these structural impediments to development such as "poor climate (arctic and tropical), landlockedness, abundant natural resources, ethnic divisions, poor institutions and bad culture."[2]

Africa's mineral and agricultural endowments are enormous and attractive for investment as well as catalysts of its development. The

---

[1] Ha-Joon Chang, *23 Things They Don't Tell You about Capitalism*, London: Penguin Books, 2010, p. 189.
[2] Ibid., p. 113.

articulated combination of the use of Africa's intellectual power and authority and its enormous mineral, agricultural and tourism endowments is the continent's best, most effective and indispensable weapon in its struggle to achieve its sustainable development. The continent's intellectuals who are experts and professionals in various fields should build a solid foundation for their leadership role in the achievement of its development. Without best and most effectively using their skills and talents in deploying mineral and agricultural resources of their countries, the continent will not achieve its sustainable development satisfying the needs and demands and interests of its people. Without its organic intellectuals committed to its development, Africa cannot achieve its strategic development objectives.

The success of development agenda of Africa is the process of socio-political, economic, cultural, human resources development, ideological, financial, trade, technological and military transformation of their countries. It depends on its leadership by its organic intellectuals in the process of achieving the strategic interests of the masses of its people. Their role is indispensable in this process. Thanks to their answer to the strategic question as to who are allies and enemies of the masses of the people in practice, their commitment to the development process, their leadership of, and role in, institutions and organisations, their individual knowledge and talents become a proud, treasured national asset through the mediation of their parties committed to their development which collectively, in this context,

> *is like one single head that thinks through a thousand brains, the cross-roads of all knowledge, of all cultures, of all specializations,*

precisely because it is called upon to know and to dominate the national and international reality in toto, to act upon it in order to transform it; it is force capable of lifting the masses up to the highest degree of a vanguard intellectual consciousness; a sort of collective man or homogeneous intellectual force susceptible of articulating the complex relationships: masses-party-leadership.

Viewed from this perspective, the "collective intellectual" must strive to educate, to turn each follower into an intellectual. Thanks to a well-designed resocialization program, each member is prepared to assume leadership. In other words, the party must create the conditions for the political man and woman to be transformed into an expert, a specialist or, if you prefer, a cadre, a skilled person. [1]

Thus, the role of intellectuals in the production of leaders, experts, specialists or skilled individuals is indispensable in the society. It is through this role that development as an intellectual process of production or creation of resources essential for human progress can best understood, highly appreciated and treasured.

Intellectuals play a leadership in representing the masses of the people on a global scale in the strategic area of development. This role is tangibly articulated by Edward Said in his view of the role of the intellectuals in representing the people in their development process. He represented the

---

[1] Antonio Gramsci, "The Modern Prince," quoted in Makidi-Ku-Ntima, "Class Struggle and the Making of the Revolution in Angola," in Bernard Magubane and Nzongola-Ntalaja, eds., "Proletarianization and Class Struggle in Africa," *Contemporary Marxism*, No. 6, Spring 1983, p. 139.

people of Palestine as an intellectual producing and disseminating knowledge by conducting research and lecturing at the universities in the United States of America until he passed away on 25 September 2003 and as an independent member of the Palestinian National Council from 1977 to 1991. According to him, the intellectual is

> *an individual endowed with a faculty for representing, embodying, articulating a message, a view, an attitude, philosophy or opinion to, as well as for, a public. And this role has an edge to it, and cannot be played without a sense of being someone whose place it is publicly to raise embarrassing questions, to confront orthodoxy and dogma (rather than to produce them), to be someone who cannot easily be co-opted by governments or corporations, and whose raison d'eter is to represent all those people and issues that are routinely forgotten or swept under the rug. The intellectual does so on the basis of universal principles: that all human beings are entitled to expect decent standards of behaviour concerning freedom and justice from worldly powers or nations, and that deliberate or inadvertent violations of these standards need to be tested and fought against courageously.* [1]

Said points out further that

> *In the end it is the intellectual as a representative figure that matters — someone who visibly represents a standpoint of some kind,*

---

[1] Edward Said, *Representations of the Intellectual*, London: Vintage, 1994, pp. 11-12.

> and someone who makes articulate representations to his or her public despite all sorts of barriers. My argument is that intellectuals are individuals with a vocation for the art of representing, whether that is talking, writing, teaching, appearing on television. And that vocation is important to the extent that it is publicly recognizable and involves both commitment and risk, boldness and vulnerability. [1]

Said is articulating the leadership of intellectuals as producers of knowledge on the global scale and as social agents through presentations of their papers at conferences, symposiums, seminars, workshops other forums, their books, journal articles, monographs, policy briefs, interviews and as social actors dominating the possession and utilisation of human capital speaking on behalf of those their works structurally represent. Their structural commitment to speak on behalf of particular social forces through their works is central in their universal role which is that no organisation and social force can achieve and sustain its strategic objectives without the organic input of intellectuals. It is for this reason that:

> In dark times, an intellectual is very often looked to by members of his or her nationality to represent, speak out for, and testify to the suffering of that nationality … To this terribly important task of representing the collective suffering of your own people, testifying to its travails, reasserting its enduring presence, reinforcing its

---

[1] Edward Said, *Representations of the Intellectual*, London: Vintage, 1994, pp. 12-13.

memory, there must be added something else, which only an intellectual, I believe, has the obligation to fulfil. After all, many novelists, painters, and poets, like Manzoni, Picasso, or Neruda, have embodied the historical experience of their people in aesthetic works, which in turn become recognized as great masterpieces. For the intellectual the task, I believe is explicitly to universalize the crisis, to give greater human scope so to what a particular race or nation suffered, to associate that experience with the suffering of others ... This does not at all mean a loss in historical specificity, but rather it guards against the possibility that a lesson learned about oppression in one place will be forgotten or violated in another place or time. [1]

Central to Said's position is that intellectuals are the dominant actors in the production of knowledge vital to development of the world and its people. They are dominant in the production of knowledge humanity requires to understand the present situation it is confronting for the achievement of its sustainable development. The task of the production of knowledge is not purely an academic task. It is a task specified by practice of those who organise and use knowledge in achieving particular developmental objectives. By producing knowledge vital to human development, intellectuals provide the humanity with power it organises in achieving its objectives.

Intellectuals play a strategic universal role in representing not only

---

[1] Edward Said, *Representations of the Intellectual*, London: Vintage, 1994, pp. 43-44.

members of their race, nation, country, region, continent, ethnicity, linguistic group and religion and other related socio-historical affiliations in the strategic area of development.

The transformation of the structure of the African economy through industrialisation and beneficiation

There is a fundamental and structural need for the continent to transform the structure of its economy through industrialisation and beneficiation. It should move away from a resource-based economy to a knowledge-based economy whose key component is a greater reliance on intellectual capabilities or knowledge-intensive activities than on natural resources.

The role of the continent's intellectuals who are experts committed to the realisation of its development through deployment of its mining and agricultural resources is indispensable in this task. Their commitment to this developmental task, and their leadership in the production of knowledge should be organised to achieve its development objectives.

Africa is facing challenges in its efforts to contribute towards the creation and sustenance of employment, wealth and development opportunities through the articulated combination of exploitation of its natural resources and utilisation of its human capital. It should solve the problem of its natural resources not being used to put itself and its people first through the implementation of its industrialisation and beneficiation development policy measures. Its poverty, unemployment and inequality challenges are linked in part to the bulk exploitation of its natural resources.

The beneficiation of its mineral resources is of vital importance in solving problems of poverty, unemployment and inequality. Its economy should be based on knowledge essential to convert its enormous primary products into finished products. By firstly contributing towards employment and wealth opportunities of the people of the continent, knowledge-based economy will be indispensable in the journey Africa is travelling in solving problems of poverty, unemployment and inequality.

Development as an intellectual process: the case of Namibia and South Africa

Namibia represents African countries consuming most of goods they do not produce. Eighty percent of products consumed in Namibia are from South Africa.[①] It has a limited capacity to produce finished goods. It remains in a situation where it consumes most of what it does not produce. It is used by South Africa as its captive market. South Africa has enormous ability to produce finished goods. This is a key challenge Namibia is confronting in its relations with South Africa and other countries, especially outside the continent. It should create its own value chain based on its raw materials. It exports beef to South Africa. It imports the very same beef from South Africa back into its national economy. It has a significant fish industry. It exports its fish to Spain where it helps to create about thirty-one thousands of jobs. It should ensure that it produces this fish internally

---

[①] This percent of products produced in South Africa consumed in Namibia was given to the author by four senior officials of the Namibian state during a fieldwork research interview in October 2011 in Windhoek, Namibia.

within itself and then export it as finished products for its fish industry to significantly contributes towards the creation of jobs. It exports copper. It does not transform copper into finished products. It exports all its manganese without any form of transformed manganese into finished products.[1] Namibia tangibly represents African countries just exporting their raw materials and importing finished products. This problem as faced by Namibia led Tjekero Tweya as its Deputy Minister of Trade and Industry to maintain that:

> *Namibia has been insane for 21 years of independence without a production capacity to produce even a tooth pick. The same reason why we import tooth picks from China is because we need them, so we need to work on our production capacity and improve ways of collecting revenue.*[2]

Nahas Angula, as Namibia's Prime Minister,[3] proposed the solution to this problem faced by Namibia. His proposed solution is of strategic importance to Namibia particularly given the position articulated by Tweya that it has no capacity to produce even a tooth pick. According to Angula, technological readiness, business sophistication and innovation are some of the key missing links in Namibia's economy compromising its growth and

---

[1] The representatives of the Namibia state, including those who requested to remain anonymous, interviewed by the author in October 2011 in Windhoek, Namibia.
[2] Tjekero Tweya, quoted in Tirivangani Masawi, "Namibia's revenue collection in dilemma," *The Villager* (Windhoek), Vol. 1, No. 8, August 8 to August 14, 2011, p. 4.
[3] Nahas Angula is a former Minister of Science and Technology of Namibia.

development potential.① He emphasises that Namibia has technologies to "transform" its "raw products into manufactured products." What is "missing" to convert its primary products into finished products is "a system of leveraging and adopting or adapting existing technologies." To solve this "lack of technological readiness" it has to acquire the capacity to "leverage and adapt existing technologies." This means investing into research and development, having quality scientific research institutions and developing its "human resource capable of knowledge production and diffusion." Its investment into knowledge production, distribution and exploitation is critical particularly given the fact that its economy is based on "extraction, trading and public service." The fact that it is an extractive economy whose extraction of its strategic raw materials is done by transnational corporations is such that while the transformation of the ownership of its national economy is critical, its transformation from resource-based economy into knowledge-based economy is of long-term strategic importance for the utilisation of its natural resources for the popular national development and progress. Knowledge is a powerful resource when organised and used to achieve particular strategic objectives. This reality is supported by Angula when he maintains: "Today the wealth of nations is built on knowledge and less on raw materials."②

South Africa, Africa's relatively and qualitatively largest and diversified economy, is fundamentally or in essence not different from problems other African countries are facing in the utilisation of their natural resources for

---

① Nahas Angula, "Enhancing Namibia's Potential for Growth." p. 7.
② Ibid.

their development needs and demands. Its unemployment problem is linked in part to the systematic bulk exploitation of its natural resources. Its sustainable development depends on the resolution of this problem in the link between unemployment and the exploitation of its natural resources. This is one of the key problems South Africa is confronting in its development agenda. Jean-Marie Jullienne articulates this reality tangibly when he maintains that:

> *it is ... becoming abundantly clear that the future depends on our ability to establish joint ventures in the field of processing our resources. South African iron ore converted into pig iron billets and further processed into rods, bars and sheets. This same process should be applied to diamonds, coal, chrome, manganese, gold and platinum. South Africa produces 75% of the world's platinum but fewer than 15% of the world's catalytic converters.*
>
> *A simple product like granite is being shipped in bulk to Italy before being offloaded onto trucks taking it to factories in Carrara and Verona to be cut and polished by Italian labour before being shipped again to the rest of the world.*
>
> *This is an absurdity when seen in the light of a world held to ransom by oil cartels, yet nothing of the sort exists in regards to mineral resources. If established here, we could ensure that local labour is not taken advantage of and paid in a currency subject to devaluation. Foreign companies reporting profits in foreign in currencies are always keen to devalue the Rand, thereby reducing labour costs and maximizing profits in their own currencies.*

It is interesting to note that as soon as South African democracy was born, a number of large mining houses moved their holding companies offshore. The concept of a devalued Rand based on our inability to compete in certain industries associated with developing nations, such as textiles, ignores the industries in which we have the greatest advantages, those based on the country's natural resources.

Countries trade on their strengths so focusing on a resource we have in abundance can make us strong and competitive, provided this comes with beneficiation. It is therefore very encouraging to see that at the last ANC National General Council meeting, a resolution was taken to increase the beneficiation of our products from 10% to 50% by 2030. This is the sensible road to prosperity, job creation and a strong and equal partnership with growing powers like India and China, whose appetite for our natural resources is unquenchable in the foreseeable future. [1]

He continues:

A small island nation like Japan, with the world's third-largest economy despite an almost total lack of natural resources, imports everything it needs and utilises its strengths to produce end products.

Imagine the joint ventures South Africa could embark on with countries like Japan. It is important for us to as a nation to take stock

---

[1] Jean-Marie Jullienne, "We must benefit from our wealth: Greater beneficiation of our natural resources to put the people of South Africa first," *The New Age* (Johannesburg), 2 February 2011, p. 13.

of what we have been blessed with in natural resources and set out how best to utilise these to maximise the benefit for the people of South Africa.

This must be a dispassionate decision based on sensible assessments of South African realities. We can only succeed if we place our nation as the primary beneficiary of the system and not be concerned with the international conglomerates' need to show profits in international currencies. [1]

The discovery of mineral resources in South Africa has been the continued process of digging and shipping of raw materials by Africans for the benefits of Europeans.

The essence of the problem faced by South Africa in the exploitation of its natural resources raised by Jean-Marie Jullienne is articulated by Ben Turok in speaking during hearings on the industrial policy action plan before the National Assembly Trade and Industry Committee in November 2012. Pointing out that the continued separation of the roles of the mining sector from the manufacturing sector of the South African economy has resulted in de-industrialisation of the country, he told Members of Parliament that everyone he spoke to told him that the beneficiation strategy document of the Department of Mineral Resources is "seriously inadequate." Central to its serious inadequacy is the fact that it does not produce a vision on how South Africa could use its mineral resources — even in some cases where it

---

[1] Jean-Marie Jullienne, "We must benefit from our wealth: Greater beneficiation of our natural resources to put the people of South Africa first," *The New Age* (Johannesburg), 2 February 2011, p. 13.

enjoys a monopoly — to "maximum benefit" of the economy.① His proposed solutions to this separation or "wall" between the mining sector and the manufacturing sector and the high input costs of electricity in the manufacturing sector include pricing arrangements, "limited protectionist arrangements applied to by government, co-operation in skills development, positive procurement measures to favour domestic industry and clear taxation policies to encourage localisation."② He continues pointing out that:

> *This separation of the roles of mining from manufacturing leads to the suggestion that mining contributes to the economy by way of foreign exchange, taxes and employment, while manufacturing in the mineral value chain should stand alone, possibly with state subsidies.*
>
> *Crucially [the mining sector] objects to any obligation ... to supply processed minerals to [national] manufacturing at anything less than international price levels. However, the result of this policy is that South African manufacturers operating in the mineral value chain have to pay import parity prices for steel, for example, which prices them out of competition.*③

Turok concludes that the country is faced with "a curious anomaly" in that it exports its resources in raw form "to be beneficiated and fabricated elsewhere and the final product is imported back ... with most of the value

---

① Ben Turok, quoted in "State beneficiation plan is 'inadequate,'" *Business Report* (Johannesburg), 8 November 2012, p. 1.
② Ibid.
③ Ibid.

added abroad."[1] He points out that "the result of the fact that even inputs into the mining sector of its economy such as machinery are largely imported" is "de-industrialisation."[2]

What Turok refers to as separation or "wall" between the mining sector and the manufacturing sector of the South African economy is the level of the forward and backward linkages[3] in production or solidarity and unity between them. To what extent is the South African economy articulated or coherent or disarticulated or incoherent given the degree of linkages between its main sectors. As a result of disarticulation or incoherence between the mining sector and the manufacturing sector of its economy, South Africa exports its mineral resources in raw form. They are converted externally into finished products and imported back to it where they are bought at a relatively high price compared to that of their export. In the process, it contributes towards the creation and sustenance of employment and wealth opportunities as well as development in the countries where its raw materials are converted into finished products. The solution to this problem is the structural and fundamental need for South Africa to have a solid articulated or coherent economy with sectoral complementarity and reciprocity of exchanges or unity and solidarity between main sectors of its economy, especially mining, agriculture and manufacturing.

Roman Grynberg regards this process as the task by Africa of digging

---

[1] Ben Turok, quoted in "State beneficiation plan is 'inadequate,'" *Business Report* (Johannesburg), 8 November 2012, p. 1.
[2] Ibid.
[3] For a detailed analysis of forward and backward linkages in the case of Africa, see, Claude Ake, *A Political Economy of Africa*, Harlow, Essex: Longman Group Limited, 1981, pp. 43–46 and pp. 88–93.

holes for the West which he maintains that it should be discontinued or stopped. Some of the Africans who have not been digging these holes in the interests of the West having been ensuring the continuity of this process. These Africans have been "keeping Africa in its place on the raw materials end of the value chain."[①] He maintains that "the World Bank, the Organisation for Economic Co-operation and Development (OECD) and even the African Development Bank, along with a gaggle of well-funded think-tanks, have developed a more subtle approach" to support their position that developing countries are simply not able to break out of their current place on the commodity value chain. He provides some of the aspects of the justification of their position when he maintains that:

In the recent case of Zambia, the World Bank in 2011 produced a report attacking that government's ongoing attempt to add value to its copper. It has, together with UK Aid, advised Zambia that adding value to copper is not worth it, it will get few jobs, no one will buy its copper semifabricates and it does not have the other resources such as nickel and metal scrap. What is more, Chile, the world's biggest producer of copper, sells almost no fabricated copper products and therefore Zambia should not even try.

Recently, the OECD and African Development Bank researchers told African countries that they should export copper concentrate and not even try to go as far as producing pure copper cathode because the Chinese have massively invested in refining and smelting capacity,

---

① Roman Grynberg, "Stop digging holes for the West," *Mail & Guardian* (Johannesburg), April 19 to 25 2013, p. 12.

making competition next to impossible. ①

Grynberg continues pointing out that:

At no point, of course, does the World Bank ask whether value addition would work if the Zambian state behaved like Indonesia and imposed a World Trade Organization (WTO)-compatible export duty tax on unprocessed copper concentrate. Or, what if Zambia was able to work closely with Chinese or Indian firms that do produce a semifabricates so that there was a way of exporting more processed copper products?

Those who are opposed to value addition to Africa argue that Africa should simply export unprocessed raw materials and use the revenue this generates to educate people and develop sectors in which they have a comparative advantage. The only connection to the mining sector should be through upstream connections such as inputs into the mining process. Put in other words, Africans should be working to make their "ivory porters" more efficient.

Of course, this model, proposed by the think-tanks of the international community, is precisely the path that was taken by Botswana with its enormous diamond resource base. For three decades, it tried to develop a good environment for business to invest, and used diamond revenue to educate its population and give them

---

① Roman Grynberg, "Stop digging holes for the West," *Mail & Guardian* (Johannesburg), April 19 to 25 2013, p. 12.

good healthcare and a decent infrastructure, just as it was told. It abandoned any major subsidies to industry more than a decade ago.

And what happened? Almost nothing. Over the past decade, the country has experienced economic growth, but has remained with a stubbornly high 18% rate of unemployment and no real transformation or diversification of its economic base.

That was until Botswana decided that exporting jobs to Europe and India by "carrying the ivory to the coast" was simply not a sustainable development model. It has begun to work with De Beers and its sightholders, telling them that diamond buyers need to process a part of their diamonds in Botswana. This has created the country's largest manufacturing industry today with 3,200 workers, which is not insignificant in a country of two million. [1]

Grynberg concludes that

The future of Africa belongs to those who refuse to continue to dig holes in the ground to make others rich, to those leaders who know their economics, understand the value chain and the high price that will need to be paid to work with business to move down those value chains to where people have productive and meaningful jobs.

Those who try to sell development models to 55 fragmented African countries with almost one billion people and relatively small national resources, based on the experience of small countries with

---

[1] Roman Grynberg, "Stop digging holes for the West," *Mail & Guardian* (Johannesburg), April 19 to 25 2013, p. 12.

giant natural resource bases such as Australia, Canada and Chile, are peddling illusions. [①]

These are social forces contributing towards change from the exploitation of Africa's mineral resources primarily in the interests of the countries outside the continent to their exploitation in the advancement of its popular strategic and tactical interests. This "300-year model of African natural-resource development" that was based on Africans, "originally as slaves and later as paid porters, carrying ivory to the coast for Europeans and Asians to cut and process" has not changed. The products whether copper, gold or coffee have not materialised in adding value to raw materials. The advice of external actors to Africans that they should continue applying it is a self-serving tactical means advancing their interests at the expense of Africans. It must no longer be used in the efforts to achieve Africa's development and progress.

Conclusion and Recommendations

Development as an intellectual process will be best and most effectively served in terms of its achievement and sustenance if political leaders of African countries are elected on the basis of knowledge, skills and talents, not personalities and constituencies. Obsession with personalities and constituencies in electing individuals into leadership positions should be brought to an end if African societies are to achieve sustainable development

---

① Roman Grynberg, "Stop digging holes for the West," *Mail & Guardian* (Johannesburg), April 19 to 25 2013, p. 12.

satisfying the needs and demands of their people. African societies should be led not only by those who are committed to their development, but also by those who are knowledgeable, skilled, talented and experienced. These leadership qualities are of crucial importance for the intellectuals do best, most effectively and efficiently play their leadership role in representing the people in the development agenda. The articulated combination of this political leadership and intellectual leadership will transform their societies into social formations well-placed in research and development and the resultant advanced technological, information, management, marketing and transportation techniques or advanced science-based production methods for the operation of their economy.

This process will lead to a structural change of their place in the global value chain. Thanks to this transformation of their place in the global value chain they will add value to their raw materials and stop digging and shipping raw materials for the West. The utilisation of raw materials of African countries primarily for their internal employment, wealth and development opportunities is critical in their journey towards their control over their national economy, and thereby the pursuit of the development strategy and tactics of their choice. This is in essence the meaning of economic independence:

Namely, control over economic decision making and the national economy; the establishment of a firm industrial structure, leading to a self-generating and self-sustaining growth; and a diversification of external economic contacts consistent with the nation's interests. [1]

---

[1] Justinian Rweyemamu, *Underdevelopment and Industrialisation in Tanzania: A Study of Perverse Capitalist Industrial Development*, Nairobi: Oxford University Press, p. 38.

This realisation of economic liberation will be the achievement of the right of African countries to their national self-determination and the free, independent exercise of their sovereignty and domestic and foreign policies in the interests of the masses of their people. Their possession of science-based production methods for the operation of their economy and their deployment in using their natural resources primarily for their internal needs and demands will be such that this right will effectively be respected in practice by countries beyond the continent.

关于中非职业教育合作及相关问题

王 南

内容摘要：随着中非合作的扩大和深化，包括中非职业教育合作在内的中非教育合作早已展开，并且不断发展，现已具备了一定的基础。非盟《2063愿景》和中国"一带一路"倡议的提出为中非全天候战略合作伙伴关系的发展带来了新的发展契机，也给中非职业教育合作提供了新的启示。本文结合中非职业教育合作的现状，对中国在职业教育领域的对非合作提出了若干建议。

关 键 词：中非；职业教育合作；机遇；建议

作者简介：王南，上海师范大学非洲研究中心研究员

一、中非职业教育合作的意义和作用

中非职业教育合作是中非教育合作的有机构成，同属中非合作的一部分。加强中非职业教育合作，既是推动中非教育合作的一个重要方面，也能为中非双方在其他领域的合作发挥积极作用，包括在经贸领域的合作，进而为中非

传统友好合作关系添砖加瓦。

对于中国来说,加强中非职业教育合作,有利于扩大中国在非洲的影响,提升中国在非洲的声望,以及增强非洲国家和民众对中国的认可度,具体包括中国产品、中国品牌和中国标准等。

对于非洲而言,加强中非职业教育合作,有助于促进非洲职业教育的发展,为非洲培养经济增长、社会发展和国家建设的能工巧匠,使非洲进一步了解、学习和分享中国发展的成功经验,促进非洲的对华合作,特别是经贸领域的合作。

二、中非职业教育合作已有一定基础

随着中非合作的扩大和深化,包括中非职业教育合作在内的中非教育合作早已展开,并且不断发展,现已具备了一定的基础,如中非双方举办职业培训、中方派出援非职业教育师资、邀请非方职业教育教师来华进修、在非洲兴办职业技术学校等。

在中非职业教育合作方面,天津职业技术师范大学就是一个积极的先行者和推动者,并且在这方面已经取得了突出的成绩。作为教育部首批设立的"教育援外基地",自 2007 年起受教育部委托,该校参与"埃塞—中国职业技术学院"的建设工作及后续办学工作,已派遣援外教师 200 余人次到埃塞俄比亚、坦桑尼亚、也门等国家援教,培养、培训当地师生 2 万余人;为埃塞俄比亚、肯尼亚、坦桑尼亚、苏丹等 60 余个发展中国家开展各类职业教育培训,培训学员 1 100 余人次。

当然,热衷中非职业教育合作的不只是天津职业技术师范大学,还有中国其他的单位、机构和企业等。2016 年 4 月 7 日,南非教育代表团一行到访深圳国泰安教育技术股份有限公司(以下简称"国泰安"),双方就国泰安在南非开展职业教育培训、创业教育、师资培训、搭建教育信息化平台、合作开发实训教育软件等合作方向进行了深入探讨与沟通。2016年10月18日,"中非(贝宁)职业技术教育学院"成立暨揭牌仪式在非洲国家贝宁的科托努市隆重举行。这所学院由宁波职业技术学院与贝宁CERCO学院联合举办。该学院将以贝宁为中心,为西非各国和在非中资企业培训各类实用的技能型人才,并举办中外合作办学项目,输出中国理念和职教技术,助推中国企业"走出去",成为高职院校国际化发展的一张崭新名片。2017年3月,重庆工业职业技术学院领导及其一行,前往埃塞俄比亚,与在那里投资兴业的力帆汽车集团,共同成立了"中埃人才培养基地",旨在为力帆埃塞市场提供技术支持,对力帆当地员工提供技术培训等。

三、中非职业教育合作迎来新机遇

2013年5月,非洲联盟第21届首脑会议提出了"2063年愿景"发展战略,表示"到2063年,必要的基础设施将会促进非洲一体化、技术转移、贸易增长和经济发展。基础设施包括高铁系统、公路、航运、海空联运以及完善的信息通信技术和数字经济"。同样是在2013年,中国提出了"一带一路"倡议。"一带一路"提出的合作领域对于实现"2063年愿景"的总体发展目标具有十分积极的意义。"一带一路"的实施,必将进一步推动中非合作。

2015年12月,在中非合作论坛约翰内斯堡峰会上,中国领导人习近平主席发表了题为《开启中非合作共赢、共同发展的新时代》的重要讲话,宣布未来三年中方将着力实施"十大合作计划"。其中的中非工业化合作计划、中非农业现代化合作计划、中非基础设施合作计划、中非绿色发展合作计划等,都需要各种各样的职业技术人才。

相信,随着非盟"2063年愿景"发展战略和"一带一路"倡议的落实和推进,以及中非合作的深入发展,各类人才的需求将会日益显现,包括中非职业教育合作在内的中非教育合作,也会因此迎来新的机遇。

四、加强中非职业教育合作的建议

（一）多渠道开展中非职业教育合作

除了政府部门和公立院校外，也应允许和鼓励民间组织和私立院校等参与中非职业教育合作。还有那些已经进入非洲的中资企业，以及中非双方成立的合资/合作公司，也都是中非职业教育合作的重要"阵地"和参与方，应该加以鼓励、支持和引导、指导。甚至某些国际组织和机构，以及第三方的相关部门等，只要对中非职业教育合作持积极态度和看法，并且愿意参与或是提供支持，也都可以将其吸收进来。

（二）鼓励驻非中资企业开展职业教育

随着中非经贸合作特别是产能合作的发展，前往非洲发展的中资企业将会越来越多。在职业教育方面，中资企业本来就有这方面的传统和优势，加之这些中资企业进入非洲后，本身就需要非洲本土的各类职业/技术人才。以苏丹麦洛维大坝建设为例，参与承建该工程的中方企业就为苏丹工人传授了相关职业技能。此举博得了苏丹方面的高度赞赏。苏丹有关部门一位负责人就曾这样表示：中国人不仅为苏丹修建了麦洛维大坝，还帮苏丹培养了一批职业技术人才。他们对苏丹未来经济增长、社会发展和国家建设的重要作用，将是难以估量的。所以，在中非职业教育合作方面，驻非中资企业完全可以发挥积极和重要的作用。

（三）增加中非职业教育和培训合作的内容

鉴于非洲的人才需求十分广泛，中非职业教育和培训合作的内容，也应该增加和扩大，特别是那些在非洲具有较大需求、对中国而言又属于强项的专业和技能，例如，中餐烹饪、中国农艺、牧渔养殖以及养生、保健等。这些技能既有中国特色，又在非洲拥有现实和潜在的需求。

（四）借助现代方式促进中非职业教育合作

不可否认，学校的课堂教育和企业的师徒传授，在中非职业教育合作过程中发挥了重要的作用，收到了良好的效果，它也是迄今为止中非职业教育合作的主要方式和渠道。然而，随着现代科技的发展和通信方式的便捷，借助互联网、手机和电视等现代化方式和手段，来促进中非职教育合作。这样不仅成本相对低廉、便利快捷，而且效果也不会差。

（五）建立相关档案和资料库

凡是通过中非职业教育合作机制接受过职业教育或职业培训，并且考试合格的非方人员，哪怕是接受过中方师傅"传、帮、带"过的非方徒弟，都是可资利用的人才资源，对于非洲来说尤为如此。有关部门应该为此建立相关档案和资料库，以便中非双方以及第三方的用人企业、机构和部门等查询，或是向其进行推荐和介绍。在促进非洲经济发展、社会进步，推进中非合作，特别是中非经贸/产能合作，助力"一带一路"建设方面，这些非方专业、技术人才一定会发挥出重要和独特的作用。

儒家教育思想和中非教育交流与合作

周志发　魏　莎　温国砫　郝子怡

内容摘要：与西方国家相比,中非教育交流与合作领域,教育思想层面的交流一直较为欠缺。基于儒家教育思想"分享错误"对坦桑尼亚三谷中学的师生做了访谈,对坦桑尼亚、喀麦隆的部分大学生做了问卷。访谈与问卷表明,"分享错误"的教学理念得到了众多师生的认同,加深了其对"孔子思想"的认识,而不仅限于汉语文字教学。基于"分享错误"的教学理念,在雅温得第二大学孔子学院课堂上进行了教学实践,为进一步让非洲学生深入了解中国的教育思想与现代化道路打下良好基础。

关键词：儒家教育思想;分享错误;中非教育;孔子学院

作者简介：周志发,浙江师范大学非洲研究院副研究员、博士;魏莎,浙江师范大学非洲研究院硕士生;温国砫,雅温得第二大学孔子学院汉语教师,坦桑尼亚达累斯萨拉姆大学发展学院博士生;郝子怡,坦桑尼亚达累斯萨拉姆大学孔子学院汉语教师

20世纪50年代以来,中国与50个非洲国家建立了教育交流与合作。从1956年根据签署的文化合作协议,中国

接受4位埃及留学生到中国学习美术、哲学和农业,至2005年11月首届"中非教育部长论坛"在北京召开,标志着中非教育交流与合作从无到有,从单一形式、领域向多层次、多领域、多形式的深入合作方向发展。[1] 从国际话语权的角度来看,中非教育交流与合作可分为三个阶段:第一个阶段是20世纪50年代至70年代末。这段时间主要表现为非洲国家摆脱殖民统治,谋求独立自主探索现代化道路。中非教育交流与合作规模较小,主要处于起步阶段。第二阶段是20世纪80年代初至90年代末期。70年代末、80年代初,英国首相撒切尔夫人、美国总统里根开始推行新自由主义政策,并利用非洲自身的危机,将新自由主义政策与对非援助挂钩,导致众多非洲国家重新失去"话语权",被迫推行结构调整计划(Structural Adjustment Program, SAP)。直至20世纪90年代末,"结构调整计划"彻底失败之后,美国和国际组织才开始反思新自由主义在非洲的适切性,但其对非洲造成的伤害已难以弥补。这段时期,中非教育交流与合作更加务实。比如1991年10月,浙江农业大学为喀麦隆雅温得第一大学理学院建立微生物实验室,并派遣教师开设微生物课程,指导和培养研究生。截至2003年年底,中国相继在非洲的21个国家实施了43期高等教育与科研项目合作,帮助喀麦隆、马里、刚果、乍得、科特迪瓦、布隆迪、塞内加尔、埃及、苏丹、坦桑尼亚、赞比亚、加纳、津巴布韦、肯尼亚、纳米比亚、毛里求斯、尼日利亚等国家的高等学校,在生物、计算机、物理、分析化学、食品保鲜加工、材料、园艺、土木工程与测量、汉语教学专业,建立了21个较为先进的实验室。[2] 第三阶段是2000年首届中非合作论坛召开迄今。这一阶段非洲国家不断对过去20多年来实行新自由主义政策造成的恶果进行反思,同时也是新自由主义从占据绝对话语权到快速衰落乃至崩溃的过程。其标志性的事件是2008年美国引发的金融危机。21世

---

[1] 贺文萍:《中非教育交流与合作概述——发展阶段及未来挑战》,《西亚非洲》2007年第3期。
[2] 《中非教育交流与合作》编写组:《中国与非洲国家教育交流与合作》,北京:北京大学出版社2005年版,第29—31页。

纪初,中国模式、中国道路或中国经验开始被非洲国家所重视,中非治国理政经验的交流变得更为密切。①

然而,就教育思想而言,非洲教育主要受到西方教育思想的影响。中国学者"以我为主",主动与非洲交流"中国特色、普遍性"的教育思想,目前还尚未开展。孔子学院的专职教师和志愿者在国内的培训活动过程中,亦缺乏这一块内容。有鉴于此,我们先做儒家教育思想"分享错误"理念在非洲的认同度研究,所选择的国家分别是坦桑尼亚和喀麦隆。

一、儒家教育思想"分享错误"与党建教育思想"公开自我批评"的融通

孔子是我国古代伟大的思想家和教育家。他顺应当时"学术下移"的大趋势,实行"有教无类"的教育宗旨,创立了规模颇大的私学。孔子最早阐述了教师也是学习者的思想,即"三人行,必有我师焉"②。他在教学法方面颇有建树,其中首推"启发式"教学:"不愤不启,不悱不发,举一隅不以三隅反,则不复也。"③其次是因材施教。其由朱熹概括的:"孔子教人,各因其材。"④其是儒家重要的教学原则。而教学相长则体现了孔子教学的民主思想。对孔子教学思想研究的历史源远流长,三种教学法颇受世人称道,古为今用。孔子教学思想虽然强调反省⑤,但其内蕴的"教师主动和学生分享自身错误",即"分享错误"的理念,却被后人所漠视。

儒家、科学哲学家波普尔等均强调从错误中学习的重要性。"错误人人

---

① 罗建波:《非洲国家的治理难题与中非治国理政经验交流》,《西亚非洲》2015 年第 3 期。
② 《论语·述而》。
③ 同上。
④ 《论语集注》,朱熹:《四书集注》,长沙:岳麓书社 1985 年版,第 153 页。
⑤ 《论语·学而》。

皆有,各人大小不同。"[1]从儒家代表人物孔子到王侯将相,从平庸之人到成就伟大事业的人,均从错误中学习、成长。而"分享错误"的教育理念早就蕴含在传统儒家教育思想之中。儒家强调"自我反省或自我批评":"曾子曰:'吾日三省吾身,为人谋而不忠乎?与朋友交而不信乎?传不习乎?'"[2]"过则勿惮改。"[3]从而达到自我纠错的目的。君子作为道德模范,是如何对待自己之"过"呢?子贡曰:"君子之过也,如日月之食焉。过也,人皆见之;更也,人皆仰之。"[4]君子反思自己的错误时,非但不隐瞒自身的错误,而且其错误会像日月之食一样为人所知。子贡之言对君子提出了两方面的要求:第一,"分享错误"是君子道德修养的内在要求。君子如果没有分享错误的精神,其错误不可能像日食、月食那样为人所知;第二,君子要具备"改过"的能力,最好能做到"不贰过"[5]。那么,孔子在教育学生的过程中,是否践行了"分享错误"之精神呢?答案是肯定的。孔子主要在三种场合与学生分享错误:(1)老师不说,无论学生是否在场,他们可能永远都不知道老师犯错了。老师该如何对待自己的错误?(2)师生均在场,学生通过辩护说明自己是对的,老师是错的。老师该如何对待自己的错误?(3)当别人指出其几乎不能"过而改之"的重大错误时,老师该如何应对?[6]

毛泽东对圣贤的认识更进一步,说:"古语说'人非圣贤,孰能无过'。我看这句话要改一下。人,包括圣贤在内,总是有过的,有过必改就好了。"[7]孔子被视为一代圣贤,其之过,"人必知之"。就像子贡所说的一样,作为君子的错误,就像天上的日食、月食一样清清楚楚。所以,毛泽东不认同"圣贤无过"

---

[1] 《毛泽东文集》(第3卷),北京:人民出版社1996年版,第360页。
[2] 《论语·学而》。
[3] 同上。
[4] 《论语·子张》。
[5] 《论语·雍也》。
[6] 周志发:《教学"新"理念:分享错误》,《上海教育科研》2007年第1期。
[7] 《毛泽东文集》(第6卷),北京:人民出版社1999年版,第346—347页。

的说法,而是强调圣贤"有过则改"。毛泽东在《主动权来自实事求是》一文中谈道:"不犯错误的人从来没有。郑重的党在于重视错误,找出错误的原因,分析所以犯错误的客观原因,公开改正。"[1]此言与子贡对君子的阐述相似。毛泽东总结出游击战原则:"敌进我退,敌驻我扰,敌疲我打,敌退我追。"问题是他是如何总结出来的? 与孔子总结出"学而不思则罔,思而不学则殆"一样,通过试错加以总结。毛泽东说自己所犯的错误,"从来没有想到自己去搞军事,要去打仗。后来自己带人打起仗来,上了井冈山。在井冈山先打了个小胜仗,接着又打了两个大败仗"。毛泽东自己带人打起仗,意思是说对部队指挥的试错权掌握在他手中。经过试错之后,毛泽东"于是总结经验,总结了十六个字的打游击的经验:'敌进我退,敌驻我扰,敌疲我打,敌退我追'"。[2] 这精辟的十六字游击战方针,并非毛泽东生而知之,而是在试错实践中总结出来的。可以说,毛泽东在民主革命时期,经过失败、胜利、再失败、再胜利的过程才最终认识了中国革命的规律,于是撰写了一系列具有历史意义的作品,比如《中国革命战争的战略问题》、《论持久战》、《新民主主义论》等。[3] 争夺中国发展的试错权以及通过"公开自我批评或分享错误",来教育阶级和群众,从而不断壮大自身。错误的代价和价值非常巨大,但接受过这些"失败、挫折'给予'的教育"的党,其战斗力明显得到提升。这就回答了什么样的党、军队更加强大。党在土地革命时期,红军发展到三十万人,经过长征仅剩不足3万人。"究竟是那三十万人的军队强些,还是这不到三万人的军队强些?"[4]从是否接受过失败、挫折的角度来看,毛泽东认为,"我们受了那样大的挫折,吃过那样大的苦头,就得到锻炼,有了经验,纠正了错误路线,恢复了正确路线,所以这不到三万人的军队,比起过去那个三

---

[1] 《毛泽东文集》(第8卷),北京:人民出版社1999年版,第197页。
[2] 同上,第392—393页。
[3] 同上,第299页。
[4] 同上。

十万人的军队来,要更强些"。① 其中,通过公开自我批评教育自己的队伍,至关重要。

孔子的教育思想中,教师主动与学生"分享错误"是君子的表现,代表着高尚的道德。而党建教育思想"公开自我批评"——与"分享错误"同个意思,既强调作为资源教育阶级与群众,更强调其是一种义务。既然公开自我批评、纠正错误是党的义务,那么党就应有试错权。所以,革命是争夺试错权的进程。拿到国家发展的试错权,党才能教育自己的阶级与群众。从中可见,党建教育思想"公开自我批评"与儒家教育思想"分享错误"相比,前者更具现代性,即从权利与义务的角度阐述教育。要实现为无产阶级服务的教育,首先代表无产阶级的政党要掌握试错权,否则无法教育阶级与群众。所以说,教育与政治是密切联系的,而且教育受制于政治,为掌握试错权的政党和阶级服务。而且,毛泽东对"进步"作出了新的解释:进步是发现错误并且公开自我批评:"在审查干部工作中,对被搞错了的人承认错误,赔一个不是,这是我们的进步,是我们全党的一个进步。"②

在西方,"分享错误(sharing mistakes)"的教学实践通常在临床医学中较多。③ 由于医生工作的特殊性,其所造成的错误往往直接伤害个人身体,所以众多医生怕担责任,彼此之间倾向于隐瞒医疗事故。另一方面,不少医生出于良知,认识到与同行尤其是资历尚浅的同行"分享错误",有助于减少医疗事故。爱荷华大学的眼科实习项目主任托马斯·奥廷(Thomas A. Oetting)说道:"分享我们的错误一直伴随我们的职业生涯,而多媒体网站真正帮助我们传播这一传统。"范德堡大学眼科研究所珍妮丝·劳(Janice Law)说:"如果我们不分享我们集体的经验,我们将不断地重复我们的错误。"所以珍妮丝·劳愿意坐下来,与同事共同探讨他们所犯的所有错误。其

---

① 《毛泽东文集》(第8卷),北京:人民出版社1999年版,第299页。
② 《毛泽东文集》(第3卷),北京:人民出版社1996年版,第262—264页。
③ 此处从广义的角度理解教学实践。

口头禅是,"是的,错误已经发生,让我们一起从中学习吧"。而且,珍妮丝将分享错误的教育理念与终身学习联系起来。① 美国圣托马斯大学法学院的朱莉·奥赛德(Julie A. Oseid)和院长斯蒂芬·伊斯顿(Stephen D. Easton)将"分享错误"的理念用来培养未来的律师。② 斯塔巴克(Starbuck)认为,一个组织不善于从他们自身的错误中学习,导致其执行力差。③ 侯斯玛(Homsma)则强调,雇员不愿意分享错误是因为他们想逃避潜在的责备。④ 森滕(Tseng)等认为,当雇员感觉到组织内对错误不够宽容时,错误便会发生。⑤ 在国内,我们探讨了孔子对待错误的态度,总结其"分享错误"的教育思想。康玉玲、李秋玲将"分享错误"的教学理念引入至手术室。⑥ 李金春、左秀琴将其用于安全护理。⑦ 田自美将"分享错误"的教学理念用到中职财会课堂上。⑧ 吕松杰将其用到科学教育领域。⑨ 在教学实践层面,"分享错误"的案例越来越丰富,但就教育学原理本身而言,其对该理念关注不够,更谈不上将其系统化。

---

① https：//www. aao. org/young-ophthalmologists/yo-info/article/how-sharing-your-surgical-mistakes-can-make-you-be.
② https：//www. questia. com/read/1G1-371969837/and-bad-mistakes-i-ve-made-a-few-sharing-mistakes; https：//www. lexisnexis. com/legalnewsroom/lexis-hub/b/careerguidance/archive/2012/09/18/learning-and-teaching-by-sharing-mistakes. aspx? Redirected=true.
③ W. H. Starbuck, "Unlearning What We Knew and Rediscovering What We Could Have Known," *Scandinavian Journal of Management*, Vol. 25, No. 2, 2009, pp. 240-242.
④ G. J. Homsma, C. Van Dyck, D. De Gilder, P. L. Koppman & T. Elfring, "Learning From Error：the Influence of Error Incident Characteristics," *Journal of Business Research*, Vol. 62, 2009, pp. 115-122.
⑤ F. Tseng & F. Kuo, "The Way We Share and Learn：An Exploratory Study of the Self-regulatory Mechanisms in the Professional Online Learning Community," *Computers in Human Behaviour*, Vol. 26, 2010, pp. 1043-1053.
⑥ 康玉玲、李秋玲:《分享"错误文化"在手术室安全管理中的应用》,《医学信息(上旬刊)》2011年第2期。
⑦ 李金春、左秀琴:《分享错误文化以加强护理安全》,《首都医药》2013年第20期。
⑧ 田自美:《中职财会课堂教学"新"理念——分享错误》,《科技信息(科学教研)》2007年第13期。
⑨ 吕松杰:《科学教师应学会和学生分享错误》,《现代中小学教育》2010年第2期。

从上述分析可知,"分享错误或公开自我批评"的教学实践,既是儒家教育思想的精髓,亦是党建教育思想的核心,同样是西方大学在医学、法学等领域颇为流行的教学实践理念。"分享错误或公开自我批评"将中国传统、党建教育思想和西方教学实践联系起来。从逻辑上讲,人类是从错误中学习的。学生可以从自身的错误中学习,那么学生能否从教师的错误中学习呢?答案无疑是肯定的。这一逻辑是具有普遍性的。而儒家传统、党建教育思想和西方教学实践都体现了这一点。但该理念在教育学理论体系之中,尚未得到应有的重视。

二、儒家教育思想"分享错误"理念在坦桑尼亚、喀麦隆的认同度研究

研究生郝子怡在坦桑尼亚三谷中学(Sangu Secondary School)做了问卷和访谈,在姆贝亚科技大学(Mbeya University of Science and Technology)、坦桑圣奥古斯丁大学姆贝亚分校(ST Augustine University of Tanzania Mbeya Center)和特库大学(Teofilo Kisanji University)做了问卷调查。汉办专职教师温国砡在喀麦隆杜阿拉大学(University of Douala)、泛非发展大学(Panafrican Institute for Development)和雅温得第二大学孔子学院(Confucius Institute of University at Yaounde Ⅱ)做了问卷调查,并在孔子学院教学实践中,围绕儒家教学思想"分享错误"写了教案,进行了授课。[①]以下是问卷调查的结果。

---

① 坦桑尼亚小学七年,中学六年。其中初中四年,高中两年。中学六年级相当于国内中学高三,中学五年级相当于国内高二。以下是对坦桑尼亚贝亚市三谷中学(Sangu Secondary School)师生的访谈。该中学较为偏远,学生英文水平较差,所以只能选择高年级的学生访谈。对该校进行大面积的问卷几乎不可能,因为每一份问卷都需要访谈者反复解释才能被高年级的学生所理解。我们对该校的中学生做了 50 份访谈,对该校 10 教师做了访谈。在坦桑尼亚和喀麦隆的大学各做了 100 分问卷,在浙江师范大学做了 810 份问卷。

第一题：在你的多年求学中，是否有老师主动与你分享过老师自身的错误？

（1）有，经常（小学、初中、高中、大学）；

（2）有，偶尔（小学、初中、高中、大学）；

（3）没有。

表1

选项 \ 师生来源	三谷中学教师	三谷中学学生	坦桑尼亚大学生	喀麦隆大学生	浙江师范大学大学生
第一选项	0%	6%	24%	23%	7.7%
第二选项	100%	58%	31%	57%	56.8%
第三选项	0%	36%	45%	20%	35.5%

三谷中学的10位中学教师（分别在数学、英语、历史和生物等学科领域）拿到这份问卷之时，虽然他们对于教师主动与学生分享错误的教学理念是陌生的，但在实践层面教师均"被动"与学生分享过错误。[1] 受访的教师说，他们在课堂上会偶尔和学生分享，但并不经常。因为犯错是一件很正常的事情，老师也不例外。地理教师 Florida Yusuph 说她偶尔与学生分享错误，比如有一次在上课的时候不小心讲错了一个知识点，学生发现了问题，课后问她，她才意识到错误，等下次去班级的时候告诉学生正确的答案。她还鼓励学生在课堂上发现错误，及时提醒老师。数学教师 Ester Andron 说："在讲课或讲解试题的过程中，为防止学生犯错，我偶尔会告诉学生某个试题我曾经作为学生的时候也做错过。"但她在教学过程中所犯的错误一般不会重提，因担心学生认为她不是一个好老师。在课堂上出现一些小错误，她会鼓励学生提出来，而且她会很乐意学生这样做。

教师偶尔与学生分享错误的过程中，学生是否认为教师与其分享错误了

---

[1] 坦桑尼亚三谷中学的师生通过孔子学院对孔子之名有所耳闻，但对孔子的教育思想却一无所知。

呢？在接受访谈的50位中学生之中,58%的学生选择了"教师偶尔与学生分享错误",有36%的学生认为教师从未与其分享错误,有6%的学生认为教师经常性地与学生分享。中学五年级男生 Urace Kinumba 说教师偶尔会和学生分享错误,包括一些行为习惯和知识上的错误。[①] 比如教师和学生说,"我以前有一些不好的行为习惯,你们不要再做。"五年级男生 Thomlen Thomas 说教师偶尔会分享一些无关紧要的小错误。他认为,很多教师担心如果和学生分享错误的话,会降低其在学生心中的威信。五年级女生 Tumaini Mhalule 说道:"当学生对一些问题不理解时,有些教师会提到他们当年和学生一样犯同样的错误,并且告诉他们怎样思考才是正确的,但这样的例子并不多,可能是教师无意中提到的。"Hebrony Faitony 却认为,教师之所以偶尔与学生分享错误,是因为分享错误令其感到羞耻。但受访的教师中没有哪位教师承认分享错误是一件令人羞耻的事情。五年级男生 Given Mwanyika 说,教师愿意与学生分享错误,学生能更加自由地讨论。四年级女生 Pamela Robert 说教师在课前偶尔会与学生主动分享错误,但她认为教师经常这样做并不好,因为很多时候会浪费时间,一节课只有40分钟。

六年级女生 Jesca Christopher 认为,一般教师可能都是无意识地分享错误,只是为了给学生一点启发或引导,并不会把分享错误作为一种系统的教学方法。五年级男生 Leonard Osward 表示,有时候教师为提高学生的自信心,会和学生分享自己的错误,但这是教师无意识的举止。Tumaini Mhalule 和 Jesca Christopher 等学生已认识到,教师只是"无意识"地与学生分享错误,其并未成为她们教师的教学理念。事实上,整个西方教育学体系尚未"有意识"地系统阐述"分享错误"的教学理念。西方虽然在医学、法学领域"分享错误"的实践尤其丰富,但医学院的医生从未认识到,病人接受医生的治疗,是将试错权让渡给了医生,而众多医生却试图掩盖或迟疑着是否履行分享错

---

① 以下"中学五年级学生"简称"五年级学生",省略中学两字。

误的义务。同理,课堂上由教师主导,同样隐含着家长将母权试错权让渡给教师。但在西方自由主义教育理论影响下,教师不知其拥有了母权试错权,更不晓该履行"分享错误或公开自我批评"的义务。①

四年级女生 Sitia Mwansite 说她的教师从未主动与学生分享错误。她认为教师一般都是高高在上的,和学生不是平等的关系。所以这些教师认为他们不能够犯错误,即使有错误,也不能把它暴露给学生。五年级女生 Aisha Dusto 说教师在学生面前通常会尽力掩盖自己的错误。五年级女生 Unique Noah 说教师在课堂上教生词的时候发音错了或拼错单词,学生发现了并提出来,教师随即改正了这个错误。这种情况偶尔会发生,但那种教师主动和学生分享深层次的错误却没有。② 六年级女生 Minza Njombe 认为教师不是经常犯错的,因为他们是经过认真备课才给学生上课的,所以会尽量避免在课堂上犯错。不愿意承认自己错误的教师和愿意承认自己错误的教师她都曾遇到过。例一,有一次在课堂上,她当堂指出小学数学教师的一个错误,结果教师挺不高兴的。后来,在课堂上即使教师不小心写错了,也没有同学指出来。例二,高中英语教师则不同,他会鼓励学生如果发现了教师的错误,学生应该马上指出来。她认为有些时候教师会故意写错,然后让学生发现问题。她从未遇到教师专门把自己的错误系统地以教学案例的方式呈现给学生。她猜想,教师不愿主动与学生分享错误是怕丢脸,影响自己的权威。五年级男生 Dennis Nixon 认为,教师觉得自己比学生更强,分享自己的错误会让他觉得丢面子。众多学生认为教师不愿意分享错误,是因为教师怕

---

① 2011 年年底,本人前往喀麦隆参加中喀建交 40 周年的学术交流会议。在学术会议上,本人基于新权利范式认为,美国、法国"拿到"攻打伊拉克和利比亚的试错权,但最终并未承担"公开自我批评和修正错误的义务"。西方的外交通常是有权力而无义务,于是其所拥有的权利或权力亦属于非法。美国的外交政策打着人权的旗帜,其实是允许美国金融资本家以侵犯人权的方式追求利润的最大化——东南亚的金融危机便是凭证。所以说,美国的外交政策从本质上讲不具备"软实力"的功能。

② 众多学生谈到教师偶尔主动与学生分享错误时,常提到英语教师。其在讲解一个词的时候告诉学生,教师之前由于不了解这个单词的用法,结果用错了,然后告诉学生正确的用法。

丢面子，怕被学生轻视，得不到学生的尊重，所以教师不敢主动分享自身的错误。中学三年级的男生 Cinosye Eliaseme 则认为，教师知识渊博，对其所教科目都很熟悉，所以不会犯错。而认为教师经常主动与学生分享错误的三位学生，谈到众多教师会主动和学生共同讨论问题，通过分享自身的错误，帮助学生更加全面地思考问题。学生倾听教师的错误之时，往往更加聚精会神，学习效果远比从自身的错误中学习更佳。

坦桑尼亚三谷中学教师100%选择了"偶尔会与学生分享错误"，给学生的印象是6%的教师会与学生分享错误，58%的学生认为教师偶尔与其分享错误，36%的学生认为教师拒绝与其分享自身的错误。这一结果与我们对"浙江师范大学大学生"所做的问卷结果是一致的：7.7%的学生认为教师会主动与学生分享错误，56.8%的学生认为教师偶尔与其分享错误，35.5%的学生认为教师拒绝与其分享错误。接受问卷调查的喀麦隆大学生之中，有57%认为教师偶尔与其分享错误，其余的问卷结果和三谷中学的问卷结果差异较大。我们认为这是合理的，因为教师是偶尔与学生分享错误，所以接受问卷调查的学生有的遇到教师分享错误的次数多一些，有的较少，差别大是合理的。

上述谈到教师是否会主动与学生分享自身的合理性错误，关键在于教师和学生如何理解"教师"这一基本概念。第二题便是考察教师和学生对"教师"概念的理解。

第二题：以下对教师的三种概念，你觉得哪一种最能体现教师内涵（可多选）

（1）教师是学生的引路人，学生智力的开发者；

（2）教师是"传道授业解惑者"；

（3）教师是先于学生犯错的，了解自己学科领域大部分几乎可能错误的人，并通过恰当的方式，分享自身经历所产生的错误，帮助学生取得学习进步的人；

(4) 自定义。

表 2①

师生来源 选项	三谷中学教师	三谷中学学生	坦桑尼亚大学生	喀麦隆大学生	浙江师范大学大学生
第一选项	100%	94%	55%	56%	45.2%
第二选项	10%	6%	25%	8%	56.2%
第三选项	0%	6%	16%	46%	56%
第四选项	0%	0%	5%	4%	2.1%

选择第一选项的三谷中学教师为100%，第二选项为10%，第三选项为0。可以说教师认同"教师是学生的引路人，学生智力的开发者"。教师是在其学科中比学生掌握更多知识的人，其任务是引导学生学习，把自己所知道的知识传授给学生，促进学生智力发展。生物教师Enock Ukali认为，教师的有些知识是先于学生犯错的，但并不是全部。与第一题联系起来，我们就知道，就整个西方教育学理论而言，鲜有从错误的角度界定教师的概念。所以说，这10位受访教师不接受第三选项是合理的。教师未曾从错误的视角界定自身，所以其也就没有理由与学生分享错误。

教师对"教师"概念的认识，直接影响中学生对教师这一职业的理解。访谈中学生的结果表明，选择第一选项占学生总人数的94%，第二和第三选项占总人数的6%。四年级女生Lindu Michael认为，教师主要的责任是准确地向学生传授专业知识。当然，教师也会犯错，但并不会犯所有的错误。Jesca Christopher认为，教师是为了传授学生知识，引导学生思考的人，是带领学生进行探索和发现的人。她认为，第二选项中教师解惑的功能不太认可，因为教师也有很多不能回答的问题。对于第三选项她认为，教师不能仅仅局限于自己的领域和自己所犯的错误里面。六年级女生Ruth Kazimoto认为，很多教师对于学科领域的许多知识并不会犯错，并不能知道所有的错

---

① 由于是多选，所以总百分比会超出100%。

误。六年级男生 Amani Mwamba 选择从错误的视角界定教师。他认为,这样的教师能够知道问题之所在,帮助学生减少错误的发生。因为教师也经历过学生时代,他已经克服了很多学习上遇到的大部分困难,知道如何去规避它们。五年级男生 Nathaniel Ambele 认同"分享错误型"教师是一位好老师,有助于学生学习教师的解决方法,促进学业进步。

中学生面临升学考试的压力,所以他们绝大多数选择了第一个选项"教师是学生的引路人,学生智力的开发者"。只有6%的中学生选择第三个选项,即愿意接受从错误的角度界定教师的内涵。而一旦中学生变成大学生之后,第一选项的百分比就会下降——参与问卷的喀麦隆、坦桑尼亚和浙江师范大学的大学生均如此。就从错误的角度界定教师而言,浙江师范大学的大学生更愿意接受之,喀麦隆的大学生次之,坦桑尼亚大学生目前的认同度则明显不足。

在实践层面,教师偶尔与学生分享自身的错误,其源于教师对自身形象的认识,从而直接影响学生对教师角色的认同。那么,教师和学生究竟是否认同"分享错误"的教学理念呢?第三题便是考察这一问题。

第三题:你对教师主动与学生分享错误的教学行为持何种态度?

(1) 很好,这样的老师是一位好老师;

(2) 不好,作为一个老师,在课堂上就不应该分享错误;

(3) 不好说。

表3

选项\师生来源	三谷中学教师	三谷中学学生	坦桑尼亚大学生	喀麦隆大学生	浙江师范大学大学生
第一选项	100%	76%	87%	70%	78.8%
第二选项	0%	24%	7%	18%	2.1%
第三选项	0%	0%	6%	12%	19.1%

受访的10位教师100%选择了第一选项,而且他们表示学校绝大多数

教师都会选择第一个选项。他们都认为，教师主动与学生分享错误，说明其是一位好教师。历史教师 Robson Kyungu 说，承认教师自己的弱点，比如和学生说"我的英语不太好"，能够给学生自信心。其次，在教学过程中，通过分享教师自己的错误，强调错误容易出现的地方，让学生有效避免相同错误的发生。教师认同主动与学生分享错误的教学形式，是认同以下逻辑：学生可以从自身的错误中学习，学生同样可以从教师的错误中学习。教师们认为，愿意分享错误的教师，让更多的学生参与其中，课堂教学会显得更加轻松，学生能更容易地理解问题。此处便出现了一个问题：教师100%认同"分享错误"的理念，但在实践层面却偶尔与学生分享自身的合理性错误，更别奢谈系统化地与学生分享了。原因何在呢？在问卷之前，"分享错误"的教学理念对于教师而言完全是陌生的或者说被遮蔽的，当教师开始思考"分享错误"教学理念之时，便开始认同之。所以，10位受访教师认同"分享错误"的教学理念，但其并未付诸教学实践。

在课堂上，教师长期以来只是偶尔与学生分享错误，那么，学生对突然间要与其分享错误的教师持欢迎还是持否定态度呢？有76%的学生选择第一选项，认为主动与学生分享错误的教师是一位好老师；24%的学生选择了第二选项，认为教师不应该在课堂上与学生分享错误。Tumaini Mhalule 认为，实践分享错误教学理念的是一位好教师。这样的教师是诚实的，敢于承认自己的不足，因而也是勇敢的。她会很尊敬这样的教师，而且教师自己的例子比较真实，具有说服力，能够让学生对这个话题记忆深刻。五年级男生 Timota Samsoni 认为，教师与学生分享错误，可以创建一个轻松的学习氛围。学生思考教师的错误时，更加专注、认真，也会变得更有自信心。皮亚杰力图避免在学生错误的时候提出质疑，是怕学生听到教师提问时，就意识到自己可能错误了。但在教师与学生分享错误的背景下，皮亚杰的担心是多余的。Ruth Kazimoto 认同分享错误的教学理念，是因其促进学生积极思考。六年级女生 Minza Njombe 认为，主动分享错误的教师会让学生觉得教师也是人。认识到老师也会犯错,学生的自信心会提高很多,让他们养成知错就改的优良品格。但 Minza Njombe 同时认为,这样并不说明没有主动与学生分享错误的教师就不是好教师。教师在课堂上长期展示其正确而鲜有犯错,犯错的主要是学生,以至于学生常常感觉到教师与学生是不同的。Minza Njombe 从教师展示错误的过程中,意识到教师是人。那么,人的基本特征是什么?"错误人人皆有,各人大小不同"。[①] 而且,当我们跟 Minza Njombe 等中学生介绍中国古代的人物孔子,他把"分享错误"视为教师拥有优良的道德品德时,她更加喜欢这位中国老者的思想了,甚至更爱学习汉语了。所以我们认为,孔子学院介绍孔子之时,从探索通往未来的试错实践和"分享错误"的角度来谈各国文明——中非不同文明——的交流与合作是恰当的切入点。

Lindu Michael 总结了教师与学生分享错误的两大益处:一是学生知道教师犯错后,知道在学习上犯错误不是一件不可原谅的事情,是可以理解的;二是学生可以从教师分享错误的案例中获取经验,并反思自己的错误进行改正。Sitia Mwansite 认为,勇于与学生分享错误的教师能够意识到自身的不完美,这种不完美可以帮助其与学生建立友好的关系。众多学生将教师与学生分享错误,视教师为真诚和勇气的化身,有利于获得学生的尊重和信任。四年级男生 Humphrey Eliezery Kisima 从师生平等的角度理解教师与学生分享错误的意义。Jesca Aseth 认为该理念有助于学生提高学习成绩。

Cinosye Ella Seme 和五年级男生 Agustino Myamba 等认为该理念不好。学生是依靠教师获得知识的,如果教师和学生分享错误,很有可能会使学生学到教师犯过的错误,会误导学生,不利于学生提高学习成绩。Aisha Dusto 不赞同该理念。她把教师的错误视为教师的弱点,而其主动展示个人的弱点是不明智的。相反,教师应该树立一个良好的形象。五年级男生 Michael Karinga 认为分享错误不利于建立良好的师生关系。五年级男生

[①] 《毛泽东文集》(第 3 卷),北京:人民出版社 1996 年版,第 360 页。

Gilbert Ezekia 说教师经常犯错,就证明其没有足够的能力,并不是一个好教师。

就第三题而言,三谷中学的中学生、坦桑尼亚大学生、喀麦隆大学和浙江师范大学生(此处指的是接受访谈和参与问卷的学生,而非指坦桑尼亚、喀麦隆全体中学生和大学生。)对"教师主动与学生分享错误的教学行为"大多持肯定态度,百分比达到70%以上。持否定评价的,浙江师范大学大学生最低,仅为2.1%。喀麦隆大学的大学生持否定态度的达到18%。但处于"不好说"阶段的大学生中,浙江师范大学的大学生达到了19.1%。总体而言,有10%—30%的参与访谈或问卷的中非学生对"教师主动与学生分享错误的教学行为"处于"不好说"的阶段。

第四题:在你的观念中,怎么样的老师才算是一个好老师?(可多选)

(1) 知识渊博,善于帮助学生提高学习成绩;

(2) 善于与学生分享自身错误,能培养学生自信心的老师;

(3) 个性开朗,能接受学生的意见,同时和学生打成一片的老师。

表 4

师生来源 选项	三谷中学教师	三谷中学学生	坦桑尼亚大学生	喀麦隆大学生	浙江师范大学大学生
第一选项	100%	80%	65%	60%	66.7%
第二选项	10%	26%	19%	34%	66.9%
第三选项	0%	14%	18%	25%	66.2%

受访的教师100%选择了第一选项,认为学校的首要任务是教给学生知识,提高学生成绩。所以,教师必须具备渊博的知识,才能教给学生更多的知识,促进智力的发展。只有 Robson Kyungu 还选择了第二选项。他认为教师不仅要传授学生知识,提高学生成绩,还应该能够培养学生的自信心,教会学生怎样做人。2010年5月,本人与学生林斌曾想利用去阿尔及利亚奥兰大学访问的机会,到该校的课堂上交流儒家教育理念"分享错误"。遗憾的

是,奥兰大学的大学生母语是阿拉伯语和法语,大多学生无法听懂英文,所以这件事我就放弃了。后来,我们与奥兰大学(Oran University)4位科学教师进行了座谈。虽然他们认同以下逻辑:"学生从错误中学习。学生可以从自身错误中学习,那么,请问学生能否从教师的错误中学习吗?答案是肯定。所以,教师应该与学生分享错误。"四位教师觉得逻辑正确,但实际上他们从未实践过"分享错误"。其中一位科学教师从教30多年,从未实践分享错误的教育理念,最后其强烈反对分享错误的教育理念。经过近两个小时的讨论,我们达成共识:合格教师(Qualified Teacher)应该多实践"分享错误"(Sharing Mistakes)的教学理念。

就学生而言,选择第一选项占学生人数的80%,选择第二选项的占26%,选择第三选项的占14%。学生们认为,知识渊博的教师可以帮助学生学习更多的知识,从而提高学生的学习成绩,顺利通过考试。六年级男生Daniel Kipanta说,学校把学习成绩好的学生视为好学生,大学的好坏也取决于学生的国考成绩,所以帮助学生提高学习成绩的是好教师。至于教师是否与学生分享错误,一方面很少教师实践这一教学理念;另一方面他马上要面临国考,他不在乎其是否分享错误。Daniel Kipanta的话是六年级学生普遍的心声,因为他们马上面临国考的压力。

Timota Samsoni和Minza Njombe等选择第二选项的原因是,实践分享错误教学理念的教师既能提高学生成绩,同时也有利于培养学生的自信心。Lindu Michael和Humphrey Eliezery Kisima认为上述三个选项都有道理。他们认为,教师首先必须是知识渊博的,这样学生才能学到更多的知识。其次教师善于与学生分享错误,学生会觉得自己与教师的地位比较平等,有利于建立良好的师生关系,以后会主动与教师探讨问题,同时提升学生的自信心。Sitia Mwansite选择第三选项。她喜欢性格开朗的教师,与她建立友好的关系。这样的教师更加了解学生的需求,同时学生通过教师了解学习生活以外的事情,使学生更加了解社会生活,提高学生的生活技能。Jesca

Christopher 则认为上述三个选项都不好。第一选项过于注重学生的学习成绩,其他方面如生活等方面也要重视。对于第二选项,她认为教师不能总是和学生分享自己的错误,况且教师也不会对所有的问题都犯错误。对于第三选项,教师与学生固然要建立良好的师生关系,但不能太亲密无间,必要时候也要有自己的权威。综上所述,合格教师应多实践分享错误的理念,是可以被认同的。

就第四题而言,中学生倾向于选择第一选项,尤其是面对国考压力的中学生。中非大学生选择第一选项的百分比有所下降,但仍旧是最重要的选项。其次,与参与问卷的坦桑尼亚、喀麦隆大学生相比,参与问卷的浙江师范大学大学生更愿意接受"分享错误型"教师,其百分比达到66.9%,而坦桑尼亚大学生和喀麦隆大学生对其的认同度仅为19%和34%。为什么中非学生会出现如此大的差异呢?是否与教师的权威相关呢?当然,在问卷设计时,即使中非学生在这项差异甚小的情况下,我们仍要追问"分享错误型"教师的权威是否受到影响。于是我们设计了第五题。

第五题:你觉得教师主动与学生分享错误,会影响到教师的权威吗?
(1) 不会。因为教师能主动分享错误本身就是一种高尚师德的体现;
(2) 会。因为教师是权威的象征,其主要的任务就是传授知识给学生;
(3) 不好说。没有思考过这样的问题。

表5

选项 \ 师生来源	三谷中学教师	三谷中学学生	坦桑尼亚大学生	喀麦隆大学生	浙江师范大学大学生
第一选项	100%	74%	62%	51%	80.1%
第二选项	0%	24%	22%	42%	6.3%
第三选项	0%	2%	16%	7%	13.6%

受访的教师100%选择了第一选项,认为分享错误不会影响教师的权威,而且是一种高尚师德的体现。Enock Ukali 选择第一选项,但他强调教师

要注意和学生分享错误的方式,有些错误是不适合与学生分享的,可能有些学生会认为这位教师和学生是一样的水平,会质疑教师的权威。教师都强调教师是人,是人就会犯错,所以分享错误更有利于赢得学生的尊重。颇为有趣的是,受访的教师平时偶尔与学生分享错误,但他们却认为分享错误更能赢得学生的尊重。也就是说,他们一直没有采用更能赢得学生尊重的教学方式。另一方面,受访的都是从事教学多年的合格教师,所以他们大多不担心实践"分享错误"教学理念可能带来的负面结果。教师很自信地说,学生信任他们,不会因为分享错误而被学生贬低。

就三谷中学的中学生而言,选择第一选项占学生总人数的74%,选择第二选项的占24%,选择第三选项的占2%。在第三题中反对教师在课堂上分享错误的学生,在第五题中选择了第二选项,因为他们认为分享错误影响教师的权威。而选择本题第一选项的学生基本上重复之前的看法,比如教师是人,是人都会犯错。或者从平等、诚实和友好等角度,说明分享错误会增强师生之间的感情。有的学生好心提醒教师,经常性分享错误会让学生认为教师不具备良好的教学能力,影响教师的权威。Amani Mwamba 认为即使是总统也会犯错,但总统犯错也不会影响他作为总统的权威。我们跟他讲了阿尔及利亚的故事:阿尔及利亚奥兰大学(Oran University)吉埃特·布菲里(Ghiat Boufelia)教授说道:"我们的总统阿齐兹·布特弗利卡(Abdelaziz Bouteflika)在电视中说:'我们错了,我们犯了错误。'老百姓听了就不干了,他们说假如你也会犯错,请你离开总统的位置。但我却认为,总统先生说他错了的时候,我们应该更加尊重我们的总统,因为这是符合人性的。"[1]Amani Mwamba 赞同布菲里教授的看法。选择第二选项的学生,比如 Michael

---

[1] 吉布提留学生 Hoche 说:"如果他们国家的总统愿意与民众开展自我批评或者分享错误,他会十分欢迎。因为这是一位充满智慧、谦卑的领导人。"当阿尔及利亚总统布特弗利卡与民众开展公开自我批评之时,民众却表现出极大的不理解,但布特弗利卡总统的行为是可以得到中国儒家教育思想"分享错误"以及党建教育思想"公开自我批评"的辩护。

Karinga 和六年级男生 Samwel Mwambene 认为教师是权威的象征,学生知道教师的错误,学生会认为教师不是一个好教师,对其丧失信心。教师不和学生分享自身的错误就不会影响其权威性。

将第五题和第三题的回答进行对比,我们发现,第三题中浙江师范大学大学生选择第一选项的学生占总人数的百分比为 78.8%,认为教师主动与学生分享错误的教学行为是一位好教师。相应地,在第五题中其有 80.1%选择第一选项,认为教师主动与学生分享错误不会影响权威。但喀麦隆和坦桑尼亚的大学生在此过程中发现了较大的变化,分别从 70%降为 51%,从 87%降为 62%,降幅分别达到 19%和 25%。也就是说,喀麦隆、坦桑尼亚的大学生虽然欣赏教师主动与学生分享错误,但还是担心教师的权威因此受到影响。

第六题:你认为"分享错误"的教学理念长期未被提及的原因是什么?(可多选)

(1) 教师自身的原因不愿意分享,对于自身错误千方百计隐瞒;
(2) 现行教师评价体系的束缚,包括社会的不认可等因素;
(3) 教育科研人员不重视;
(4) 没有提出这个理念的必要性,因为教师犯错本来就不能被人们认可。

表 6

师生来源 选项	三谷中学教师	三谷中学学生	坦桑尼亚大学生	喀麦隆大学生	浙江师范大学大学生
第一选项	40%	68%	41%	47%	49.8%
第二选项	80%	14%	20%	24%	75.3%
第三选项	10%	26%	31%	27%	29%
第四选项	0%	6%	9%	11%	19.1%

受访的教师有 40%选择了第一选项,认为教师倾向于隐瞒自身的错误,不愿意和学生分享错误。有的教师认为,如果和学生分享错误,学生会认为这位教师没有足够的能力而去质疑教师。另一个原因是教师没有分享错误

的意识,教师会想为什么要分享错误呢?但其实每个人都在学习,学生通过教师、同学、父母学习,也能从他们的错误中学习。80%的受访教师选择了第二选项,认为目前的评价体系中没有包含教师主动分享错误的理念,这导致很多教师没有这方面的意识。社会上人们认为教师都是知识渊博的,教师的知识多于学生,教师是不会犯错的。Ester Andron认为分享错误型教师理念可以推广,将其纳入现行的教师评价体系中去,促进教师更好地自我反省,建立师生间良好的沟通。英语教师Kasale Osman认为第一、第二、第三选项都有道理。有些教师由于担心学生对教师的评价,所以不敢和学生分享自己的错误。同时,现行教师评价体系也没有包含有关教师分享错误的理念。有10%的教师选择了第三选项,他们觉得教育科研人员同样没有注意到"分享错误"教育理念的必要性。没有教师选择第四选项,显然教师均认可"分享错误"这一教育理念。

就中学生而言,有68%的学生选择第一选项,远高于其他选项。中学生认为,教师不想和学生分享错误,主要是教师担心自身的权威受到影响。这与受访的10位教师都不担心分享错误会影响他们的权威形成鲜明的对比。有14%的学生选择第二选项,有26%的学生选择了第三选项,因为他们认为教师深受教育科研人员的影响。有6%的学生选择第四选项。参与问卷的中非大学生之中,有40%以上认为"分享错误"的教学理念长期未被提及,个人因素颇为重要。而浙江师范大学的大学生则认为,社会评价体系对教师的影响至深:有75.3%的学生认为,现行评价体系束缚了该理念的推广和认同。让人惊讶的是,有19.1%的浙江师范大学的大学生认为,没有必要提出分享错误的教育理念,因为教师犯错不被社会认可。这一比例远高于参与问卷的坦桑尼亚和喀麦隆的大学生。

第七题:对于学者提出"分享错误"的教育新理念,你是一种怎么样的态度?

(1)我认为很好。无论是对学生还是教师来说,该理念都是一个进步的

理念;

(2) 行不通,因为教师犯错不能被社会所接纳,大家会认为教师很差劲;

(3) 我不知道,但是持着一种观望的态度。

表 7

选项 师生来源	三谷中学教师	三谷中学学生	坦桑尼亚大学生	喀麦隆大学生	浙江师范大学大学生
第一选项	100%	74%	70%	67%	80%
第二选项	0%	26%	16%	18%	3.6%
第三选项	0%	0%	14%	15%	16.4%

第八题:从事教师教育工作时,你将来是否愿意主动与学生分享自身的错误?为什么?

(1) 会,因为我认为主动与学生分享错误是对学生尊重的体现,对学生的学习和成长都会有很大的帮助;

(2) 不会。因为如果和学生分享了错误,我作为教师的威严就没有了,就很难开展教学工作了;

(3) 不知道。没想过这样的问题。

表 8

选项 师生来源	三谷中学教师	三谷中学学生	坦桑尼亚大学生	喀麦隆大学生	浙江师范大学大学生
第一选项	100%	76%	72%	75%	79%
第二选项	0%	20%	19%	13%	5.4%
第三选项	0%	4%	9%	12%	15.6%

第七题再度考察师生对"分享错误"教学理念的认同度,第八题考察师生将来是否愿意实践该理念。三谷中学的教师在第七题中均选择了第一选项,认为该理念是一种进步的理念。其在第八题中同样选择第一选项。中学生在第七题和第八题的选择上,个人认同和实践上略有差异。坦桑尼亚大学和

喀麦隆大学的大学生对于"分享错误"教学理念的不认同的分别为16％和18％,不愿意在将来再实践之分别为19％和13％。将第七题和第三题进行对比,我们发现,在填写问卷的过程中,坦桑尼亚大学生认同"分享错误"的教学理念的在第三题达到87％,但在第七题降为70％,降幅达到17％。喀麦隆大学生认同该理念的在第三题为70％,但在第七题降为67％,降幅为3％。浙江师范大学大学生认同该理念的在第三题为78.8％,在第七题升至80％,上升了1.2％。坦桑尼亚大学生不认同"分享错误"的教学理念的在第三题为7％,但在第七题升为16％,上升了9％。喀麦隆大学生不认同该理念的在第三题为18％,在第七题仍为18％。浙江师范大学大学生不认同该理念的在第三题为2.1％,在第七题升至3.6％,上升了1.4％。这说明在深入填写问卷的过程中,有的学生对"分享错误"教学理念反复思考是否接受之。而三谷中学教师对"分享错误"教学理念的认同度较为稳定。

三、教案:儒家教育思想"分享错误"在非洲孔子课堂的教学实践

(一) **教学目的**:树立非洲学生心目中的孔子形象:孔子是"分享错误型"教师,是勇于承认自己错误的人。尤其是,要让非洲学生了解孔子的至理名言,并非生而知之,而是在试错实践的基础上总结出来的。让非洲学生了解在创新领域内不断试错、分享错误和纠错的过程是社会发展的基本演进方法,并以中国发展为案例加以解释。

(二) **教学重点**:儒家教育思想"分享错误"的理论渊源;中国近代以来落后的根源是缺乏通往未来的试错实践及相应的教育。

(三) **教材**:《教学"新"理念:分享错误》,《上海教育科研》2007年第1期;《孔子的学习观与"因材施教"新论》,《新疆师范大学学报》(哲学社会科学版)2008年第3期;《论新型大学新理念:"分享错误"》,《学术界》2011年第4期;《新自由主义的实质:"新殖民理论"——兼论非洲"结构调整计划"》,《学

术界》2015 年第 12 期。

（四）教师与教学对象：温国砫；雅温得第二大学孔子学院杜阿拉 2 级学生，共 11 人。

（五）教学步骤：通过对儒家教学理念"分享错误"的介绍，演示分享错误过程，从而延伸到试错法是人类进步的普遍方法；试错权是人类发展的母权。讨论中国的"容错机制"与现代化进程。

（六）教学过程

1. 案例启示（20 分钟）

写出汉字：先生、九十九、六十六，让学生标出拼音，然后给出错误答案：xiāng sheng、jǐu shí jǐu、liù shí liù，让学生认读。在此期间：

（1）若学生指出其中错误，教师便坦诚承认错误，并改正错误。

（2）若学生未指出错误，则在学生朗读几遍后，教师自己发现错误，并向学生们坦白，上述是教师故意犯错，考察同学们是否辨别出教师的错误。但下面的错误，并不是教师故意犯错，而是教师在做学生时经常犯的错误。

（3）写出汉字：日和曰。

小时候，作为教师的我"日和曰"分不清，甚至追问发明汉字的人，为何采用这种区分呢？最后，错多了，也就接受这种区分。此外，翘舌音与平舌音小时候学习时我并不注意，直到进行汉语发音纠正时才发现自己错了很多年。举例说明教师学习"前鼻音和后鼻音"的发声技巧，以及教师是如何犯错的。再比如，在美国学者面前，教师发 theory 的音，美国人居然听不懂，后来才知道我把 th 发成/S/音，此后很注意两者之间的区别。最后提问：教师是如何成长的？在试错中成长。

人是从错误中学习的。学生可以从自己的错误中学习，那么，学生能否从教师的错误中学习呢？同意的请举手（统计举手的人数）。然后，展示我们的问卷结果：

第九题：在你的多年求学中，是否有老师主动与你分享过老师自身的错误？

(1) 有，经常（小学、初中、高中、大学）；

(2) 有，偶尔（小学、初中、高中、大学）；

(3) 没有。

表 9

选项　　师生来源	三谷中学教师	三谷中学学生	坦桑尼亚大学生	喀麦隆大学生	浙江师范大学大学生
第一选项	0%	6%	24%	23%	7.7%
第二选项	100%	58%	31%	57%	56.8%
第三选项	0%	36%	45%	20%	35.5%

中非教师为何不愿意主动与学生分享错误？请学生分析原因。从试错到纠错的过程是人类进步的最基本方法？是否认同？

2. 儒家教育思想"分享错误"之教学（30分钟）

孔子"分享错误"的教学思想主要表现为以下三种情境：

(1) 老师不说，无论学生是否在场，他们可能永远都不知道老师犯错了。老师该如何对待自己的错误？人类进步是以犯错误为基础的，尝试了错误的方法，才能找到正确的方向。儒家教学理念分享错误的精髓就在于此。孔子是最早阐述"分享错误或自我批评"的思想，他提出了通过尝试并发现错误，然后获得新的见解。比如，孔子谈到"学与思"的关系时说："学而不思则罔，思而不学则殆。"①他告诉学生，他尝试过"终日不食，终夜不寝，以思，无益"，凭空胡思乱想，是错误的做法，还"不如学也"。② 所以说，"思而不学则殆"是孔子通过尝试，发现错误之后悟出来的道理。

(2) 师生均在场，学生通过辩护说明自己是对的，老师是错的。老师该

---

① 《论语·为政》。

② 《论语·卫灵公》。

如何对待自己的错误？子游在武城做父母官时，孔子带领弟子前往。到武城时听到弦歌之声，孔子莞尔而笑，说："割鸡焉用牛刀？"①，言鸡乃小牲，割之乃用小刀，何用解牛之大刀，以喻治小何须用大道。子游辩解说："昔者偃也闻诸夫子曰：'君子学道则爱人，小人学道则易使也。'"子游所引的，正是孔子日常所说的话。言君子、小人皆不可以不学，故武城虽小，亦必教以礼乐。孔子意识到自己刚才说错话了，当场便呼其弟子，"二三子！"提醒学生专心听他下面要讲的话。他说："偃之言是也。"做老师的，要告诉学生的，不是他的"至理名言"，而是当众承认子游说得对呀，前提却是承认自己刚才说得不对："前言戏之耳！"孔子不仅实践了"过而改之"，且当场"分享错误"，而认错之快，其心之诚，溢于言表，堪称楷模。

（3）当别人指出其几乎不能"过而改之"的重大错误时，老师该如何应对？孔子所处的时代，同姓不婚被视为基本的礼法。但身为君王的鲁昭公却娶了同族的女子为妻。所以陈司败问孔子："昭公知礼乎？"孔子却说："知礼。"孔子退后，陈司败还有话要说。他就和小孔子30岁的学生巫马期谈："吾闻君子不党，君子亦党乎？君取于吴为同姓，谓之吴孟子。君而知礼，孰不知礼？"巫马期把陈司败的话带给老师。孔子竟然没有替自己的言语辩护，而是承认自己的过错，说："丘也幸，苟有过，人必知之。"在很多情况下孔子本有多种选择，为自己开脱或避而不答，但他选择了当着学生的面承认错误。有感于孔子的认错，此评价颇高，说："讳者非讳，若受而为过，则所讳者又以明矣，亦非讳也。"

在《论语·子张》中，我们可以看到孔子分享错误或自我批评的思想被他的学生继承并发扬光大。如子贡曰："君子之过也，如日月之食焉；过也，人皆见之；更也，人皆仰之。"意思就是君子（道德楷模）的过错，好比天上的日食、月食一样，犯过的错误，人人都能看见，改正错误之后，人人都敬仰他。这是

---

① 《论语·阳货》。

一种非常高境界的自我批评,我们可以看到作为道德楷模的君子都有犯错的时候,但改正过来之后却是"人皆仰之",充分体现了孔子"分享错误或自我批评"的思想。

此处要指出英文翻译的错误:君子翻译成英文时,通常用Gentleman,但该词无法真正理解君子,因为中国的君子指的是愿意与学生分享错误的人,而英国式的Gentleman没有这一层意思。

3. 儒家教育思想"分享错误"与杜威思维五步法(10分钟)

杜威的"思维五步法":(1)学生要有一个真实的经验的情境;(2)在这个情境内部产生一个真实的问题,作为思维的刺激物;(3)他要占有知识资料,从事必要的观察,对付这个问题;(4)他必须负责有条不紊地展开他所想出的解决问题的方法;(5)他要有机会和需要通过应用检验他的观念,使这些观念意义明确,并且让他自己发现它们是否有效。

人类最初能传递的是"试错的实践或活动",但在杜威的五步教学法中,教师与学生"分享错误"的教学理念完全缺失。在该环节,教师与学生一起讨论如何将儒家教育思想"分享错误"融入教学法之中。

4. 将儒家教育思想"分享错误"与"容错机制"强调的试错权联系起来(20分钟)

让学生三人一组,选出一位组长,让组长代表三人上台做一道难题较高的题目——题目是从汉语水平考试的试题中选出来的。允许换一次人,即每组有两次机会答题。答对了,全组学生奖励三份礼物;答错了,全组学生每人做20个俯卧撑。因而,三个人中必然选出汉语水平最高的一位即组长前去答题。但另外两个人并不能保证选出来的这个人能够答对题目,因此他们必须共同承担答错题目的后果。

一旦选出来的组长试错失败了,他有义务回来把为什么答错了题目告诉另外两个人(此处讨论:代表三人试错的组长做错了,能否拒绝与另外两位"分享错误"?)。他们三个人可以互相商量,最后再次推出一人答题。由于此前答错题目的人汉语水平最高，那么他经过了分析错误之后，就更有可能答对题目。三人都有1/3的机会通过试错答题。每个人都有试错的资格即拥有试错权，但每个人的试错权都是不完整的，只有1/3。所以，三人必须将每个人1/3的试错权交给其中一人去试错，否则被视为无效。而试错完之后其中一人得回来与另外两人"分享错误"，进而纠错，最后尝试更为合理的试错。

5. 中国的试错实践及其教育（20分钟）

我们知道，中国是文明古国。中国古代科技曾一度独领风骚，比如"四大发明"为人类文明的进步和发展作出了巨大的贡献。但是，从近代鸦片战争以来，中国却在科技发展中远远落后于欧洲各国。随之而来的是一系列屈辱的岁月，中华民族走到了"最危险的时候"。近代中国为何会走到这一步？英国学者李约瑟曾提出了"李约瑟难题"：尽管中国古代对人类科技发展作出了很多重要贡献，但为什么科学和工业革命没有在近代的中国发生？（此处与学生展开讨论）

在试错的角度看，我们会看到另一种令人豁然开朗的答案：从古代通往近代的路上，中国缺少的是通往未来的试错实践。缺少了这种试错实践，"传递这种试错实践的活动"即教育亦无法展开，或者说"分享通往未来的试错实践"处于缺失状态，所以中国落后了。中国航海曾经领先世界，但明朝的海运，阻碍了进一步的试错实践。瓦特花费了10年时间不断试错，从自身的试错中学习，终于改良了蒸汽机，使之具有实用价值。瓦特的试错实践在当时无疑是迈向未来的试错实践，所以英国率先发起了工业革命（此处与学生讨论非洲在哪些领域的试错实践指向未来）。经历了"三千年未有之变局"之后，无数的中国仁人志士开始学习世界先进国家的试错经验，以图"师夷长技以制夷"。从洋务运动到戊戌变法，从辛亥革命推翻帝制到军阀割据，再到日本帝国主义的入侵，无数中国的精英和普通百姓们付出了鲜血的代价，捍卫了国家的主权和民族的尊严后，才迎来中华人民共和国的成立。

在建设社会主义的道路上，中国共产党进行了诸多试错实践。改革开放时期,邓小平等同志提出了"摸着石头过河"的渐进试错原则,并以"试点"的方式来进行经济体制改革,取得了成功(此处讨论非洲20世纪80年代以来被迫接受了美国的新自由主义,失去了独立探索非洲现代化道路的机会)。"试点"的思想开创了在创新领域下一切从实际出发、积累试错经验从而找到正确发展道路(讨论哪些非洲国家学习中国"试点"的思想发展经济)。2006年7月,深圳市制定了"试错条例",建立了"容错机制",为在创新领域从事改革的官员保驾护航,同时及时地将试错实践公之于众即与民众分享错误,以便教育官员与群众。至2017年年底,全国31个省、自治区和直辖市相继出台"容错机制",为中国进一步探索通往未来的试错实践提供法律保障。

6. 围绕问卷与学生交流儒家教育思想"分享错误"(20分钟)

7. 学生提问。学生提到了两个重要问题:老师,你认为容错机制具有普遍意义性,那么容错机制能否解释非洲的发展?如何解释容错机制与中国现代化道路?

8. 总结、布置作业

(1)儒家教育思想"分享错误"是一种道德实践吗?(2)儒家教育思想"分享错误"与喀麦隆传统文化之间能否融通?该思想是否对喀麦隆课堂教学有促进作用?(3)中国的历史发展表明,通往未来的试错实践的缺乏是导致中国近代以来落后的主要根源,喀麦隆甚至非洲近代乃至现在落后于世界潮流是否也是同样的原因?

四、儒家教育思想"分享错误"在非洲的认同度

对坦桑尼亚三谷中学教师访谈结果表明,儒家教育思想"分享错误"作为教学法对于他们而言完全是陌生的,所以教师除了被动与学生分享错误之外,真正主动与学生分享错误的教学实践颇为稀缺。但受访的教师均认同"分享错误"这一教学理念。对中非大学生的问卷表明,大多数学生亦认同主

动与学生分享错误的教师。绝大多数中非学生认为，教师主动与学生分享错误将有助于提高学生的学习成绩、自信心，更是实践了勇于承认错误，有错就改的高大形象。中非学生之中，仍旧有部分学生反对该理念，因其担心教师的权威受到挑战，以及教师可能无法承受社会的压力。随着该理念的传播和推广，越来越多的学生会认可之。在我们访谈的过程中，谈到教学理念"分享错误"是孔子教育思想的精髓时，坦桑尼亚和喀麦隆的师生都表示他们对孔子充满尊敬，希望有机会到孔子学院学习。所以我们认为从儒家教育思想"分享错误"的角度，更能在中非之间搭起交流与合作的桥梁。而从西方传来的教育学理念来看，从苏格拉底、柏拉图、亚里士多德，到近代的夸美纽斯、洛克、卢梭乃至赫尔巴特、杜威的教学论之中，众多的教育名家均未将教师与学生主动分享错误视为重要的教育理念。所以，通过中非儒家教育思想"分享错误"的交流，有助于中非师生从新的视角重新审视西方教育理论体系。

汉办专职教师温国砡在孔子课堂上讲述儒家教育思想"分享错误"之时，11位喀麦隆学生从最初未曾听说过这一教育理念到后来特别认同这种教学方法，并表现出极大的兴趣。这11位学生听说2500年之前的孔子便实践了"分享错误"的教学理念，自然而然认为这种教学理念非常值得提倡，因为该思想经受住了时间的考验。但这11位喀麦隆大学生显然不能理解"分享错误"是一种美德。喀麦隆人注重亲情，愿与和他人分享食物，亲人之间可以分享财富，但彼此之间分享错误则颇为罕见。从喀麦隆整个文化来讲，缺乏长辈（包括教师）与晚辈（包括学生）分享错误的传统。我们提出的假设："法属殖民地更强调权威，不容易接受分享错误的教育理念，而英属殖民地更能接受分享错误的教育思想。"这一观点再度在这11位大学生身上得到验证。基于儒家教育思想"分享错误"，温国砡与非洲学生一道，重新思考西方思想家比如赫尔巴特、杜威等教育理论存在的问题，其中最关键的是修正赫尔巴特教学形式阶段和杜威的"思维五步法"。参与上课的11位学生积极参与修改，表现出极大的热情。上完课后，这11位大学生对中国的"容错机制"颇感兴趣,那么容错机制能否解释非洲的发展?如何解释容错机制与中国现代化道路之间的关系?从上述问题可以看出,非洲学生对汉办教师提出了很高的要求,不仅要通晓孔子的教育思想,还要对中国现代化道路给出能与世界对话的解释。我们认为,从儒家教育思想"分享错误"的角度,让非洲教师重新认识教育、教学、教师的内涵。其次,通过儒家教育思想与党建教育思想的融通性,让非洲人认识中国革命的艰辛,以及改革开放所取得的成就。最后,共同研究非洲传统文化与儒家教育思想"分享错误"的融通性。

中国对非洲教育援助项目中的人类学角色

牛忠光

内容摘要：从 20 世纪 60 年代初我国向非洲派出第一批医疗援助团队迄今，我国对非援助已经形成了独具特色的援助体系和政策理念。国内与之相关的学术研究成果不仅深化了人们对援助非洲的认识，而且很大程度上也驳斥了西方的"中国威胁论"等。然而，从文献研究角度来看，这些研究大多集中于政治学、历史学、经济学等领域，而缺少人类学学科视野下的反思。事实上，西方人类学自其建立伊始是为便于欧洲殖民者对其非洲殖民地的管理，即使西方殖民体系土崩瓦解之后，人类学中延伸出来的应用人类学、发展人类学等学科分支也大多关注于西方国家对非洲或其他发展中国家的援助项目。鉴于此，我们从发展人类学的视角，通过对西方人类学在非洲发展研究所扮演角色的反思，以及对我国某个援非项目的分析，认为在当前"一带一路"大背景下我国人类学学者需要更多地批判性地引介西方人类学在此方面的成果，深入我国对非教育援助项目之中开展田野调查，扮演好和处理好研究与咨询的双重角色，为我国对非援助的顺利实施提供参考。

关 键 词：中国；非洲；援助；人类学；角色

作者简介：牛忠光，江汉大学外国语学院讲师

一、引言

中国对非洲大陆的援助最早可以追溯到 20 世纪 60 年代,当时中国政府向阿尔及利亚派遣了第一批医疗援助队。而后,1964 年周恩来总理访问非洲各国,并在加纳和马里阐明了著名的"对外经济技术援助八项主张",这八项主张至今依然是中国对非外交政策的基石。中非关系渡过了 50 多年的风雨历程,历经了 5 个 10 年的不同发展阶段;或者简单而言,改革开放之前和之后两个一脉相承但也特色鲜明的重要时期[1]。无论哪个时期,[2]中国对非援助都具有自身特色,与西方对外援助实践或学术话语理论体系存在明显区别。

20 世纪晚期西方人类学界曾经针对西方殖民统治、西方在第三世界国家实施的发展援助项目、援助政策的形成和实施过程进行了持续深入的反思和批评。而相比之下,我国人类学家对中国对外援助实践的关注较少。那么,他们又该如何借鉴西方人类学家们的反思和批评,来界定他们自身在中国对非援助实践中的角色呢?或者,从多大程度上而言,中国的援助项目能够接纳人类学家的参与?在援助实践这样一个涉及不同利益主体的复杂权力关系网络之中,他们又如何摆脱一种两难的境地,即一方面按照援助者和受援助当局的意愿和计划将援助项目顺利执行,而另一方面又需要根据客观中立的学术和道德要求来保护当地被援助者的利益呢?

---

[1] 贺文萍:《中国援助非洲:发展特点、作用及面临的挑战》,《西亚非洲》2010 年第 7 期,第 12—19+79 页。
[2] 即西方学界例如 Brautigam(2008)曾将中国对非援助分为"安全与社会主义时期"(1950—1963)、"领导第三世界时期"(1964—1977)、"合作共赢时期"(1978—1994)和"走出去时期"(1995 年至今)。

二、中国人类学与对非项目援助研究

随着中国企业人员和资本不断涌入非洲大陆,来自西方社会的批评声音也纷至沓来。西方社会认为中国是在利用援助来掠夺非洲的自然资源、导致贸易不平衡、进行新殖民主义,等等。[①] 还有一些批评认为,中国企业为了挣钱而污染和破坏环境以及向非洲输入中国劳动力等[②]。但是,与这些批评相对照的则是中非合作稳步不断深入的发展。当然,中国和非洲各国也并非无视这些批评的存在,相反,自上而下的政府关切一直持续不断地进行着,而且中国本土人类学学者对于这些问题的关注也开始出现。但是,比起西方人类学家们对非洲援助和发展问题的深入而广泛的反思和研究成果,国内学界的非洲研究或者援非研究大多集中于政治学、历史学、经济学等学科领域,只有少几位学者如潘华琼[③]、蒋俊[④]、马燕坤[⑤]和徐薇[⑥]等从理论层面阐述过人类

---

① Robert I. Rotberg, "China's Quest for Resources, Opportunities, and Influence in Africa," In R. I. Rotberg, ed., *China into Africa: Trade, Aid, and Influence*. Washington, D. C.: Brooking Institution Press, pp. 1-20; Jeremy. Kelley, "China in Africa: Curing the Resource Curse with Infrastructure and Modernization," *Sustainable Development Law & Policy*, Vol. 12, No. 3, 2013, pp. 35-60.

② Naidu, S., & Davies, M. China fuels its future with Africa's riches. *South African Journal of International Affairs*, Vol. 13, No. 2, 2006, pp. 69-83; Zhao, S. A neo-colonialist predator or development partner? China's engagement and rebalance in Africa. *Journal of Contemporary China*, (ahead-of-print), 1-20. http://www.soderbom.net/Roads_Enterprises.pdf, accessed on May 20, 2014.

③ 潘华琼:《非洲人类学研究:希望与困难并存》,《西亚非洲》2000年第3期,第47—51+77页。

④ 蒋俊:《非洲人类学:演进、实践与启示》,《西亚非洲》2010年第3期,第68—72页。

⑤ 马燕坤、刘鸿武:《自我表述与他者表述整合的非洲图景——兼论非洲研究的视角与方法》,《西亚非洲》2009年第9期,第15—19+79页;马燕坤:《记忆、想象与重构:人类学对非洲形象的创造》,《北方民族大学学报(哲学社会科学版)》2010年第1期,第117—122页;马燕坤:《人类学非洲研究及中国学科建构的现实诉求》,《西亚非洲》2010年第7期,第26—31+80页;马燕坤:《人类学对非洲的发现与重现》,《世界民族》2011年第2期,第50—54页。

⑥ 徐薇:《人类学的非洲研究:历史、现状与反思》,《民族研究》2016年第2期,第111—120+126页。

学与非洲研究之间的关系。近两年,专门针对我国对非发展援助的研究田野式调查成果才开始出现。① 这些研究主要关注于中国企业在非洲的发展以及中国对非洲农业发展的援助项目,具有浓厚的人类学实证色彩。但是,整体来看,我国学界对于人类学和人类学家在中非发展援助项目中所扮演的角色仍缺少反思,并且目前来看相关研究依旧局限于农业领域和非洲中资企业方面,而对于诸如教育领域广泛存在的多方位援助项目仍缺少相关研究。

究其原因,从历史的角度来看,是由于从 20 世纪 50 年代到 70 年代,人类学学科被取消。直到 80 年代末,"人类学"才开始在高校机构中出现,一些年轻的人类学学者开始引进西方人类学理论,开展与国外的学术交流②。此后,我国人类学经过二三十年的发展,出现了包括发展人类学、经济人类学、工商人类学等人类学分支学科。然而,我国人类学特别是发展人类学仍然是处于不平衡发展阶段,其研究对象依旧是关注国内少数民族地区的经济发展问题或民族地区的经济研究,进入 21 世纪之后相关研究议题也拓展到了我国城市商业发展、市郊农村都市化、农村发展和农村扶贫等方面③,也有一些学者基于中国的发展实践反思"发展主义"④,或者对西方的发展人类学理论进行总结和反思⑤。

---

① 徐薇:《中国与非洲:能否跨越制度与文化的边界——基于某中博合资玻璃厂的工商人类学考察》,《青海民族研究》2016 年第 3 期,第 43—48 页;卢琰:《国家与个人:中国援非农业专家的身份研究》,中国农业大学 2016 年博士论文;雷雯、王伊欢、李小云:《制造"同意":非洲如何接纳中国农村的发展经验?——某中坦援助项目的发展人类学观察》,《广西民族研究》2017 年第 3 期,第 91—98 页;王伊欢、雷雯:《中国企业跨国互动策略及其社会责任研究——基于对某中坦农场的工商人类学考察》,《西南民族大学学报(人文社科版)》2017 年第 5 期,第 8—14 页;陆继霞、李小云:《中国援非农技专家角色分析——以中国援非农技组派遣项目为例》,《外交评论(外交学院学报)》2017 年第 4 期,第 85—105 页。
② 胡鸿保:《中国人类学史》,北京:中国人民大学出版社 2006 年版。
③ 朱晓阳、谭颖:《对中国"发展"和"发展干预"研究的反思》,《社会学研究》2010 年第 4 期,第 175—198+245—246 页。
④ 叶敬忠、孙睿昕:《发展主义研究评述》,《中国农业大学学报(社会科学版)》2012 年第 2 期,第 57—65 页。
⑤ 潘天舒:《发展人类学概论》,上海:华东理工大学出版社 2012 年版。

实际上,与西方学界从20世纪末对"发展"问题的广泛批评反思相比,我国人类学者对关于"发展"的批评关注较少。其原因一方面,20世纪至今早期我国人类学所秉持的"学以致用"、"改造社会"的知识传统,具体而言便是帮助中国快速实现经济和社会发展的知识取向[①];另一方面,作为第三世界国家,我国经济发展的成功以及曾经作为西方援助对象的经验,都使得无论是官方还是民众相信"发展是硬道理"。在这种情况下,我国人类学家如同其他领域的知识分子一样,在对城市和农村经济发展建言献策方面被寄予厚望。然而,近些年来随着我国经济遭遇到了发展转型的瓶颈,发展人类学作为一种分析工具或反思角度,较之以前也受到更多的关注[②]。与此同时,中国实施的"走出去"战略以及新近的"一带一路"倡议,我国对非援助关系的深入发展,使得我国对非洲的发展援助遭遇到社会政治、文化、环境等问题的挑战,我们更应该思索的是国内人类学家们要如何适应新形势,在这一领域扮演重要的角色。

基于西方发展人类学近40多年的理论知识,笔者认为,面对我国在非洲发展进程中的广泛参与,我国人类学家们应该主动反思其应该在其中所要扮演的角色。具体而言,他们如何看待我国的对非发展援助与西方对非援助的关系?我国政府或者援助项目的实施者是否欢迎人类学家的参与?当政府邀请人类学家参与项目咨询或研究时,他们又如何界定自己的身份?人类学家又如何看待当前中国发展理念对于非洲的影响或者移植?针对这些问题,笔者所要反思的是人类学究竟是扮演"实用性的项目参与者",还是"不带任何偏见的批评者"呢?

---

① 引自加州大学伯克利分校人类学华裔教授刘新于2014年4月16日在中国人民大学人类学研究所进行的题为《中国人类学的昨天与今天》的讲座。(中国人民大学人类学研究所通讯,《人类学记事》,第三卷第二期总第十期,2014年4月,第11页。)
② 罗康隆、黄贻修:《发展与代价:中国少数民族发展问题研究》,民族出版社2006年版;陈刚:《发展人类学视野中的文化生态旅游开发——以云南泸沽湖为例》,《广西民族研究》2009年第3期,第163—171页。

其实，这一反思脱胎于人类学传统上对于"学术"、"应用"和"实践"（practicing）的争论。西方大多数人类学家认为，与研究对象的内在事物保持一定距离对于保持相对中立的立场非常必要，从这个意义上，他们与另外一些真正实际参与到项目之中的人类学家不同，后者志于将知识应用到项目实践当中。相应地，人类学在西方学界被细分为三类，即学术人类学、应用人类学和实践人类学（Nolan，2002）[①]。这三者的关系在20世纪西方人类学界被称为"距离与参与之舞"（dance of distance and embrace）[②]，并且强调与发展项目的"距离"，而非实际"参与"。然而，这一人类学方法论上的争论，在其他发展中国家则"相对温和甚或根本不存在"（Hill & Baba，2006：8）。我国情况亦是如此，即我国人类学传统强调"应用研究的价值"，因为"传统中国知识分子秉持着学以致用的理念"[③]。在这一传统影响下，我国的发展人类学研究更多是应用型的，即人类学研究者"在大多数情况下从事学术研究"，"也从事学校以外的项目咨询等实用性工作"[④]。因此，我们倡导人类学研究者应该在进行参与式观察研究之外，在条件许可的情况下，也有必要参与到所研究的发展援助项目中去。

但是，在这一过程中，由于人类学家扮演研究者和项目执行者双重角色，他们便更应具有强烈的警惕性，警惕滑入西方人类学家对非殖民时期或者20世纪50年代之后西方对非发展援助中所产生的"西方中心主义"强势霸

[①] Nolan, R. W. (2002). *Development anthropology: Encounters in the real world*. Cambridge MA: Westview Press.

[②] Hill, C. E., & Baba, M. L. (2006). "Global Connections and Practicing Anthropology in the 21st Century". In: Hill, C. E., & Baba, M. L. (eds). *The globalization of anthropology*. NAPA Bulletin, Vol. 25, pp. 1-13.

[③] Wang, Jianmin and Young John A. (2006). "Applied Anthropology in China". In: Hill, C. E., & Baba, M. L. (eds). *The globalization of anthropology*. NAPA Bulletin, Vol. 25, pp. 70-81.

[④] Venkatesan, S., & Yarrow, T. (Eds.). (2012). *Differentiating development: beyond an anthropology of critique*. New York and Oxford: Berghahn Books.

权话语。这里我们仅以马林诺夫斯基对西方在非洲的殖民管理的研究为例，展开进一步的探讨。

三、马林诺夫斯基的教训

事实上，人类学的"工具性"，即成为一个服务性学科，是由现代人类学的开创者马林诺夫斯基在 20 世纪 20 年代早期所最先倡导的。当时，面对西方学界对于英国和法国在其殖民地的殖民行政管理的争论，马林诺夫斯基提出了"实干家"（practical man）的概念，认为在"野蛮人法律（savage law）、经济、习俗和制度"方面，实干家需要人类学家们参与到殖民管理中，"不了解这些知识会使得他常常在黑暗中摸索"①。"只有当实干家意识到他不能在黑暗中辗转摸索，意识到他需要人类学知识，他才能变得对（人类学）专家有利，并且反过来，人类学专家也会对他有用。"（同上：37）那么，"人类学家必须直接去研究现存正在运作的本土制度，他必须集中关注针对正在变迁的非洲以及白人和有色人种的接触、欧洲文化和原始部落文化之间的人类学研究"（同上：22）。具体而言，人类学家"必须拓展他的研究兴趣，将之适应与他一起工作的人和当地人的实际需求"（同上：22）。客观而言，马林诺夫斯基所倡导的人类学参入殖民政府管理，对后来应用人类学的建立起到了重要作用。但是，他的这一做法也受到了后世的严厉批评，当时的人类学被普遍批判为殖民主义的"共谋"。

这里之所以重提 20 世纪初马林诺夫斯基的观点，我们想要强调的是我国对非援助与早期西方在非洲的殖民统治以及后来西方对非援助在本质上截然不同，我国人类学家在对非援助项目参与和研究中的角色应该是作为不同利益相关者之间的中介者（mediator），而非是某一方的"共谋"。从马林诺

---

① B. Malinowski, "Practical Anthropology," *Journal of the International African Institute*, Vol. 13, No. 1, 1929, pp. 22 - 38.

夫斯基时代算起,殖民主义已经瓦解了半个多世纪,人类学面对其内部反思和外部批评,也历经了多次范式转换。今天的人类家们已经不再会天真地去选择为某一个目标群体服务,特别是像具有制度性权力的政府或国际援助组织等,来操作本土"发展",而是充分地认识到了通过考察一个发展项目的方方面面来探究其是否可行或有意义。然而,无论人们如何努力寻求世界的平等,至今不平等的政治和经济权力依旧充斥于全球各个角落,人类学家们也不可避免地被卷入其中。当我国人类学家开始从事非洲研究,对中国援非政策和实践或者中国企业在非洲大陆的实践进行调查分析时,将近一个世纪之前马林诺夫斯基对他们而言依旧是一个警醒。我国人类学研究者要清醒地意识到面对西方的激烈批评,需要秉持道德、实用和相对主义立场。中非政府层面的政策话语均强调相互合作和平等交流是双方合作的主流,同时任何一方也都有各自不同的政治经济利益诉求。例如,早在 2009 年广州举办的一场"中国海外研究"会议上,中国社会学、人类学学者严海蓉便指出,中国学者不仅要反驳西方对于中非关系的错误认知,而且也要明确指出中国对于非洲的援助并非是完全慈善性的捐助[1]。而实际上,变化中的现实要比预想的更复杂。当私企工人、小生意老板、非法移民等中国民众涌入非洲,并不断出现与非洲本地民众的冲突时(例如,中国人在加纳的非法采金等问题),我国政府也开始意识到已经很难像以前那样完全运用行政权力去维护和经营中国在非洲的良好形象。[2] 这一问题也已经引起有关学者的注意和研究[3]。对于参与其中的我国人类家而言,他们又该如何处理与政府之间的关系呢?而当中国私企意识到需要寻求人类学家的帮助来避免或解决与非洲当地

---

[1] 刘小枫等:《中国海外研究(上)》,《开放时代》2010 年第 1 期,第 5—62 页。
[2] 2012 年我国外交部非洲司一位官员在中央民族大学民族学与社会学学院的一次学术讲座中也曾指出,近年来由于一些中国商人和工人在非洲触犯当地法律,给我国在非洲人民中的良好形象带来了极大的负面影响。
[3] 沙伯力、严海蓉:《非洲人对于中非关系的认知(上)》,《西亚非洲》2010 年第 8 期,第 13 页。以及沙伯力、严海蓉:《非洲人对于中非关系的认知(下)》,《西亚非洲》2010 年第 11 期,第 11 页。

民众的冲突时,人类学家们又该如何界定他们的角色？这些都是需要我国人类学研究者们所需要思考的。抛开其他不讲,单有一点是需要警惕和避免的,即不要成为某些牺牲当地民众利益的糟糕援助项目或私企发展项目的"共谋"。

四、一个中国对埃塞俄比亚的教育援助发展项目案例分析

论及人类学家在援助发展项目中的角色问题,西方人类学家们的研究大多基于人类学家本人对援助项目的参与观察式的田野调查,另外也有一些人类学家根据自身参与发展援助项目的经历,展开相关项目研究。如上所述,近年来我国的非洲研究特别是我国对非援助项目研究中业已出现人类学方面的研究成果,然而作为援助项目参与者的研究者的反思性研究还鲜见。鉴于此,笔者将以中非教育援助项目"当事人"身份或佛古森所谓的"前线工作者"(frontline worker)[①]身份,以及作为一名人类学研究者的双重身份视角,基于我国对埃塞俄比亚的一项职业教育援助项目的分析,对援助项目本身以及人类学家的角色问题进行回顾性反思,这有助于再次确定人类家们扮演实际参与者或不带偏见的批评者过程的重要性和积极意义。

2008年,笔者与其他同事由我国教育部派遣,与埃塞俄比亚教育部签订劳务合同,参与援助一项高等职业教育援助项目。我们对外的职业身份为国家公派"援外教师",而外方即埃塞俄比亚的接纳身份为外国专家雇员。

一项援助项目的开展往往前后会持续许多年,牵涉许多利益相关群体,涵盖方方面面。笔者的研究视野限定在项目所实施的两年(2008、2009),所关注对象是包括前线参与者在内的相关行动者,聚焦于他们之间相互交织的社会网络。具体而言,该项目涉及两个层面的利益相关者,即中方和埃塞俄

[①] Ferguson J. (1994) The Anti-politics Machine: "Development", *Depoliticization and Bureaucratic Power in Lesotho*. Minneapolis: University of Minnesota Press.

比亚方,其中双方所牵涉的都是一些与项目相关的政府组织。

该援助项目包括了两个阶段。第一个阶段是基建方面的援助,即规划和建立校园内的办公楼、教学楼、大礼堂、操场等基础设施。这些设施由我国商务部具体负责实施和项目招标,中资企业承建,根据两国政府间协议,建好之后,整个校园以及其中的建筑全部免费捐献给埃塞俄比亚方,其所有权全部归属埃方。第二个阶段是两国教育合作框架之下的人力资源援助,应埃塞俄比亚教育部请求,中方决定继续向埃塞俄比亚捐献办公家具、教学和培训设备,并提供人力资源援助;埃塞俄比亚教育部为中方援助师资提供基本工资,而我国教育部则按照援外政策为援外人员提供相关补助。在这种情形下,中方一线援助人员既是我国对外援教专家,又是埃塞俄比亚方聘用的雇员,他们便肩负了两种职责,同时需要满足中方和埃塞俄比亚方的双重要求。另外,除了受两国政府的领导之外,他们的援教行为也受限于我国国内相关组织机构,显而易见经常面临具有不同要求的不同利益相关者们的协商和约束。从某种意义上而言,该教育援助项目在技术和知识援助之外,也处于一种复杂的"权力博弈"之中。

首先,在中方援助话语体系中,一方面,中国援助人员和专家被认为是技术传授者(technological transferor),即参照中国职业教育的经验,帮助埃塞俄比亚方培养职业技术人才;另一方面,相关的中方各相关政府部门期待中方一线援教人员成为中埃双方的友谊"大使",能够促进两国人民之间的交流和友谊。因此,尽管该援助像任何其他对非援助一样不设有任何政治性条款限制,但是政治性"期待"却弥漫在援助项目的方方面面。

而相比之下,埃塞俄比亚方在该项目实施过程中也有自身不同的期望。他们的主要目的是邀请中方专家传授技术知识,希望借此能够提升埃塞俄比亚职业教育质量,最终能够满足埃塞俄比亚工业和经济发展需求。另外,其中一个隐性目的是希望能从中方获得更多的援助,从而确保该职教学院的顺利运行。例如,为了满足埃塞俄比亚建筑和基础设施领域的劳动力市场需求,埃塞俄比亚方试图说服中方能够帮助他们成立建筑系。但是,各种渠道的努力最终均没有获得中方积极回应。后来,埃塞俄比亚教育部转而转变学院职能,提升该学院办学层次,即从培养职业技术人员(相当于我国职业技术学院)转变为培养职教师资(相当于我国师范类大学)。①

除了以上这种政府之间的高层交流,基层的行动者,即主要是学院之中的双方一线员工也处于文化交流的相互适应和碰撞之中。对于中方一线工作人员而言,其能动性促使他们坚持依靠其专业知识以及基于此的专业理解去执行教育援助,而中方政府层面则好像更多希望他们能够强化中方在埃塞俄比亚的存在,树立中国促进埃塞俄比亚教育和经济发展的"友谊使者"形象。不同的期待和理解,在学院运行过程中出现了不同程度的碰撞。尽管该学院在双方努力之下最终开张运行,并培养了第一批毕业生,但是在某些场合,国内相关部门对该项目的运行效果仍存有微词。其中最重要一点便是,他们认为中方一线援助人员没有成功地在该项目运行过程掌握主导权。然而,中方一线援助人员则持有不同看法,认为来自不同方面的权力干预不可避免会出现许多意想不到的后果。特别是我们国家在实施该教育项目援助过程中没有完全充分地考虑埃塞俄比亚社会的现实,以及埃塞俄比亚对自身职业教育发展的理解和规划。

从人类学的外部、整体论视角来看,最为吊诡的是,从一开始人类学家或者其他专家均没有被邀请评估该教育援助项目的实施效果。所有的评判都局限于非正式或非官方层面。具有限资料可见,针对该项目的所谓官方评估,也只是每一位中方一线援助人员提交的一份工作总结报告。该援助项目目前仍然按照埃塞俄比亚方的教育发展计划和中方的援助继续运行,但是其

---

① 实际上,埃塞俄比亚教育部在对该教育援助项目的规划上表现出太大的灵活性,甚至令人感觉很随意。最开始,埃塞俄比亚教育部请求中方帮助其建立一所中等职业学校,但是当校区基建完成之后,他们又决定将其升格为高等职业学院。然而,当该学院运行4年,刚完成两届学生的培养之后,埃塞俄比亚教育部再次决定转变其职能,而升格为联邦职教师资培训学院。

中任何一方均没有迹象邀请人类学家或其他学科专家的参与。

从以往研究文献来看,没有什么知识分子会真正地受到政治家们的欢迎,被邀请参与发展援助项目。在《真理与权力》(1980)一书中,福柯阐述了两种知识分子,即"一般"知识分子和"具体"知识分子,两个概念分别类似于"体制内知识分子"和"体制外知识分子"[①]。这一分类主要基于科学的政治性以及其潜在的意识形态功能。一般认为,后一类知识分子置身于政治权力体系之中,而常常需要及时地参与到政治活动之中,帮助制定特定政策,并确保政策的执行和实施。毫不奇怪,在当前这个资本横行的世界,后者占了很大一部分,他们的行为受到特定意识体系的限制,其政治限制之下的意识形态因素充斥于西方意识形态的发展或援助实践和研究之中,这与人文科学研究所一直追求的价值中立想背道而驰。

面对这样一种矛盾困境,人类学家在发展援助项目中如何摆正他们自身的位置呢?毫无疑问,殖民时期马林诺夫斯基们的所作所为,以及20世纪七八十年代的发展项目,已经广受后现代主义者或解构主义者的批评,它们已不可能在今日重现。然而,时至今日,人类学家在发展援助项目中的角色也从未被动摇,或者使他们自己远离这些项目,而是以整体论分析视角对他们在其中的角色进行着重塑。具体而言,他们的目标群体面向所有的参与者,而非仅仅是过去人类学田野调查中的本地人。因此,从事发展援助项目研究的人类学者需要承担两种角色,一是他们自身需要成为有能力理性地发现问题和解决问题的参与者,直接地审视整个项目,以发现如何使得社会文化因素能够确保项目实施,而非成为其羁绊。而这并不能简单地被认为是人类学

---

① 叶敬忠:《发展的西方话语说——兼序〈遭遇发展〉中译本》,《中国农业大学学报(社会科学版)》2011年第2期,第5—15页。For more discussions about Chinese intellectuals' roles in contemporary China, please see Gu and Goldman (2004). Gu, E. and Goldman, M. (eds). (2004) *Chinese Intellectuals between State and Market*. London: Routledge Curzon.

家又重回到了像殖民政治权力的"共谋者"角色,①特别是针对其中捐赠者的权力。其中,人类学的角色所强调的依然是人类学知识的实用性和适用性,而其最终要看的是如何推动发展项目的实施能够平衡每一位利益相关者的利益。另一方面,参与发展援助项目时,人类学家需要抱有一种批判的眼光,甚至在"伙伴关系"、"平等"和"不附带任何政治条件"等这样的援助话语之下,能够认识到"一套理性化话语的背后暗含着官僚权力或霸权(dominance)意图,其中发展援助的真正政治目的是隐藏在理性规划的外衣之下的"②。进一步而言,需要进一步说明背后隐含的政治目的从某种程度上是无害或者没有剥削性的,而有时只是与捐助国自身的国家利益相关,或者有时只是受到某个权威参与者的个人偏好所致。然而,权威参与者个人偏好对于发展项目的计划、执行和评估好似并没有引起发展人类家的更多关注,而这也正是笔者所建议的,即将对"权威参与者"作为一个关键变量或因素去揭示中国对非援助的实践。

莫斯赛(Mosse)认为在发展政策上存在着工具性和批评性两种截然相反的主导观点,而这在他看来是了解政策话语和援助实践之间关系的障碍。正如他所言:"发展进行极富洞察力的民族志调查能够打开项目实施的黑匣子,从而解决政策与实践之间的关系问题,但是这些截然相反的工具性和批判性观点却阻碍了这一进程。"③然而,笔者却不认为这两种观点无法调和。人类学家并非不可能在参与发展援助项目时,采纳这两种观点或者说担当两种角色。人类学传统上的文化相对论和整体论视角,使得人类家们更易于听

---

① 事实上,很多西方学者对于中国在非洲发展的参与的批评,也片面地回到了20世纪末反思人类学对于西方殖民权力的批评的窠臼里面,特别是那些以"新殖民主义"批评中国对非援助的论调。
② D. Mosse, "Is good policy unimplementable? Reflections on the ethnography of aid policy and practice," *Development and Change*, Vol. 35, No. 4, 2004, p. 641.
③ D. Mosse, "Is good policy unimplementable? Reflections on the ethnography of aid policy and practice," *Development and Change*, Vol. 35, No. 4, 2004, pp. 639–671.

取利益相关各方的观点,特别是对于当地人的诉求,并且他们也更能考虑到"非技术性"的文化因素[①]。以教育援助项目为例,从工具性的角度而言,人类学家之所以能够在其中找到一席之地,是因为中国的发展经验从某种意义上而言对于非洲发展有借鉴意义,由于两者共享着类似的历史遭遇和某些文化特质,并且具有相同的减贫和经济发展诉求。中国对非援助实践的实施也正是基于此种期望。然而,与此同时,需要给予更多关注的还有兼容性问题(compatibility),即中国的发展模式是否适合所有非洲国家。在援助项目实施和评估过程中,人类学对于所有利益相关者们的细致入微的民族志调查和对比分析,在这个意义上大有裨益。

五、结语

毫无疑问,中国的经济发展对发展中国家或欠发达国家产生了持续影响,特别是那些致力于减贫和推动国民经济繁荣发展的非洲国家,更是如此。中国的经济成功发展对于非洲国家而言,最明显的意义则在于印证了发展人类学家们所一直努力打破的偏见,即西方对于第三世界国家的偏见,认为在西方发达国家主导之下第三世界国家或发展中国家无法获得充分发展,最终会不可避免地沦落为西方主导的全球不平等经济体制的牺牲者。的确,在这样一个不平等的全球市场体制之内中国的成功发展经验,使大多数非洲国家获得了发展其自身经济的信心和动力。中国与非洲在诸多方面的利益需求,促使两者在众多领域正在开展深入地援助项目合作。但在这一过程中,人类学对援助发展项目的参与调查研究和深入反思还比较欠缺。

众所周知,包括人类学家在内的大多数知识分子也一直不断努力维系其对社会问题的批评反思立场,他们期待能够有助于构建一种相对平等、多样

[①] 潘天舒:《发展人类学概论》,上海:华东理工大学出版社 2012 年版,第 122 页。

化和互尊互重的社会,而非充满明显或隐形的不平等和剥削。这也从某种程度上使得援助项目实施的中外双方对研究者存在或隐或显的"警惕"。但是,学术研究者本身不是"麻烦制造者"(trouble-maker),而是"解决问题者"(trouble-shooter)。因此,人类学本身的知识体系有助于人类学研究者成为在两种文化之间发现问题和解决问题的援助项目参与者,推动援助项目顾及各方利益相关者的利益和立场,并且能够从整体性角度对项目进行评估式研究,从而为今后类似援助项目的进一步开展提供借鉴。

埃塞俄比亚留学生价值观实证研究
——基于天津职业技术师范大学的数据

王 慧 翟风杰

内容摘要：为了解埃塞俄比亚留学生价值观特点，以期为跨文化管理提供依据，本文运用施瓦茨价值观理论对埃塞俄比亚留学生和中国学生的价值观进行了实证研究和对比分析。结果显示，埃塞俄比亚留学生与中国学生在价值观方面存在较大差异。这启示我们在埃塞俄比亚留学生管理过程中要提高跨文化敏感性和移情能力，善于从价值观角度思考问题，并对埃塞俄比亚留学生跨文化适应给予关注。

关 键 词：施瓦茨价值观理论；埃塞留学生；肖像价值观问卷；SSA地图

作者简介：王慧，天津职业技术师范大学助教。翟风杰，天津职业技术师范大学教授

　　来华留学生管理本质上是一种跨文化管理，属于跨文化交际的范畴。而价值观则"可以说是跨文化交际的核心"。本文拟采用目前发展较为成熟、应用较为广泛的施瓦

茨肖像价值观问卷(Portrait Value Questionnaire,以下简称PVQ)对天津职业技术师范大学埃塞俄比亚来华留学生(以下简称"埃塞留学生")的价值观进行实证分析,了解其基本取向、特点及结构,并将其与相同层次中国学生的价值观进行比较研究,明确差异所在,以期为相关院校完善埃塞留学生跨文化管理制度、提高跨文化管理效率提供基本依据。

一、施瓦茨价值观理论

(一)价值观类别

施瓦茨(Shalom H. Schwartz)于1992年对来自20个国家的样本进行了经验分析,并在此基础上提出了人类基本价值理论(Theory of basic human values)。该理论源于人类的三种基本需求:个人作为生物体的需求,协调地进行社会交往的需求和群体得以存续和发展的需求。根据对这三种需求的不同回答,推导出十种价值观类别,即自我导向、刺激、享乐主义、成就、权力、安全、遵从、传统、仁爱和普世主义。每一种价值观类别各自对应的核心动机目标如表1所示:

表1 价值观及其核心动机目标

价值观	核心动机目标
自我导向	独立思考和行动;选择、创造和探索
刺激	追求生活中的兴奋、新奇和挑战
享乐主义	追求个人的快乐和感官满足
成就	根据社会标准,通过证明能力来实现个人成功
权力	社会地位和声望,控制或主宰人或资源
安全	安全,和谐,社会关系及自身的稳定
遵从	对有可能伤害他人或违反社会期望及规则的行动、倾向和冲动的约束
传统	尊重,信奉,对于传统或宗教给予自己的风俗及观念的接受
仁爱	对群体内与自己有频繁接触的人的福利加以保障和强化
普世主义	理解、感激、包容,保护所有人和所有文明的福利

(二)价值观结构

施瓦茨(1994)根据上述价值观所体现的核心动机目标之间的协调或冲突关系,采用最小空间分析法(Smallest Space Analysis,SSA)对其进行了结构分析,10种价值观类别按照各自核心动机目标之间的相关系数被由近及远地排列于环状结构(Circumflex)中,相互冲突的价值观类别被置于相反的位置而相互协调的价值观则被置于相邻的位置,位置越近彼此的动机目标越相似,反之亦然。

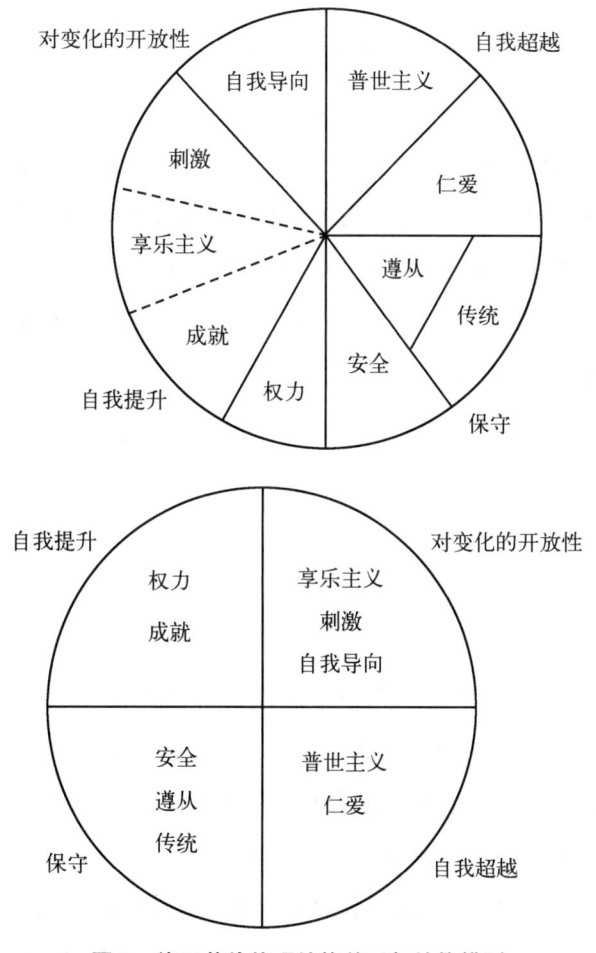

图1 施瓦茨价值观结构关系与结构模型

根据上述结构关系,施瓦茨进一步建立了"开放"对"保守"、"自我超越"对"自我强化"的二维度四分区的价值观结构模型。"开放"追求的是个体独立的思想和行为以及有益的改变,包括"自我导向"、"刺激"、"享乐主义";"保守"表征的是自我约束、维护传统以及保持稳定,包括"遵从"、"传统"与"安全";"自我超越"讲求人际平等、关心他人,包括"普世主义"和"仁爱";"自我强化"则与"自我超越"相反,追求个体自身的成功和对他人的控制,包括"成就"和"权力"。

(三)肖像价值观问卷

在价值观研究过程中,施瓦茨先后发明了两种价值观测量工具:施瓦茨价值观量表(Schwartz Values Survey,简称 SVS)和肖像价值观问卷(Portrait Value Questionnaire,以下简称PVQ)。其中,PVQ是根据价值观类别的内涵,设计出40项价值观条目,每一项都描述了一个具有某种特征的人物肖像,与上述价值观类别内涵的动机目标相对应。每种价值观类别对应3—6个问题,问题的多少取决于此种价值观内涵的宽泛程度。以六级量表的形式由高到低反映被调查者与问题所描述人物的相似程度。被调查者的不同回答会获得不同的分数,从而反映出不同的价值观取向。

二、研究方法

(一)问卷调查

采取课堂发放和电子邮件两种形式向天津职业技术师范大学埃塞俄比亚留学生(含往届学生)发放了PVQ问卷。鉴于埃塞留学生均具有较高的英语水平,因此使用英文原版问卷。其中,课堂发放是主要的问卷发放形式,占比88%。两种方式均在发放前对调查目的、匿名性、填写时间作了明确说明。本次调查总计发放100份问卷,回收86份,其中,8份全部答案均相同,作为无效问卷予以剔除,有效问卷共计78份。为最大限度剔除管理制度、校园文化等外在环境变量的影响,减少误差,本文选择天津职业技术师范大学的100名中国学生作为参照对象。问卷为中文版本,调查方法同上,其中,4份问卷未能完成,因此,有效问卷共计96份。

（二）分析软件

本文所采用的分析工具为 IBM SPSS Statistics 19.0。

（三）研究方法

本文首先问卷结果进行信度分析,发现测试结果均为有效。其次用均值排序及多维尺度分析两种方法对埃塞俄比亚留学生和中国学生的价值观进行了比较分析,发现两者在价值观认同度和价值观结构上均存在较大差异。

三、实证研究

（一）变量选取

本文选择施瓦茨价值观理论中的10种价值观作为研究变量,即自我导向、刺激、享乐主义、成就、权力、安全、遵从、传统、仁爱和普世主义。

（二）信度分析

本文选择目前最常用的克朗巴哈系数作为信度系数,分别计算埃塞留学生及中国学生的克朗巴哈系数,得到表2结果。信度分析结果显示,问卷调查的数据可靠,可用于进一步的分析。

表2 中埃学生的克朗巴哈系数

价值观	克朗巴哈系数	
	埃塞留学生	中国学生
权　力	0.801	0.736
成　就	0.776	0.758
享乐主义	0.821	0.635
刺　激	0.779	0.789

续　表

价值观	克朗巴哈系数	
	埃塞留学生	中国学生
自我导向	0.788	0.712
普世主义	0.82	0.808
仁　爱	0.808	0.75
传　统	0.606	0.717
遵　从	0.858	0.779
安　全	0.833	0.819
总　体	0.916	0.885

(三)价值观类别排序分析

1. 埃塞俄比亚留学生的价值观类别排序分析

将埃塞留学生10种价值观均值从高到低排序,其价值观划分为三档:第一档均值在5分以上,表明埃塞留学生对该类价值观的认同度很高,包括仁爱、自我导向、普世主义和安全;第二档均值小于5分但接近5分,意味着埃塞俄比亚留学生对这几种价值观有较高的认同度,包括享乐主义、遵从、刺激和成就;第三档是均值在5分以下,表明埃塞俄比亚留学生对这种价值观类别的认同度较低,包括传统和权力。

价值观是在个体社会化的过程中逐步形成的,个体生存发展所处的生活环境必然会对其价值观的形成及变化产生重要影响。故本文通过分析埃塞留学生的生活环境,对其价值观顺序加以解释:

第一,本文的研究对象大部分出生于20世纪90年代,1991年以后出生者占被调查者总体的79.5%。1991年是埃塞俄比亚国家发展史的分水岭。埃塞俄比亚政权也在这一年发生了更迭,废除了一党制,实行联邦制和多党制,并于几年后实施了新的宪法。一般而言,宪法体现了民众意志的最大公约数,也体现了一个国家的主流意识形态,因此无疑是影响价值观的重要环境变量。"体现在新宪法中的最重要的原则有:(1)埃塞俄比亚是一个多民族国家,各民族拥有直至分离权在内的自决权;(2) 实行联邦制,中央和地方分享国家权力;(3) 强调民主权力和人权"。[①] 试看贯穿于其中的关键词——自决、分享、民主、人权,对比埃塞留学生认同度最高的价值观及其内涵——"仁爱:对群体内与自己有频繁接触的人的福利加以保障和强化"、"自我导向:独立思考和行动"和"普世主义:理解、感激、包容,保护所有人和所有文明的福利",其中的一致性一目了然。"仁爱"价值观对原则(1)和(2)是支持的,"自我导向"可以视作是原则(1)的价值观基础,"普世主义"体现在政治理念中无疑就是"民主"、"平等"。由此也能对埃塞留学生认同度较低的价值观加以解释。"权力"价值观所体现的"控制或主宰人或资源"的动机目标与权力的分享原则是相抵触的,而"传统"所追求的"对于传统或宗教给予自己的风俗及观念的接受"无疑不利于自决、民主、人权等原则的实现。

第二,埃塞俄比亚的经济社会发展状况则可以对埃塞留学生较为认同的"安全"价值观作出解释。埃塞俄比亚是联合国公布的最不发达国家之一,经济发展水平总体较低。医疗卫生水平低下,人均预期寿命短,传染性疾病高发。施瓦茨认为,安全价值观受阻时,人们会对其更加关注。因此,埃塞俄比亚留学生对于"安全价值观"的认同度很高是有充足理由的。

第三,从埃塞留学生的社会背景来看,他们普遍较年轻(平均年龄 24.18 岁),大多来自亚的斯亚贝巴等埃塞俄比亚较大的城市,大部分属于奖学金生,财产较为独立,观念较为开放。研究发现,年龄与"自我导向"、"刺激"、"享乐主义"等价值观呈负相关,即越年轻的群体越容易认可这三种价值观,而有收入相对独立的群体如自由职业者更倾向于追求"自我导向"的价值观。

2. 与中国学生价值观类别排序的比较分析

从表3可以看出,埃塞留学生认同度居于前三位的价值观分别为"仁爱"、"自我导向"和"普世主义",而中国学生分别为"遵从"、"成就"和"安全"。

[①] 钟伟云:《列国志:埃塞俄比亚,厄立特里亚》,北京:社会科学文献出版社2006年版,第114—125页。

除了排序最低的"传统"和"权力"价值观以外,两者的价值观取向没有相似之处。

表3 埃塞俄比亚留学生与中国学生价值观排序之比较

价 值 类 别	埃塞俄比亚留学生均值排序	中国学生均值排序	差 距
仁爱	1	8	7
自我导向	2	5	3
普世主义	3	6	3
安全	4	3	−1
遵从	5	1	−4
享乐主义	6	7	1
刺激	7	4	−3
成就	8	2	−6
传统	9	9	0
权力	10	10	0

中国学生的价值观特征体现了传统的影响。中国人最重视"平安",认为"人无远虑,必有近忧",主张"三思而后行","小心驶得万年船",凡事以规避风险为基本原则。另外在传统伦理道德和社会结构的深刻影响下,中国人倾向于以满足社会期待作为评判事物的标准,大而言之讲求"为国争光",小而言之讲求"光耀门楣"。

与中国学生相比,埃塞留学生更认可追求精神愉悦、追求自我实现的价值观,其动机源于满足自我而非满足社会期待,更崇尚变化而非稳定。在与埃塞留学生进行交往的过程中可以发现,无论选择课程还是在运动会中选择比赛项目,他们考虑的往往是过程与兴趣,而非结果与能力。

四、价值观结构分析

施瓦茨价值观理论除了要考察各价值观类别的顺序外,还要分析它们之间的相互关系,以掌握价值观的整体结构。本文采用多维尺度分析工具(PROXSCAL)来测量中埃学生各价值观类别之间的相似性,进而绘制各自的价值观 SSA 地图,建立各自的价值观结构模型。参数设置如下:数据格式:从数据中创建近似值,源的数目:一个矩阵源,模型:恒等函数、区间,选项:初始配置为 Torgerson。结果如表4和图2所示:

表4　应力及拟合度量

指　标	埃塞留学生	中国学生
标准化初始应力	0.013 35	0.091 71
D.A.F.	0.986 65	0.908 29

其中,埃塞留学生 Stress 值为 0.013 35,小于 2.5%;D.A.F 值为 0.986 65,趋近于1;中国学生的 Stress 值为 0.091 71,D.A.F 值为 0.908 29,表明两个模型的拟合效果都很好。

从价值观结构图来看,埃塞留学生与中国学生不但对各价值观类别的认同度存在极大差异,价值观结构即价值观类别的内部关系也很不一致。

埃塞留学生处于第一象限的价值观类别包括"刺激""自我导向"和"仁爱",对于埃塞留学生来说,保护他人福利与思想行为的独立以及追求新奇和改变是基于同一动机的;而中国学生的"仁爱""自我导向"则与"安全"紧密联系,表明在中国学生眼中,无论是追求思考或行为的独立性,还是关怀他人,都是基于和谐、稳定的目标。对于中国学生而言,"刺激"与"享乐主义"属于同一类别,而绝对不会与"仁爱"联系在一起,这个类别的价值观在中国语境中甚至是含有贬义的。

埃塞留学生的"享乐主义"和"成就"价值观处于同一维度,表明其成就是与自我满足相联系的;而中国学生的成就价值观则体现在社会层面,所为之奋斗的群体的规模与成就感的大小是成正比例的。

埃塞留学生"权力"与"传统"价值观同处第三象限,表明追求权力和尊崇

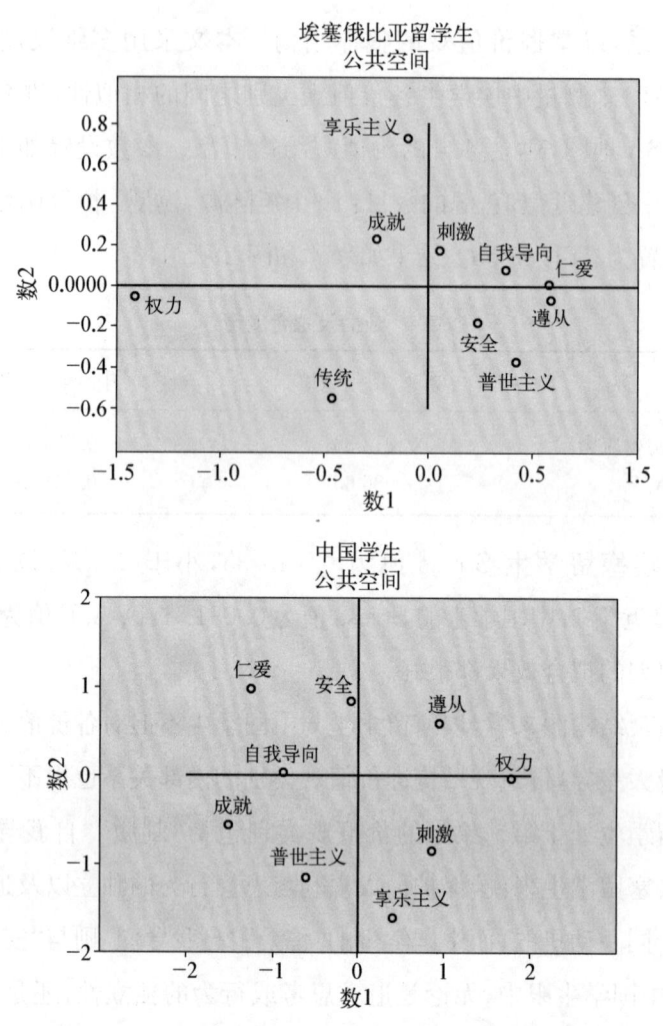

图 2 埃塞俄比亚留学生和中国学生价值观 SSA 地图

传统对于埃塞留学生来是一致的；中国学生与此类似，又加入了"遵从"价值观，反映了传统社会结构与权力等级观念、服从意识之间的一致性。

"普世主义"、"遵从"和"安全"居于埃塞留学生价值观结构的第四象限，说明追求平等、公义、自我克制以服从社会希望与和谐、稳定三者的深层动机是一致的；而如前所述，中国学生的"遵从"和"安全"则是与"权力"相联系的。

与施瓦茨价值观结构图相比，埃塞留学生价值观结构呈现出价值观类别沿逆时针方向向相邻价值观维度移动的态势，"权力"进入了"保守"维度，"遵从"和"安全"进入了"自我超越"维度，"仁爱"进入了"开放维度"，"享乐主义"则进入了"自我强化"维度。可以看出，埃塞留学生的价值观结构与施瓦茨价值观结构的差异并不大。这种差异是由个别价值观类别向相邻维度移动所引起的，并未改变施瓦茨价值观结构所基于的那种兼容对立关系。而中国学生的价值观结构与之相比则有本质差异。不仅体现为价值观类别的变动，还体现为价值观维度的变化。某些在施瓦茨价值观结构模型中处于同一维度的价值观如"自我导向""刺激"和"享乐主义"甚至处在了对立位置上。这有可能是中国社会转型期的复杂社会结构和多元思想文化交织状态在大学生价值观上的一种反映。比如"自我导向"与"刺激""享乐主义"处在对立位置上，唯一的解释是，随着市场经济的发展，自主、自立作为改革开放的主题词已经为中国大学生所认同，而"刺激"、"享乐主义"则既为传统文化所排斥，又被主流价值观所摒弃而与之发生了对立。

另外，施瓦茨价值观结构模型是施瓦茨基于亚洲、非洲、拉丁美洲、中东、东欧、西欧以及大洋洲的13个国家和民族的样本而制定的，代表了一种普遍或者平均的价值观结构。而埃塞留学生价值观结构与施瓦茨基础价值观结构的相似性则可能印证了"文化趋同"的观点，这种观点认为政治、经济和社会领域的深远变革以及全球资本市场整合会导致世界文化趋同。当然，这种趋同只会是弱势文化向强势文化的趋同，是世界其他国家价值理念向以美国为代表的发达国家价值理念的趋同。中国学生的价值观结构则可能是中国经济快速发展、社会结构急剧变化的背景下各种观念相互角力、相互渗透的一种复杂结果。比如上文所做的价值观结构分析显示，"开放"维度的价值观类别并没有被中国学生作为一个整体认同，而是按照中国主流价值观标准作出了相互对立的区分。"文化趋同"并没有在中国学生身上发生。这给我们的启示是，在全球化背景下，如果想要保护自己的文化，维护文明多样性，只能通过不断增强自身的经济文化实力来实现，对于发展中国家来说，这一点尤为重要。

五、结论

　　本文基于施瓦茨价值观理论、运用"肖像价值观问卷"对埃塞留学生和中国学生的价值观进行了调查。调查结果具有较高的信度并且与研究对象社会化过程中所处的政治、经济、文化环境所反映出的价值观信息较为一致。

　　调查结果显示，埃塞留学生与中国学生的价值观差异较大。不仅价值观取向不尽相同，价值观结构也有明显差异。与中国学生相比，埃塞留学生更崇尚平等、自主、变化，其价值观动机是源于内部的自我满足需要而非外部的社会期待。这对于埃塞留学生管理具有如下启示：

　　首先，管理教师要正确认识并深入了解埃塞留学生与我们在价值观取向及价值观结构方面存在的差异，提高跨文化敏感性和移情能力，防止程式化的思维和简单化的工作方式，重视采取平等的沟通姿态和民主的解决方式。

　　其次，管理教师要善于从价值观角度思考管理问题产生的原因和解决问题的办法。比如，欲达到使埃塞留学生踊跃参加某项活动的目标，应避免采用"展示留学生良好形象""为班集体争光"等中国式的鼓励方式，而应着力描述活动本身的趣味性。

　　最后，埃塞留学生和中国学生反映了中埃之间的"文化距离"。而"文化距离"则是影响跨文化适应的重要变量。因此，管理教师要把价值观差异作为跨文化适应的预测指标，对埃塞留学生特别是新生的文化不适给予关注，降低其"文化休克"的发生概率。

中非教育交流与产能合作的战略对接

中非产能合作：挑战与对策

姚桂梅

内容摘要：国际产能合作是新时期中国政府扩大对外投资与对外输出优势产能的一项重大倡议，是"一带一路"建设的重要内容之一。非洲是中国实施国际产能合作的重要地区，中非产能合作具备了一些有利条件，同时面临一系列新的问题与挑战：非洲多党政治出现水土不服，局部国家政局动荡、不安稳状态空前，政治安全风险提升；经济增速放缓背景下，不仅"安哥拉模式"遭遇空前挑战，而且债务风险趋升；中国企业"走出去"乱象带来的不利影响凸显；对非援助工作亟待改进；西方对中非关系的防范和干扰力度加大；在非洲的舆论环境需要改善。对此，需要中非双方携手从构建中非命运共同体的长远利益和共同利益出发，尽快化解或消弭上述问题与挑战，为中非产能合作顺利进行扫清障碍。

关 键 词：非洲；产能合作；问题；对策

作者简介：姚桂梅，中国社会科学院西亚非洲研究所研究员、南非研究中心主任、创新项目《中非产能合作重点国别研究》首席研究员国际产能合作是新时期中国政府扩大对外投资与对外输出优势产能的一项重大倡议。它的提出和实施,对于促进国内经济增长和结构调整升级、加强与世界不同发展阶段国家的发展战略对接和产业互补衔接、深入推动全球产业链高中低端深度融合、不断增强中国对"一带一路"沿线重点国家和地区经济辐射力和影响力、有效促进世界经济持续稳定复苏具有十分重要的意义。非洲是中国实施国际产能合作的重要地区。目前,中国已把埃塞俄比亚、肯尼亚、坦桑尼亚等国列为先行先试示范国家,把南非、埃及、安哥拉等国列为重点对象国;以设施联通和园区建设为主要内容的产能合作正在一些非洲国家重点推进,业已取得良好的阶段性成果。但同时也面临着来自非洲、中国和国际层面的新问题与新挑战。

一、中非产能合作面临的问题和挑战

2015年12月,中非合作论坛约堡峰会确立了中非全面战略合作伙伴关系。中非确定的"十大合作计划"为中非产能合作创造了良好条件,指明了前进的方向。但随着一些产能合作项目的实施,越来越多的非商业性因素困扰着项目的顺利推进,造成不利影响,需要中非双方努力化解。

(一)非洲大陆政局总体趋稳,但局部不安稳状态空前,政治安全风险提升

首先,尽管多党政治已在非洲落地生根,但西式民主与非洲本土政治交融而经常出现水土不服问题。当前最突出的就是"第三任期"问题。在"多党民选"这条红线难以逾越的情况下,非洲执政者尝试通过修宪突破任期限制成为延续和巩固政权的迂回之策。这种变革已在多国引发骚乱,殃及政局稳定性。2014年10月,执政27年的布基纳法索总统孔波雷,欲推动议会表决修宪草案,取消总统任期制,最终引发军事政变。2015年4月,布隆迪总统恩伦齐扎第三次参选总统并于7月再次当选,遭到欧美集体制裁,并引发严

重社会动荡。2015年,刚果(布)、卢旺达先后就取消总统任期限制举行了修宪公投,均已绝对多数获得通过。修宪后卢旺达总统卡加梅理论上可以执政到2034年。刚果(布)总统萨苏则在2016年3月的大选中胜出,实现再次连任。2016年9月,刚果(金)首都金沙萨也因现任总统约瑟夫·卡比拉试图通过修宪、推迟选举等方式延长其执政时间而发生大规模骚乱。

其次,肯尼亚大选出现重选闹剧,反映出肯国内政治部族化与民主化交织纠葛。2017年的肯尼亚大选可谓一波三折。虽然肯雅塔在总统重新选举中获胜,但二次投票过程动荡、冲突频发。据外媒统计,自8月8日首次大选投票至今,因选举政治引发的暴力冲突已造成约50人死亡。更为严峻的是,反对党至今仍拒不接受重选的结果,在其势力占优的基苏木等地区可能继续出现骚乱,也不排除出现暴力冲突升级的可能,从而肯尼亚政局和社会安全风险提升,对该国政经发展和吸引外资产生负面影响。

再次,非洲经济的下滑导致非洲政治与社会形态出现空前的不稳定,令投资者充满戒备。2014年以来,非洲经济增速放缓;2016年,更是迎来增速的低谷(1.7%),低于2.6%的人口增速。非洲国家外汇的减少、本币贬值、通胀攀升、失业人口的增加导致本就存在很多严重政治和社会问题的非洲国家增添了一系列的不稳定因素。党派纷争、国内战乱、游行示威、罢市罢课、武装抢劫、恐怖袭击等现象均能在非洲发现踪迹。例如,南非在经济下行背景下,不断爆发排外骚乱、学生运动等社会冲突事件,对社会稳定与治安造成了一定冲击。影响更大的是,2017年3月31日,南非总统祖马宣布改组内阁,撤换了包括财政部长戈尔丹在内的多名部长。受此影响,南非多地爆发抗议游行,4月3日和7日,国际著名评级机构标准普尔(Standard & Poor)和惠誉(Fitch Ratings)相继下调南非主权信用评级。内阁重组和降级事件将导致南非外部融资成本上升,影响投资者信心,并增大南非经济发展的不确定性。另外,在布隆迪、刚果(金)、津巴布韦、埃及等国政局或安全形势不稳,政策连续性受到挑战,再加上非洲国家固有的基建赤字、就业赤字、劳动观念、治理问题、恐怖袭击、社会冲突等复合问题,中国在非洲的人员安全问题日益突出。中非互利发展的战略目标与非洲的现存的真实环境出现相当反差,需要中非携手共同化解挑战。

(二)经济增速放缓背景下,不仅"安哥拉模式"遭遇空前挑战,而且债务风险趋升

近年来,曾深受非洲国家欢迎的资源—信贷—项目的"安哥拉模式"适用范围越来越窄。安哥拉和赞比亚与中国合作领域相对集中,模式比较单一,对华经济关系处于失衡状态。安哥拉政府用石油供应来换取中国在资金及大型基建项目方面的支持,但以市场为导向的中国民企投资十分有限。特别是受能矿等大宗商品价格持续走低的影响,安哥拉等国财政收入减少,基建投资匮乏,新上马的项目减少,在建项目也出现停建、缓建、工程款支付延迟的情况,导致2016年中国对非工程承包新签合同额和完成营业额同比增速双双放缓现象。

与此同时,一些非洲国家的债务负担加重,令人担忧。就政府债务与GDP的比例这一指标而言,2016年非洲国家的中位数为48%,相比2014年升高了10个百分点。特别是近年来,中国向埃塞俄比亚、肯尼亚、坦桑尼亚、莫桑比克、赞比亚、安哥拉、刚果(布)、津巴布韦、吉布提都提供了巨额贷款,且都与基础设施建设项目相关。根据2017年6月麦肯锡研究报告《龙狮共舞》指出,2012—2016年,中国对非政府贷款额已翻3倍。仅2015年,中国贷款占撒哈拉沙漠以南非洲国家政府当年新增债务总额的1/3。未来,如果世界经济继续低迷,大宗商品的需求没有提振,非洲国家极有可能出现对华债务违约问题。与此同时,中国还要面临"中国加剧非洲债务负担"的指责。

(三)中国企业"走出去"乱象带来的不利影响凸显

中国政府鼓励和支持企业"走出去",到非洲开展经贸合作。但随着"走出去"规模日益扩大,一系列问题和乱象显现出来。中国在非洲的企业大多从事一般商品贸易、工程承包和资源开发等较低端领域,国企、民企和私企一

拥而上,出现盲目、短视、无序或恶性竞争;只追求短期效益,忽视履行劳动保护等社会责任;有的企业不顾环境保护,对非洲资源进行粗放式开发等一系列问题;甚至还有出现了问题也未能得到有效解决的现象。

（四）对非援助工作亟待加强与改进

中国对非洲援助大幅增加,有力促进了中非关系,同时一些问题日益显现。一是在援助立项上,存在不科学、不合理、与受援国实际需求错位、与中国外交战略结合不紧密等情况。例如,有的大型公共设施华而不实,利用率低;有的援非农业项目与受援国农业发展规划脱节,成为当地的农业"孤岛",虽是样板工程但非实效工程,对当地农业的带动作用非常有限。再有一些老的援助项目,如以坦赞铁路、友谊纺织厂为代表,问题积重难返。另外,援助宣传不到位,既包括内宣,也包括外宣,造成中国百姓认为对非洲援助过多而非洲人民受惠不多的尴尬局面。

（五）西方对中非关系的防范和干扰力度加大

西方长期把非洲视为势力范围和"后花园",宁愿非洲长期贫穷落后,也不愿他人涉足。西方对快速发展的中非关系深感忧虑,认为其利益受到威胁,遂千方百计地挑拨中非关系,干扰和阻挠中国在非洲的发展,"新殖民主义论"、"中国威胁论"、"资源掠夺论"等恶毒论调由此而生。在遏制不成之后,西方转而寻求同中国进行对话与合作,提出所谓"三方合作",一为参与到中非合作中来,二为试图约束和"规范"中国在非洲的行为。由此,中非关系中的西方因素和中西关系中的非洲因素成为绕不开的议题。

二、保障中非产能合作顺利进行的对策建议

综上所述,中非产能合作面临的问题与挑战,既有政治、经济、外交、舆论方面的问题,又有中国和非洲双方之间的问题,也有外部世界的因素。中非关系中这些新问题与挑战的出现,归根结底是因为时代发生了变化,中非关

系从未像今天这样紧密而又复杂。为此,我们双方需要把握好中非关系发展的规律和趋势,从长远和全局利益出发,设计和构建好符合时代特征的合作共赢、共同发展的中非新型友好关系,为中非产能合作顺利进行扫清障碍,创造良好条件。

第一,秉持"真实亲诚"对非政策理念,维护中非高度政治互信。通过加强高层互访等方式做好非洲新一代领导人的工作,增加他们对中国的认同感和信任度,做到无论领导人怎样更换,中非友好的大局保持不变。逐步改变中国对非外交"重政府、轻民间"的状况,努力推动中非各领域、各层次的交往,积极培育非洲对华友好的民间力量,使中非友好具有广泛社会基础。对于老一辈领导人缔造的中非友好遗产,需要深入挖掘、扩大宣传、发扬光大,不能埋没遗忘。在国际事务中更多地照顾非洲国家关切的事务,积极稳妥地参与非洲和平安全事务,妥善处理非洲热点敏感问题,树立和维护中国负责任大国形象。继续坚持不干涉内政原则,但在新时期宜赋予其新内涵,需要灵活把握和运用。政治互信是中非友好的基石,为中非产能合作保驾护航。

第二,倡议在中非合作论坛框架下,设立"中非经贸合作论坛"。当前,复杂的国际经济环境下,与时俱进的中非关系出现许多新变化,尤其在经贸合作领域面临着许多新的机遇与挑战,需要重点研讨。目前的中非合作论坛框架下,在部长级会议召开前后虽然有企业家大会、智库论坛等帮衬,但尚缺乏专司经贸合作事宜的论坛辅佐。为此,倡议建立长久的、机制化的"中非经贸合作论坛"。除配合领导人峰会或部长级会议召开全议题的研讨外,还应根据新形势每年设立1—3个专项议题进行集中研讨,快速解决实践中的问题,助推共赢发展。中非经贸论坛可由商务部或由其责成某个省商务厅具体承办。

第三,非洲国家经济发展的多样化要求快速出台精细化国别对策。近年来,非洲经济发展过程中国别差异性愈发突出,这就要求中方的对非战略不仅有统筹全局的整体考虑,而且还要有精准的国别对策。例如,政府引导的对非投资领域不仅要有农业、制造业、服务业,而且要细化为食品行业、纺织服装业、建筑业、公用事业、信息技术、金融业和零售业等消费导向型行业;而国别对策中就更要有靶向指引。例如,在肯尼亚,应利用肯尼亚在东非区域的优良区位优势,开发跨区域电力、通信、港口、公路干线、航空等基础设施项目,关注农业经济作物种植加工、医疗卫生、保障性住房等农业民生领域合的优势;开拓旅游地产、互联网金融、零售等具有良好发展基础和资源优势的现代服务业领域。在安哥拉,除了投资石油外,还应关注电力、物流等基础设施项目,此外还要重视种植、养殖和加工制造业等优先领域和关乎民生的领域。在卢旺达,应持续关注基础设施、信息通信、绿色能源、产业园区,以及现代农业、旅游、会展经济等领域的合作机会,找准时机跻身重点项目。

第四,创新合作模式,加大重点领域的市场开发力度。首先,中国要探索新的市场进入策略。目前,中国在非投资项目大多为绿地投资,只有12%是合资项目,未来可考虑通过合资、并购等方式加速进入市场并扩大规模,特别是面对消费者的行业。其次,创新投融资模式。在埃塞俄比亚、肯尼亚、刚果(布)、安哥拉等中非产能合作先行先试或重点合作对象国家,可结合中国优势产能与当地发展诉求,以产业园区、自由贸易区、经济特区等模式,推动我优势产能行业的龙头企业,协同上下游企业赴非投资;在涉及种植、养殖和加工制造业等优先领域和关乎民生的领域,要发挥好投援结合、投扶结合的优势。

第五,加大金融支持力度,引导支持产能合作。跨国投资企业对股权投资、信贷、结算、汇兑等金融服务需求不断增加,但中国金融机构"走出去"的步伐落后于企业,金融服务不能满足企业需求。针对中非产能合作需求,建议:一是加大与非洲国家的货币互换力度和运作模式,缓解中资企业汇兑和汇率风险,推动双边贸易以人民币结算;二是促进国内商业银行为在非中资企业提供金融服务,推动商业银行在某些非洲国家设立分行;三是完善信贷支持政策,增强政策性贷款的作用力,针对非洲项目和市场环境的特殊性,对用于非洲的中长期贷款给予一些专项政策安排,放宽"内保外贷"和项目融资的限制,解决目前境外资产不能抵押、项目融资难等问题。四是密切关注非洲外债问题。非洲日益凸显的债务问题可能会拖累非洲国家的基础设施建设与产能合作,也将对中非合作模式产生深远影响。应跟踪研判非洲债务问题发展趋势,对重点国别作精准评估分析,在此基础上提出有效、可行的建议。

第六,改进对非援助工作,使援助更好地为外交大局和中非产能合作服务。认真践行习近平主席提出的正确义利观,在力所能及的范围内增加对非援助。进一步完善援外机制,科学审慎选定援助项目,把好立项关;将援助与中国外交大局紧密结合起来,防止为援助而援助;将援助与受援国实际需求紧密结合起来,更多地向民生领域和惠民项目倾斜;将援助与企业发展结合起来,鼓励中国带资参与援助项目。加强援外项目监督管理,严把工程质量关,杜绝形式主义。做好援外项目评估工作,完善后续跟踪机制,确保援助达到预期目的。目前中国尚无对外援助立法,重大项目可请人大代表参与,做好监督工作。改进对外援助宣传工作,掌控援助话语权,让国内民众理解和支持外援工作,让受援国民众切实感受到援助效果,为中国援助叫好。从长远和大势来说,制定有中国特色的对外援助立法,设立与中国负责任大国地位相符的专门对外援助机构,已是势在必行。确保对外援助更好地为中国外交大局服务,为中非产能合作服务。

第七,整治"走出去"乱象,推动中非产能合作顺利实施。中国"走出去"战略迫切需要顶层设计,出台"走出去"立法,完善"走出去"机制,既要加强支持与服务功能,又要加强管理与监督功能。引导中国合法、有序、有力地走出去,在非洲诚信经营,良性竞争,履行企业社会责任;将企业利益与国家利益结合起来,不以损害国家利益为代价获取企业利益;将企业命运与驻在国命运结合起来,不以漠视驻在国命运而试图独善其身。可考虑建立企业黑名单制度,被列入黑名单的企业一定时期内不得到海外经营。加强对中国赴非洲公民的教育,要求他们切实遵纪守法,尊重当地习俗,平等友好对待当地人民,维护国人良好形象。新形势下中非产能合作为中国"走出去"战略注入新的活力,"走出去"战略则为中非产能合作顺利实施铺平道路。

第八,加强在非洲的领保工作,为中非产能合作创造和平安全的环境。如果没有一个和平安全的环境,产能合作就无法展开。安全工作预防为上,中国在"走出去"之前应进行国别安全形势与项目安全风险评估,避免进入存在严重安全隐患的地区,重大敏感项目宜执行安全"一票否决"制。已进入非洲的企业和人员必须增强安全防范意识,付出相应的安全成本,切实采取安全措施,做好安全防范工作,同时遵守当地法律,避免授人以柄。从政府层面来说,针对当前有的非洲国家会发生集中抓捕外国非法移民的情况,需要通过官方渠道做好驻在国政府工作,敦促对方依法行事,防止规模性地非法抓捕中国公民,以免引发群体性事件,给两国关系带来不利影响。

第九,提升在非洲的软实力,为中非产能合作创造友善的舆论环境。产能合作过程中不可忽视文化软实力建设,中非文化交流需要同步跟上,扩大双方人民之间的友谊和理解,减少跨文化差异和误解,为中国在非洲发展创造良好条件。通过办好孔子学院、增设中国文化中心等举措,努力提升中国在非洲的软实力。全方位、多层次、多渠道开展外宣工作,密切与非洲国家主流媒体的联系,更多地邀请非洲记者访华,为申请在中国设立常驻机构的非洲媒体提供便利和支持。切实重视对非洲国家非政府组织的工作,通过提供资助和访华机会等手段增加对其影响力,为它们与中国有关部门和团体开展交流创造条件,培养一批知华、亲华的非政府组织。

第十,妥善应对中非关系中的西方因素,为中非产能合作排除干扰。对于中非产能合作,西方必定会极尽干扰甚至破坏之能事。坚决反对西方挑拨中非关系,散布"中国威胁论"、"新殖民主义论"等攻击性论调;严密防范西方对中非产能合作可能进行的阻挠甚至破坏,将其负面影响降至最低。既然中非关系中的西方因素已难避开,宜审时度势,适当回应其诉求,在坚持以我为主的前提下，尝试在农业、医疗、卫生、教育等非涉我重大核心利益且西方较为擅长的领域开展多边合作，树立中国开放、开明、合作的形象。

综上所述，中非产能合作面临的问题与挑战，既有政治、经济方面的，也有人员、舆论方面的，既有双方之间的问题，也有外部干扰因素。我们需要把握好中非关系发展的规律和趋势，从长远和全局利益出发，设计和构建好符合时代特征的中非新型友好关系，为中非产能合作顺利进行扫清障碍，创造良好条件。

中非海洋产业合作的对策建议

张振克

内容摘要：非洲国家拥有丰富的海洋资源，发展海洋经济的条件得天独厚。由于历史原因，非洲国家的海洋产业和海洋经济发展相对落后。中国海洋产业发展比较成熟，具有较为丰富的海洋产业和海洋经济发展经验，也存在非常旺盛的市场需求。目前，随着非洲国家对海洋经济的日益重视，中国和非洲国家已经迎来了开展海洋产业合作的难得历史契机。中非双方应高度重视海洋合作，在互利共赢的基础上，发掘合作潜力，推动中非海洋经济的繁荣发展。

关 键 词：中国；非洲；海洋产业合作

作者简介：张振克，南京大学非洲研究所所长，教授、博士生导师。主要从事地理学、资源环境、中非海洋合作等方面的研究

21世纪是海洋的世纪，非洲国家正迈入开发海洋资源、发展海洋产业的新时代。在中非合作不断加强的今天，中国在海洋领域有能力参与和投资非洲海洋资源开发、海洋

产业发展,如此能使中非经贸合作更加全面和平衡,进而实现中非合作共赢,服务"一带一路"建设。

一、非洲国家关注海洋经济

非洲大陆四面环海,海岸线长约 2.6 万千米,共有 38 个沿海和岛屿国家,即 2/3 的非洲国家拥有自己的海岸线。的确,非洲的海洋资源令人称羡。以渔业资源为例,2014 年,非洲国家渔业总产量为 600 万吨,其中捕捞占 83%,养殖占 17%。海洋渔业资源的开发主要是出售捕捞许可证和许可期,给国外渔业公司进行商业化的捕捞。非洲渔业产值每年达到 240 亿美元,其中养殖产值 30 亿美元;在海洋捕获量中 25% 为非洲以外国家渔船的捕捞量,价值达到 33 亿美元。

正因为非洲拥有丰富海洋资源,海洋经济有望成为推动非洲经济发展的新引擎。海洋产业、海洋经济已开始成为非盟和众多非洲国家关注的焦点。2015 年 4 月,非盟公布了《2063 议程》(非洲未来 50 年发展议程)最终版,提到非洲要走一体化的道路,其中第 15 条是关于海洋经济的内容,提出非洲要大力发展蓝色海洋经济,海洋经济是非洲经济增长和转性的重要资源基础。具体表述为:非洲拥有三倍于大陆的海域面积,非洲的蓝色经济对非洲大陆经济转型和增长是重要的引擎。海洋渔业、海洋造船运输业和深海矿产资源和相关海洋资源的开发是非洲蓝色经济的主要开发领域。

已有非洲国家制定了自己的海洋产业发展规划。2014 年,南非总统宣布南非实施 Phakisa("费吉萨")海洋开发计划。该计划主要针对南非国家海洋经济的增长及就业,指出四项产业将在海洋经济中作为优先发展产业:(1) 海上运输制造,例如沿海运输、转运、造船和船只维修及翻新;(2) 近海石油和天然气勘测;(3) 水产养殖;(4) 海洋保护和海洋治理。南非拥有东、南、西三面环海的独特地理环境,海岸线长 3 924 千米。如此广袤的海洋空间和丰富的海洋资源,其经济潜力尚未被开发。

二、非洲海洋经济与产业发展现状

尽管非洲拥有发展海洋经济得天独厚的条件和优势,但由于长期的殖民统治和独立之后的连绵战争和内乱等,目前非洲的海洋产业、海洋经济在总体上还十分薄弱。例如,虽然滨海旅游资源丰富,但开发利用有限。

在目前非洲海洋经济中占有相对突出地位的产业,主要是海洋渔业和港口运输业。对于许多非洲国家而言,海洋资源的开发,似乎仅限于渔业资源的开发,而海洋运输业、海洋船舶业、滨海旅游业、海洋油气业等其他海洋经济形式,对这些非洲国家的经济贡献率微乎其微。即便是在渔业领域,许多非洲国家的渔业资源也未得到充分开发和利用,渔业产值率非常低下。例如,非洲东部沿海坦桑尼亚、埃塞俄比亚、肯尼亚和莫桑比克的渔业/农业对GDP的贡献分别是 2.6%/25%、0.02%/39%、0.5%/27.4%、4%/28%。

再如,对许多非洲国家来说,港口运输业发挥着对外经济联系的枢纽作用,是非常重要的海洋产业。尽管近年来非洲港口发展迅速,但是,而今非洲港口的整体现代化程度、港口装卸效率普遍较低,港口基础设施建设和管理水平亟待提高。在非洲许多港口,集装箱港收费远高于世界其他地区港口;运输成本高,非洲内陆国家进口货物的跨境贸易清关程序平均超过 50 天,出口平均超过 40 天;非洲集装箱约 80% 以空箱形式出口,增加了集装箱的调运成本。所以,非洲港口设备、基础建设改造和港口管理仍有很大的提升空间。

三、中非海洋产业合作现状

改革开放以来,中国的海洋产业、海洋经济发展迅猛,开发、利用海洋资源的技术和能力日益提升,正在由海洋产业、海洋经济大国向海洋产业、海洋经济强国迈进。可以认为，在海水养殖、海洋产品加工、海上运输设备制造、海上油气勘探开采以及海洋基础设施建设等方面，中非双方有着非常好的合作条件和互补优势，因而双方在海洋产业/海洋经济合作领域存在着大量现实和潜在的机遇。

2014年12月，南非总统祖马在访问中国时表示，希望在中南海洋合作协议基础上进一步加强南非与中国在海洋领域的交流与合作。他还向中方通报了南非开放海洋经济开发的"费吉萨"计划。2015年7月，南非副总统访问中国，重点访问了深圳市，目的也是为了进一步加强南中两国对海洋资源的开发合作，学习深圳发展模式、港口物流和临港工业发展的经验。他感慨道："深圳港的高效运行方式、物流仓储配套令人惊叹，在'费吉萨'计划实施过程中，我们希望引入成熟的中国合作方为南非港口的升级换代带来更多管理经验和技术支持。"

中国积极参与中非海洋领域的合作可以说是恰逢其时。非洲沿海/海洋国家共有38个（含岛屿国家），在港口建设、滨海旅游开发和沿海城市与基础设施建设、海上油气资源勘探开发、海洋渔业资源开发与合作方面，有着极大的国际发展合作潜力。对于中国来说，是率先在南非这个在非洲有影响力的大国进行海洋产业领域的合作，还是与坦桑尼亚、肯尼亚、莫桑比克、摩洛哥、阿尔及利亚以及几内亚-塞拉利昂等国进行合作，多部门的协同和合作非常重要，需要相关部门或者研究机构做进一步的系统的规划和方案设计。

目前，中国对非投资主要集中在非洲几个主要的经济大国，85％的直接投资是采矿业、建筑、制造业、金融、制造业和科技服务业；在海洋产业领域的投资总体薄弱，主要是大型企业和集团在国家国际经济合作政策、资金扶持下在非洲海洋产业领域的规模有限的投资，涉及渔业、港口和油气资源开发。渔业方面，中农发集团（中水集团并入）1985年组织到西非毛里塔尼亚开始远洋渔业合作和渔业资源开发。主要是辽宁、山东、浙江、福建的渔业公司在非洲进行投资开发，采取中外合作分成、获得捕鱼证的方式开发海洋渔业资源,主要集中在西非国家,在国际市场有一定影响。

在港口建设方面,中水电等国内工程建设领域的企业已经参与在非洲多个国家的港口改造和建设项目中。如近几年的吉布提港扩建、阿比让港口扩建、蒙巴萨港改建、巴加莫约港口建设等。在水产养殖方面,非洲与中国江苏的合作较多,主要集中在淡水养殖方面。其他海洋产业领域的合作不多,鲜见报道。

四、关于开展中非海洋产业合作的建议

毋庸讳言,中非海洋产业/海洋经济合作应该成为未来中非经贸合作的重要内容之一,特别相关中资企业"走出去"的战略方向之一。它符合非洲发展愿景,能惠及当地民生,并且有利于"一带一路"建设。为此,特提出如下对策建议:

第一,鉴于中国海洋产业涉及较多职能部门,如交通、海洋、旅游、建设、工信等部门,建议由商务部或者海洋局出面协调相关部门,组织国内相关领域专家进行海洋产业"走非洲、求发展"的调研,对我国海洋产业发展面临的问题和挑战以及中非海洋产业/海洋经济合作等问题进行分析。安排和组织相关领域的对非考察和交流活动,由政府、企业和相关领域的专家组成考察组,联系我驻非洲使领馆,对非洲相关国家进行实地调研和考察,与非洲国家的相关政府部门进行对接,商讨合作开发海洋资源以及中非海洋产业/海洋经济合作的相关事宜。

第二,重视海洋产业领域投资环境分析、对非投资风险预测和投资回报的研究。未来的中非发展合作,不会是昔日的"无偿援助",需要更新观念,在非洲国家要积极主张和维护投资非洲的中资企业的权益。营利是对外投资的驱动力,也是企业走出去发展、投资非洲海洋产业的目的。选择社会稳定、资源丰富、投资环境良好的国家和地区,进行海洋领域的对非投资是当务

之急。

第三，在非洲国家海洋经济投资环境还不是很好的情况下，若能先走一步、占据先机十分重要。可以通过调研和评估，在非洲先期建立1—2个"中非海洋产业/海洋经济合作示范区"，兼顾区域性海洋产业结构的构建和区域经济发展，普惠民生和促进地方发展。在增加就业和承担社会责任方面做出表率，为未来中非海洋领域更广泛的合作奠定基础、积累经验。

第四，关注国际舆情动态和分析，2013年之后西方媒体对中国在非洲的海洋产业尤其是渔业合作有较多的负面报道，有夸大和歪曲之用心，应组织专业团队做认真研究，防患于未然，及时提出相关的决策咨询建议，服务于中非海洋产业合作的持续发展。

中非产能合作的法制化途径分析

朱伟东

> **内容摘要**：中非产能合作的深入必然会促进中非民商事交往更加频繁，这会导致中非之间跨境民商事争议、跨国犯罪案件、投资争议等大量发生。但中非目前现有的法律框架不足以应对和有效解决这些问题。为使这些法律问题得到有效解决，为中非产能合作创造良好的法律环境，实现中非产能合作的法制化，中国需要与非洲国家加强在双边、区域性和多边领域的法律合作。
> **关 键 词**：中非；产能合作；法制化；投资争议
> **作者简介**：朱伟东，中国社会科学院西亚非洲研究所研究员

为落实《约翰内斯堡行动计划》，进一步推动和加强中非产能合作，中国外交部已将南非列为引领非洲工业化的火车头，将埃塞俄比亚、肯尼亚、坦桑尼亚、刚果（布）等国列为先行先试示范国家，将埃及、莫桑比克、安哥拉等国列为中非产能合作重点对象。这必然会促进中国与这些国家人员、投资和经贸的往来，产生更多的民商事和投资纠纷。为

此，中国应考虑加强与非洲国家和地区的法制建设，以便为中非产能合作提供坚实的法律保障框架，将中非产能合作纳入法制化轨道，促进中非产能合作和双边民商事交往的顺利开展。根据中非之间法制建设的现状，在对中非产能合作法制化过程中，中国可首先考虑拓展与非洲国家的双边法制合作领域，加强与非洲地区性组织的法制合作与建设，在条件成熟时，考虑推动构建中非产能合作的多边法制保障体系。

一、拓展中非双边法制合作领域

虽然每届中非合作论坛会议通过的行动计划都提到中非之间应加强签署并落实投资和司法协助方面的双边条约，并推动中非之间在立法、司法和执法领域的合作，但与中非经贸、投资和人文交流的发展相比，中非目前的双边法制建设还稍显滞后，还不能为中非双边交流与合作提供切实有效的法律保障，不能为中非产能合作提供坚实的法律后盾。

例如，在投资领域，自 1989 年中国与非洲国家加纳签订第一个双边投资保护协定以来，迄今中国仅同 33 个非洲国家签署了此类协定。但在这 33 个投资保护协定中，生效的仅有 18 个。[①] 在上述中非产能合作先行先试示范国家和合作重点对象国中，中国仅同南非、坦桑尼亚、埃塞俄比亚、刚果（布）存在有效的双边投资保护协定，中国同肯尼亚在 2001 年 7 月签署的双边投资保护协定至今尚未生效。目前，中国投资已遍布非洲 50 多个国家和地区，考虑到在非投资面临很多的政治风险、法律风险等，中国应尽快同更多非洲国家签署双边投资条约，并将已签署的双边投资条约积极推动落实生效。在

---

① 这 18 个生效的双边投资保护条约是中国同下列非洲国家签订的：加纳、埃及、摩洛哥、毛里求斯、津巴布韦、阿尔及利亚、加蓬、尼日利亚、苏丹、南非、佛得角、埃塞俄比亚、突尼斯、赤道几内亚、马达加斯加、马里、坦桑尼亚和刚果（布），根据商务部条法司网站上的信息整理：http://tfs.mofcom.gov.cn/article/Nocategory/201111/20111107819474.shtml。

不存在有效的双边投资保护条约时,如果中国在非洲国家的投资被征收或国有化,就无法获得此类条约所提供的救济。西方发达国家就非常重视利用双边投资保护条约来保护它们的海外投资利益,特别是在政治动荡的非洲国家进行投资是更是如此。例如,英国与26个非洲国家签署有双边投资保护条约,其中21个已经生效。德国与43个非洲国家签署有双边投资保护条约,其中41个已经生效。当与非洲国家政府发生投资争议时,西方国家的投资者还非常善于利用双边投资保护条约规定的救济途径来保护自己的投资权益。在解决投资争端国际中心所受理的外国投资者针对非洲国家提起的投资争议中,基本上都是来自西方发达国家的投资者。[①]

在民商事领域,近年来中国和非洲国家法院受理的涉及来自对方的当事人的案件越来越多,这些案件如果不能快速有效得到解决,必然会影响中非之间正常的民商事往来,阻碍中非产能合作的顺利开展。考虑到中非双方法律制度差异巨大,双方对彼此的法律制度不是很了解,中非双方可通过双边民商事司法协助条约,对涉及另一方当事人的民商事案件的管辖权确定、法律内容的查明、司法和司法外文书送达、域外调查取证、判决和仲裁裁决的承认和执行作出具体规定,以便能够快速解决争议,防止久拖不决,或即使作出判决,而判决得不到承认和执行。但现实情况是,中国目前仅同北非4个国家即摩洛哥、阿尔及利亚、突尼斯、埃及签订有民商事司法协助条约,一些与中国有频繁民商事往来且拥有较多中国移民的非洲国家还没有同中国签署此类条约,如南非、苏丹、尼日利亚、安哥拉、几内亚、加纳、赞比亚、坦桑尼亚、埃塞俄比亚、博茨瓦纳、津巴布韦、乌干达、肯尼亚等国。这些国家中有些是中非产能合作先行先试示范国家,如埃塞俄比亚、坦桑尼亚、肯尼亚,有些是中非产能合作重点对象国,如安哥拉。在不存在此类条约时,会造成中非之间的许多民商事案件不能得到有效处理或根本无法得到解决。中非之间已

---

① 朱伟东:《外国投资者与非洲国家之间的投资争议分析——基于解决投资争端国际中心相关案例的考察》,《西亚非洲》2016年第3期,第144页。

经发生的一些民商事案件有力地说明了这一点。

例如,在2015年4月湘潭市中级人民法院受理的当事人申请承认和执行非洲国家乍得商事法庭做出的判决一案中,湘潭中院审查后以中国和乍得不存在有关判决承认和执行的民商事司法协助条约以及不存在互惠关系为由,拒绝承认和执行乍得法院做出的判决。这种情况可能使得当事人不得不在国内法院重新提起诉讼,这会造成当事人时间、金钱和精力的浪费。如果中国和乍得存在双边民商事司法协助条约,就不会存在判决承认和执行的障碍。在2013年1月浙江省乐清市人民法院受理的一起案件中,乐清市法院以当事人已在乌干达最高法院(商业法院)就同一案件提起诉讼为由,驳回了当事人的起诉。如果乌干达最高法院(商业分院)故意拖延案件的审理,而中国法院又不受理该诉讼,就可能导致案件久拖不决,当事人的合法权益不能得到及时有效的维护。针对这种情况,如果中国和乌干达签订双边民商事司法协助条约,对此类跨境民商事交往中经常出现的平行诉讼现象做出明确规定,就可以避免今后再次出现类似情况。2016年4月,在江苏省泗洪县人民法院受理的一起埃塞俄比亚人之间的离婚案件中,法院以原、被告双方均系埃塞俄比亚人,婚姻系在埃塞俄比亚的教堂内缔结,在对婚姻效力等案件事实认定及法律适用方面存在重大困难等为由,认为中国法院对该案没有管辖权,应由埃塞俄比亚法院对进行管辖。如果双方当事人已在中国长期定居,中国法院这样的判决显然会给非洲国家的当事人的生活带来极大不便。随着中非民商事往来的更加频繁,此类案件会越来越多,这就迫切需要中非之间加强民商事司法合作,签署更多民商事司法协助条约,为中非之间民商事争议的顺利解决提供法律保障。

在开展中非产能合作中,还必须注意双重征税问题。由于各国一般都是按照纳税人居住国原则和所得来源地原则进行征税,在跨国民商事交往中,就可能出现对同一纳税人重复征税的情况。双重征税加重了纳税人的负担,不利于国家之间资金、技术和人员流动。为解决双重征税问题,各国一般都会通过谈判同其他国家签订避免双重征税协定。截至目前,中国已同15个非洲国家签订有避免双重征税协定,这 15 个非洲国家分别是肯尼亚、津巴布韦、博茨瓦纳、乌干达、赞比亚、埃塞俄比亚、阿尔及利亚、摩洛哥、突尼斯、尼日利亚、南非、塞舌尔、埃及、苏丹和毛里求斯,其中中国同肯尼亚、博茨瓦纳和乌干达签订的避免双重征税协定尚未生效。[①] 在上述中非产能合作的重点国家中,只有埃及、南非、埃塞俄比亚同中国存在此类协定,与其他几个非洲国家都没有签署此类协定。显然,中国和非洲国家之间生效的避免双重征税协定的数量极其有限。相比之下,英国同 28 个非洲国家签署有避免双重征税协定,而法国同 26 个非洲国家签署有此类协定。

在刑事领域,中非之间日益增多的跨国刑事犯罪案件对中非双方人民的生命和财产安全造成极大威胁,对中非社会秩序的稳定带来了极大的隐患,严重影响了中非产能合作和人文交流的顺利开展。为此,中非双方需要建立起切实可行的双边刑事司法协助渠道。截至目前,中国仅同突尼斯、阿尔及利亚、埃及、南非和纳米比亚签署有双边刑事司法协助条约,同阿尔及利亚、突尼斯、南非、纳米比亚、安哥拉和埃塞俄比亚签署有引渡条约。在上述中非产能合作国家中,中国仅与南非和埃及签订有刑事司法协助条约,与南非和安哥拉签订有引渡条约。与埃塞俄比亚、坦桑尼亚、肯尼亚、刚果(布)这几个中非产能合作先行先试示范国家都没有签署此类条约。而中国与这些国家之间频繁发生的刑事案件,如 2016 在肯尼亚发生的跨境电信诈骗案等,表明了签署此类条约的重要性。2017 年 6 月初,在赞比亚发生的赞比亚警方和移民局拘押 31 名中国人的事例,再次凸显了中国与非洲国家加强刑事司法和执法合作的必要性和迫切性。

二、加强与非洲地区性组织的法制合作与建设

为了推动地区一体化,改善区域内的贸易、投资环境,推动区域内投资、

[①] 信息来自国家税务总局网站:http://www.chinatax.gov.cn/n810341/n810770/index.html。

贸易的发展,非洲国家创建了许多地区性组织,如东非共同体、东南非共同市场、西非国家经济共同体、南部非洲关税同盟、中部非洲经济货币共同体、非洲商法协调组织等。这些非洲地区性组织有的专门制定了区域内贸易、投资协定,对区域内的贸易和投资事项作了详细规定。同这些地区性组织展开自由贸易协定的谈判,加强与这些地区性组织的法制合作与建设,对于中非开展产能合作具有重要的意义。

首先,中国与非洲地区性组织通过谈判签署自贸协定可以推动非洲地区一体化,助力全球化的发展,实现中国和非洲大陆的共同繁荣。促进非洲地区一体化,推动中非贸易、投资的制度化、便利化,实现中非共同繁荣是中国政府近年来的一贯主张。例如,2015年12月中国政府发表的第二份《中国对非洲政策文件》明确提出:"支持非洲自贸区建设和一体化进程,积极探讨与非洲国家和区域组织建立制度性贸易安排。"

其次,中国与非洲地区性组织达成自贸协定有利于进一步扩大非洲市场,实现中非投资、贸易合作的转型升级。中国与非洲国家的投资、贸易目前都是在双边协定基础上进行的,中国还没有与任何非洲地区性组织达成更为全面的自贸协定。与非洲地区性经济组织达成自贸协定,将更加有利于中国产品进入非洲市场,扩大对非投资。

最后,中国与非洲地区性组织通过谈判达成自贸协定,有利于进一步增强中国相对于西方国家或地区在非洲的投资、贸易竞争力。西方国家或地区非常重视通过自贸协定与非洲国家或地区开展投资、贸易。例如,为了拓展非洲市场,近年来欧盟与一些非洲地区性组织展开了系列经济伙伴协定谈判,欧盟与东非共同体和南部非洲发展共同体签署的经济伙伴协定已分别在2016年6月和10月生效适用,欧盟与西非国家经济共同体和西非经济货币联盟16个成员国也已就经济伙伴协定内容达成一致,正在履行批准程序。美国也与东非共同体、东南非共同市场、西非国家经济共同体等签署了《贸易、投资框架协定》。中国如果不尽快与非洲地区性组织开展自贸协定谈判,就可能在非洲面临来自西方国家更多的投资、贸易竞争压力。由于缺乏制度性贸易安排,中国商品进入非洲市场也可能会受到更多随意的排挤和打压。

在与非洲国家或地区性组织启动自贸协定谈判时,中国可首先选择经济条件较好、市场潜力大、区域辐射性强的地区性组织开展此类谈判。例如,中国可首先考虑与南部非洲关税同盟、东南非共同市场、西非国家经济共同体等开展此类谈判。非洲大陆目前也正在推动非洲区域内贸易的发展,推动非洲统一市场的实现。例如,2015年6月,26个非洲国家政府首脑在出席非洲经济峰会时,签署协定决定整合东非共同体、东南非共同市场和南部非洲发展共同体这三大地区性组织,组成非洲规模最大的"三方自贸区"。据乌干达《新景报》12月8日报道,在非洲第四届贸易部长级会议上,与会代表审议通过了《非洲自由贸易协定》的主体框架结构,一致决定于2018年3月由各国元首共同签订该协定。一旦完成签署,该协定将成为仅次于世界贸易组织的第二大协定安排。协定的签署,意味着非洲向着自由贸易区正式建立迈进了实质性的一步。[①] 从国际、国内形势来看,可以说,在目前,中国同非洲地区性组织开展自贸协定谈判面临难得的机遇和条件。

三、构建中非产能合作的多边法制保障框架

在中非开展产能合作中,还应重视多边法制的作用。对于开展产能合作过程中出现的各类涉外民商事纠纷、投资争议等,多边法制可以提供一个便利、通畅的解决途径。例如,对于涉外民商事案件,当需要对司法文书进行域外送达或需要进行域外调查取证时,可以利用双方国家都加入的海牙《域外送达公约》和《域外取证公约》所规定的途径进行;对于外国投资者与投资东道国政府之间的投资争议,可以通过1965年《华盛顿公约》所规定的解决投

---

① 《〈非洲自由贸易协定〉将于2018年初签署》,http://www.mofcom.gov.cn/article/i/jyjl/k/201712/20171202685664.shtml。

资争端国际中心(ICSID)仲裁机制进行；对于外国仲裁裁决的承认和执行，可以按照1958年《纽约公约》的规定进行。

但就中非产能合作所能利用的现有多边法制体系来看，除对于仲裁裁决的承认和执行存在十分便利的条件外，中非双方在涉外民商事领域、投资争议领域所能利用的多边法制体系要么明显不足，要么不适合中非双方的实际需要。在仲裁裁决的承认和执行方面，非洲目前已有35个国家加入了《纽约公约》，[①]中国也是该公约的成员国，这对于仲裁裁决在彼此国家申请承认和执行提供了便捷的渠道。在涉外民商事领域，中国早已批准海牙《域外送达公约》和《域外取证公约》，但在非洲方面，截至目前，仅有摩洛哥、突尼斯、埃及、博茨瓦纳、马拉维和塞舌尔6个国家加入了《域外送达》公约，[②]仅有南非、摩洛哥和塞舌尔3个国家加入了《域外取证公约》。[③] 考虑到中非之间发生的民商事纠纷已几乎涉及所有非洲国家，利用公约来解决中非民商事案件的域外送达、域外取证显然还很不现实。

在投资争议解决方面，截至目前，已有46个非洲国家成为《华盛顿公约》的成员国，中国也是该公约的成员国。[④] 但这并非意味着中非之间的投资争议就可通过该公约规定的仲裁机制进行。首先，在中非之间已生效的18个双边投资条约中，仅有9个规定了可以将投资者与东道国政府之间的一起投资争议或征收补偿额争议提交给根据该公约设立的国际中心解决。[⑤] 而目前，中国对非投资基本遍及所有非洲国家和地区，利用这一公约解决机制显然不能满足实际需要；其次，许多非洲国家在实践中已认识到《华盛顿公约》

---

① 数据是根据来自"纽约公约"网站上的信息整理而成：http://www.newyorkconvention.org/list+of+contracting+states。
② https://www.hcch.net/en/instruments/conventions/specialised-sections/service。
③ https://www.hcch.net/en/instruments/conventions/status-table/? cid=82。
④ 参见解决投资争端国际中心网站：https://icsid.worldbank.org/en/Pages/about/Database-of-Member-States.aspx。
⑤ 这个双边投资保护条约分别是中国同下列非洲国家签署的：摩洛哥、加蓬、突尼斯、赤道几内亚、马达加斯加、马里、坦桑尼亚、刚果(布)(一切投资争议)、埃塞俄比亚(征收补偿额争议)。

的投资争议仲裁解决机制对非洲十分不利。① 例如,仲裁庭的仲裁员基本来自西方发达国家,仲裁程序基本是在欧美等国家进行的,非洲的法律文化和传统没有在仲裁程序中得到应有的重视等,因此,一些非洲国家开始对《华盛顿公约》的投资争议仲裁解决机制产生抵制情绪,如南非、埃及等,不排除以后有更多的非洲国家推出这一多边机制,这就为中非之间利用这一多边机制解决投资争议带来潜在的障碍。

因此,从长远来看,中非双方可以根据双方投资、经贸发展的现实以及相似的法律文化传统,努力构建符合双方实际情况和现实需要的多边法制保障体系。例如,在投资和贸易领域,中非双方可以考虑在中非合作论坛框架下,探讨建立自由贸易协定的可能性,并对中非经贸、投资纠纷的解决机制作出相应的规定;考虑到制定全面自由贸易协定的复杂性以及解决投资争议问题的现实迫切性,中非之间也可首先就中非投资争议的解决这一程序性问题进行协商谈判,在考虑到双方实际情况和双方法律文化与传统的基础上,可以设立一个中非投资争议解决中心;在民商事领域,考虑到非洲法律的复杂性和多样化,中非双方可以就民商事司法协助作出一个多边安排,对涉外民商事案件管辖权的确定、域外调查、域外取证、外国法内容的查明、法律信息的交流、民商事判决的承认与执行等事项作出明确规定。

四、结语

通过上述分析可以看出,虽然中非产能合作过程中中非之间的民商事、投资争议、跨国犯罪案件会大量发生,但目前中非之间并没有完善的法制框架来应对这些法律问题。从中非产能合作的长远发展来看,只有把它纳入法

---

① 朱伟东:《外国投资者与非洲国家之间的投资争议分析——基于解决投资争端国际中心相关案例的考察》,《西亚非洲》2016年第3期,第145—146页。

制化的发展轨道,它才能得到健康、良性的发展。就中非产能合作的法制化途径来看,中国和非洲国家首先可以考虑签订更多的双边条约,为跨境民商事纠纷、跨国犯罪案件、投资争议等提供便捷、高效的解决渠道。在此基础上,中国可与非洲的地区性组织进行沟通联系,以便达成地区性的经济伙伴协议或自由贸易协定,为中非产能合作奠定区域性的法制框架。当然,中国作为最大的发展中国家,非洲作为发展中国家最集中的大陆,双方可以努力构建反映广大发展中国家利益和呼声的国际经贸规则,通过谈判签订多边的民商事司法合作公约或经贸投资公约,不但有利于中非产能合作在更大范围内进行,也有助于推动新的国际经贸规则的形成。

China-Africa Industrial Capacity Cooperation: Achievements, Challenges and the Way Forward

Kabiru Adamu kiyawa & Prof. Emeritus Dr. Barjoyai Baradai

Abstract: In recent times, the relationship between African countries and China has attracted global attention as a result of its sudden rise. One of the major reasons for such global focus is the implications that are associated with this relationship on the global economy. As a result of this apprehension, China-Africa relationship is viewed by individuals, groups and other countries from different perspectives. For example, while some of the African political leaders consider China's hand of friendship across the continent as an avenue for building industrial capacity and achieve their aspiration for industrialization, others see it as another form of colonization where the continent will be turned into a source of cheap raw materials and dumping ground for old technology and finished goods from China. Against this backdrop, this paper examines the achievements and challenges associated with China-Africa Industrial Capacity Cooperation. The paper being an ex post facto research relied on published related materials. Findings of the study revealed that despite the mixed reactions that have greeted the China-Africa relations the relationship has recorded some significant achievements in its current status. A testament to this assertion is the various joint industrial projects running in billions of dollars being undertaken in different African countries by the Chinese government. In addition, findings of the paper indicate that notwithstanding the current achievements, China-Africa relations are still facing some challenges especially on the issue of trust or negative perception. Consequently, it is the opinion of the authors that more public relations should be done to correct the public misunderstanding and perception of China-Africa relations.

Keywords: Achievements; Capacity; Challenges; China-Africa; Cooperation; Industrial

Author: Kabiru Adamu kiyawa, Ph. D Candidate at the Department of Islamic banking and Finance, Faculty of Finance and Administrative Sciences AL-Madinah International University; Emeritus, Professor at the Department of Islamic banking and Finance, Faculty of Finance and Administrative Sciences AL-Madinah International University; Dr. Barjoyai Baradai, Department of Islamic banking and Finance, Faculty of Finance and Administrative Sciences AL-Madinah International University, Shah-Alam, Selangor, Malaysia

Introduction

Despite all the advances made by African countries in the post-colonial era in the economic sector, several economic development indicators shown in recent years indicated that Africa has failed to achieve its desirable level of industrialization. As a result of this unfortunate development, the continent's share of global manufacturing quota has continued to decline at an alarming rate. Thus, Calabrese asserts that the effects of the continent's deindustrialization process which began in the 1980s are still being felt. [1] For example, the value added by manufacturing sector to the GDP of African

---

[1] Linda Calabrese, "China-Africa cooperation: a new dawn for African industry?" 8 January 2016, retrieved from: https://www.odi.org/comment/10242-china-africa-cooperation-new-dawn-african-industry.

nations declined to less than 11% in 2014 while Africa provided only 4% of the global value added in manufacturing. This implies that African countries are essentially excluded from the global value chains and this occurs where the role of China as the current main economic partner comes into perspective. Although the relationship between China and Africa dates back to the pre-independence era, in 2006 the relationship between the two took a new dimension following the 2006 proclamation by the Chinese government to make the year as the "Year of Africa". This declaration was followed by an event tagged the Forum on China-Africa Cooperation (FOCAC) in Beijing and subsequently attended by 48 African leaders.

Following the 2006 proclamation, China's economic activities in the continent has accelerated significantly and China has since become Africa's major trading partner in Asia.[①] For example, the renewed relationship between China and Africa has resulted in Chinese investment growing to about USD 14 billion between the periods of 1990 and 2007 — a 300 times growth.[②] Interestingly, bulk of China's investments in Africa is tilted towards extractive industries. Others include infrastructural funding particularly road construction, railways, dams and power projects scattered across the continent. Furthermore, the relationship between China and Africa has resulted in the cancellation of nearly USD 3 billion African debt with additional pledge of USD 10 billion in concessional loans to African

---

[①] Harry G. Broadman, *Africa's Silk Road: China and India's New Economics Frontier*, Washington DC: World Bank, 2007, pp. 278 - 279, retrieved from: https://siteresources.worldbank.org/AFRICAEXT/Resources/Africa_Silk_Road.pdf. See also: Chris Alden and Ana Cristina Alves, "China and Africa's Natural Resources: The Challenges and Implications for Development and Governance", South African Institute of International Affairs, Occasional Paper No. 41, September 2009, retrieved from: http://www.voltairenet.org/IMG/pdf/China_and_Africa_s_Natural_Resources.pdf.

[②] Harry G. Broadman, *Africa's Silk Road: China and India's New Economics Frontier*, 2012 Editions...

countries.[1]

As a result of the developments, the relationship between African countries and China has attracted global attention in recent times. One of the major reasons for such global focus is the implications that are associated with this relationship on the global economy. This situation has created a sense of apprehension. As such China-Africa relationship has been viewed by individuals, groups and other countries from different perspectives. For example, while some of the African political leaders consider China's hand of friendship across the continent as an avenue for building industrial capacity and achieve their aspiration for industrialization, others see it as another form of colonization where the continent will be turned into a source of cheap raw materials and dumping ground for old technology and finished goods from China. The apprehension towards China-Africa economic relationship is not confined to the local continent's critics. Existing literature indicates that Western countries have also expressed discontent on the issue.

For example, Robinson summarized the Western countries perception of the increasing economic relationship between China and African countries in three perspectives. Firstly, China's relationship with Africa is viewed as a development partnership whose engagements are of mutual benefits. Secondly, the West thinks that of China as an economic competitor capable of undermining Africa's development. Lastly, China is seen by the West as a colonizer using long term projects to impose its geostrategic control in order to dislodge the existing influence of the Western nations.[2] In

---

[1] Loro Horta, "China-Africa: Development Partner or Neo-Coloniser?" University World News, No 0042, 29 November 2009, retrieved from: http://www.universityworldnews.com/article.php?story=20091127134020463. Deborah Bräutigam, "China, Africa and the International Aid Architecture", Tunis: African Development Bank Group, Working Paper No. 107, 2010, p. 31, retrieved from: https://www.afdb.org/fileadmin/uploads/afdb/Documents/Publications/WORKING%20107%20%20PDF%20E33.pdf.

[2] David Robinson, "Chinese Engagement with Africa: The Case of Mozambique", Portuguese Journal of International Affairs, No. 6, Spring/Summer 2012, pp. 4 - 5.

particular, critics of China's increase interest in the Africa point to the fact that most of Chinese investment in the continent are located within the mineral rich countries such as Angola, Nigeria, Zimbabwe, Niger and others. Against this backdrop, this paper examines the achievements and challenges associated with China-Africa Industrial Capacity Cooperation. The paper is structured into five sections comprising introduction, brief history of China-Africa relations, achievements, challenges, China-Africa Industrial Cooperation — The Way Forward, and lastly conclusion and recommendations.

Brief History of China-Africa Relations

Historically, although relationship between China and Africa dated back to the period pre-independence era, but formal relationship between the two can be traced to May 1956 when China and Egypt established first diplomatic relations. The period represents the beginning of African states breaking away free from the yoke of colonialism. In particular, the relationship between China and Africa during that period was basically characterized by the former supporting the later in its attempt to liberate itself from the Western colonialists. In the beginning, China's support for Africa was mainly based on its ideological differences with the West; however, as time went by, the relationship took a different dimension. A major change in the dynamics of relationship between China and Africa began in the periods of 1980s. That was when the Chinese started its "Opening up and Reform Policy" which gave birth to a wide-range of policies that culminated in the emergence of a new China as it is known today. Under the new policy, economic and geo-strategic interests became the driving philosophy for the Chinese relationship with Africa instead of the previous attempt to instill political ideology. Therefore, owing to China's increasing economic and political power as well as the hunger for resources under the new philosophy, the dynamics of relations between China and Africa also changed. On the whole, the changing dynamics in China-Africa relations following the emergence of new China in 1949 to date can be categorized into three phases.

1. Phase I (1950s – 1970s)

The first phase of relationship between China and Africa covers the period from the early 1950s to the end of the 1970s when the relationship resulted in some initial establishment and development of infrastructure within the early independent countries. During this period, the relationship was mainly focused on mutual support to the African nationalists who were struggling to liberate the continent against imperialism and colonialism as well as consolidate the gains of national independence. Two remarkable events highlighted the importance China attached to its relations with Africa in that period. First, the visit of Chinese Premier Zhou Enlai's on 3 different occasions between the year 1963 to 1965 to 11 African countries. Secondly, the construction of railway by the China linking Tanzania and Zambia. It was during those visits that the then Chinese Premier Zhou disclosed China's eight principles for providing economic and technical assistance to Africa. In fulfillment of its pledge, China ensured that the Tanzania-Zambia Railway which is today regarded as an important monument of China-Africa diplomatic history was successfully executed and completed between 1970 and 1976 at the cost of USD 455 million. In reciprocation of this friendly gesture, Africa has stood firmly behind China desire of safeguarding its national sovereignty and reunification. In addition, Africa demonstrated its desire to maintain and elevate its relationship with China by standing solidly on the side of China at the United Nations. Hence, the late Chinese leader, Chairman Mao stated that, "It is our black African brothers who carried us into (the United Nations)" when China's legitimate rights were restored on the 26th UN General Assembly Conference in 1971 with an overwhelming majority of 78 votes in favor (including 26 African votes, with 35 against,

17 abstentions and 2 absences).

2. Phase II (1980s)

The second phase of 1980s China-Africa relation marks the beginning of economic engagement between China and African countries. This is the period when China's friendly relations and political cooperation began to mature and cooperation between the two extended to economic and trade. As a result of this shift, various economic and technological joint projects were implemented based on China's principle of equality and mutual benefit in 1983. Under the new policy, four principles were introduced by China in 1983 on aspect of economic cooperation with African countries. These include, seeking equality and mutual benefit, stressing practical results, adopting various forms of cooperation and pursuing common development. These four principles expanded the previous China's eight principles of foreign economic and technical assistance and helped in adding more impetus to China's economic and trade relations development with Africa in the new era.

3. Phase III (1990s – To Date)

The third phase of China's relations with Africa began in the early 1990s and aided by the end of Cold War China adjusted its policy towards African countries. The phase of China's relationship with Africa is regarded as the stage of China's comprehensive cooperation with the continent of Africa. This is because apart from strengthening its existing economic and trade cooperation with Africa, China also made effort to boost cooperation in political, cultural and educational fields, seeking multi-channeled, multi-faceted and all-round development of the China-Africa relations. For example, the establishment of Forum on China-Africa Cooperation in 2000 provided a strategic and institutionalized platform for stepping up the bilateral exchange, communication and cooperation. Following the Forum's first meeting in Beijing in October 2000 a new impetus was injected to China-Africa Relations. For example, at the political level, President Hu Jintao and Vice President Xi Jinping have made high level bi-lateral visits to three African states of Angola, Botswana, and South Africa on six different times.

At the economic level, China's cooperation with Africa has tremendously expanded within the period of 1990s to date. China's investment stock in Africa has gone over the USD 10 billion-mark, involving mining, manufacturing, agriculture and other sectors. At present, China has become Africa's largest trading partner and Africa China's fourth largest overseas investment destination and second largest overseas labor service engineering contracting market. As a result of this development, the number of Chinese people in Africa has also grown above one million while there are more than 2,000 Chinese companies engaged in economic and trade activities in Africa. At the cultural and educational fronts, the Confucius Institute aiming to promote Chinese culture and cultural exchanges in Africa have sprung up like the wet session mushrooms. The number of African students studying in China and taking part in various types of human resources training courses has also increased. In the security field, China in recent years has actively participated in the UN peacekeeping operations in Africa, having sent more than 3,000 peacekeepers to 12 operations. Currently, there are more than 1,100 officers and soldiers still serving in active duty in eight peacekeeping districts in Africa.

Achievements

During the Forum on China Africa Cooperation (FOCAC) held in Johannesburg, South Africa in December, 2015, a series of key policy initiatives were put forward by the Chinese President Xi Jinping aimed at ushering in a new dawn in China's economic relations with Africa that were sought to result in a "win-win cooperation". Other than the sum of USD 60 billion pledged at the forum to support Africa's effort in overcoming challenges to poverty reduction, agricultural modernization, and affordable quality public health, the forum also stressed the need for increased industrialization of Africa. Prior to the Johannesburg declaration, Africa has established industrial cooperation with China and as a result of this relationship, Chinese presence in the continent has increased significantly. Presently, available data from the largest Chinese public database indicates that China is currently undertaking 3,030 developmental projects in different parts of Africa. In the same vein, the Chinese state news agency Xinhua disclosed that out of these projects, 1,046 have been completed, including the building of 2,233 kilometers railways and 3,350 km of highway roads. Likewise, trade between China and Africa has risen from the previous USD 6.5 billion in 2004 to an estimated USD 200 billion in 2013. [1]

Consequent to these disclosures, *M&G Africa Reporter* examined the major ongoing developmental projects between China and Africa in 2015. Findings of the research agency revealed that China is having 16 active development projects (worth over USD 60 billions) whose minimum value is not less than one billion USD each in different parts of Africa. These include the followings:

(1) USD 12 billion 1,402 km Coastal Railway in Nigeria aimed at linking the country's economic capital city of Lagos located in the Southwestern geopolitical zone with Calabar located in the eastern part of the country. Interestingly, this happens to be the highest single overseas contract awarded to China.

(2) USD 8.3 billion 1,124-km Lagos-Kano railway project in Nigeria, awarded to Chinese Civil and Engineering Construction Company (CCECC).

(3) USD 7.16 billion Infrastructure for mines barter deal (Sicomines) in DR Congo.

---

[1] "Commentary: China-Africa relations: something besides natural resources", 02 March 2015, retrieved from: http://www.xinhuanet.com/mrdx/2015-02/02/c_133963774.htm.

(4) USD 7 billion Mini-City Project on the outskirts of Johannesburg awarded to Chinese property group Shanghai Zendai and is considered as one of the largest real estate contract given to a Chinese company in South Africa.

(5) USD 7 billion joint Venture between China International Fund and Guinea to create a holding company for investments in development projects. Under the arrangement, Guinea has only 25% stake in the newly created Guinea Development Corporation (GDC). On the other hand, the CIF and Sonangol (a parastatal that oversees petroleum and natural gas production in Angola) would share the remaining 75% stakes. In addition, CIF was granted the rights to explore any unexploited Guinean mineral and energy resources. In return, the CIF would use some of the accruing revenue to finance infrastructural projects suggested by the Guinean government. One of the implications for this arrangement is that all iron ore and associated minerals zones that cover 7,000 square km fall under Chinese control.

(6) USD 5.8 billion contract for the construction of 200,000 bbl/day oil refinery in Angola.

(7) USD 5.6 billion 1,344-km Chad-Sudan regional Railway network project.

(8) USD 4.34 billion Regional Cement plants in Cameroon, Ethiopia, Kenya, Mali, Niger, Nigeria, Senegal and Zambia, with another in Nepal between Dangote Cement China's Sinoma International Engineering Co.

(9) USD 3.4 billion Kenya standard-gauge railway to connect Nairobi and Mombasa funded to the tone of 90% by Export-Import Bank of China.

(10) USD 3.1 billion Mepanda Nkua dam and hydroelectric station in Mozambique also funded by Export-Import Bank of China.

(11) USD 1.38 billion contract for the construction of railway from Khartoum to Port Sudan, Sudan.
(12) USD 1.23 billion Republic of Congo Capital rebuilding project.
(13) USD 1.03 billion Mtwara-Dar Es Salaam Gas Pipeline project in Tanzania.
(14) USD 1.1 billion Thermal power project in Zimbabwe.
(15) USD 1.01 billion Textile Complex project in Egypt.
(16) USD 1 billion Deep sea port in Cameroon awarded to China Harbor Engineering Company Ltd. [1]

Breakdown of the above selected projects revealed that only two i. e. USD 4.34 billion Regional Cement plants in Cameroon, Ethiopia, Kenya, Mali, Niger, Nigeria, Senegal and Zambia, with another in Nepal between Dangote Cement China's Sinoma International Engineering Company and USD 1.01 billion Textile Complex project in Egypt totaling USD 5.35 billion have direct bearing on the industrial capacity building of Africa. The bulk of USD 64.09 billion are directed towards exploration of mineral resources and other infrastructural projects. This shows that despite the huge inflow of Chinese direct investment in Africa, not much progress has been made in changing the poor industrial capacity of the continent. The current position of China's relationship with Africa in the area of industrialization is captured by Ajakaiye as follows:

China is increasing its presence in exploration and/or exploitation of oil and other mineral products all over Africa. By far the largest proportion of China's foreign direct investment in Africa is in the oil sector followed by other sold minerals. A relatively small proportion are in manufacturing sector, especially, agro-processing,

---

[1] "What crisis? 16 of China's biggest projects in Africa — it's all billion dollar territory in here." September 2015, retrieved from: http://mgafrica.com/article/2015 - 09 - 18-multi-billion-dollar-deals-chinas-27-biggest-active-projects-in-africa.

pharmaceutical and telecommunications sectors. ①

Looking at the unbalanced Chinese investment scenario, one is tempted to align with the concern by observers who hold the view that China's relationship with Africa is mainly for the exploitation of its natural resources. However, in spite of the seeming imbalance in Chinese investment spread, Africa's quest for achieving industrial capacity with the help of China is not completely lost. This is because there are some private Chinese firms that engaged in different manufacturing businesses in many African states. For example, in Nigeria, many Chinese businessmen are taking advantage of the country's expansive market to invest in the manufacturing sector such as textile industries, household appliances, automobile; consumables and iron and steel as well as ICT products. Among the notable Chinese firms operating Nigeria's industrial sector is the Western Metal Products Company Limited (WEMPCO), a multi-billion naira integrated steel mill, situated at Magboro, on Lagos-Ibadan Expressway, Ogun State, and it is the first of its kind in Africa. The sprawling steel-manufacturing plant according to available data boasts of a production capacity of 700,000 metric tonnes and a production machinery of five-stand Tandem Mill.

Others include, Nigeria-China Manufacturing Company, Nigeria Sino Trucks, Sinoma, Huawei and ZTE. Thus, while Chinese private investors mostly invest in the agro-allied industries, manufacturing and telecommunications, Chinese public FDI mainly targets natural resources and infrastructural development particularly power and transport sectors. For instance, a study conducted by African Economic Research Consortium1

---

① Olu Ajakaiye, "China and Africa — Opportunities and Challenges", *A Presentation at the African Union Task Force on Strategic Partnership Between Africa and the Emerging Countries of the South*, Addis Ababa, Ethiopia. 11 – 13 September 2006, retrieved from: https://pdfs.semanticscholar.org/a86b/f51b2144dad276215c78843abd2dbefdb098.pdf.

reveals that China has established over 30 solely-owned or joint-venture companies in the construction, oil and gas, technology, services and education sectors of the Nigerian economy. More Chinese enterprises are expanding their investments in the manufacturing sector ostensibly in the hope of transferring technologies and training personnel to increase local job opportunities. To this extent, Egbula and Zheng describe the current economic relationship between China and Nigeria, the giant of Africa in the following manner:

> *While initially driven by its vast demand for energy resources, China's involvement in Nigeria has since expanded far beyond oil. China's public and private companies are making forays into Nigeria's manufacturing and information and communication technologies sectors. They are developing two special economic zones within Nigeria and are building new roads, railways and airports across the country. China is also known for its policy of offering unconditional aid — which they calls "co-operation".* ①

In addition, China has also established a China-Africa industrial capacity cooperation fund, designed to aid Africa's development. The fund, according to Chinese state news media, Xinhua has a takeoff capital of USD 10 billion, and is solely targeting industrial sectors like manufacturing, hi-tech, agriculture, energy, infrastructure construction and finance in African countries. According to the People's Bank of China, both local and foreign investors are free to join the fund. ②

---

① Margaret Egbula and Qi Zheng, "China and Nigeria: a powerful South-South alliance", *West African Challenges*, No. 05, November 2011.
② "China-Africa industrial capacity cooperation fund starts operation", 07 Jan. 2016, retrieved from: http://news.xinhuanet.com/english/2016-01/07/c_134987683.htm.

Challenges

Although China-Africa relations have recorded some achievements, but the foregoing suggests that there are challenges to be overcome before the relationship can achieve its desired objectives. These challenges can be categorized into the following dimensions: (1) Investment Disparity, (2) Trade Balance, (3) Cost of Manufacturing, (4) Security Situation in Africa, and (5) Corruption.

1. Investment Disparity

In spite of the fact that, Chinese investment in Africa has significantly increased in recent time, existing data indicate that there is significant disparity between amount attracted by industrial manufacturing sector and that of mineral resources. For example, out of the selected 16 major selected investment currently being undertaking by various Chinese firms in various African countries amounting to over USD 65 billion, the manufacturing sector attracted less than USD 6 billion. Therefore, unless this investment trend is address, China-Africa industrial cooperation will not achieve its intended objectives.

2. Trade Balance

The most significant challenge confronting China and Africa relationship with regards to the industrialization cooperation is the issue of balance of trade arising from the fact that cheap Chinese imports are finding their ways into the many African countries. This policy is discouraging diversification of the productive based of many African economies away from crude agricultural and mineral products towards manufacturing and eventually service or knowledge intensive activities. This is seen as real challenge because cheap Chinese goods make it difficult for potential investors to engage in manufacturing business as they cannot withstand or survive the strong competition from the imported Chinese products. The consequences of this scenario is that in countries like Nigeria, Kenya, South Africa local manufacturing industries are shutting down resulting in many people losing their jobs (Wilson III, 2005; Shin, 2005; Kaplinsky, et. al, 2006).[1] Thus, instead of China-African trade partnership facilitating the transformation of African industrialization process, it is creating an impediment. As such, some observers are of the view that, instead of China, helping Africa to achieve its industrialization it is turning the continent into a dumping ground.

3. Manufacturing costs escalation

Rising production costs in many African countries occasioned by poor infrastructural development has led to importation of finished goods. Although empirical data on production costs in Africa are not easily available, several reports indicate that Africa has high cost of production. The impact of such production costs on Africa's competitiveness seems to be above and beyond what is experienced by other regions in the world. For example, Kenya's factory floor productivity is close to China's but the moment you add indirect costs, Kenyan firms lose 40 percent of their productivity advantage when compared to Chinese firms.[2]

4. Security concern

Providing a safe environment where firms can conduct their business is a key requirement for economic development. This is owing to the fact that there is a strong correlation between security and development. Thus, it has

---

[1] Ernest J. Wilson III, "China's influence in Africa: implications for US policy", 28 July 2005, retrieved from http://www.cidcm.umd.edu/wilson/wilson_congressional_testimony_2005_07_28.pdf on 8th October 2017. See also: David H. Shinn, "China's approach to East, North and the Horn of Africa", 21 July 2005, retrieved from: www.uscc.gov/hearings/2005hearings/written_testimonies/o5_07_2122wrts/shinn_david_wrts.pdf; Raphael Kaplinsky, Dorothy McCormick & Mike Morris, "The impact of China on Sub-Saharan Africa", April 2006, retrieved from: https://www.ids.ac.uk/files/DFIDAgendaPaper06.pdf.

[2] Giuseppe Iarossi, "Benchmarking Africa's Costs and Competitiveness", in *The Africa Competitiveness Report 2009*, World Economic Forum, World Bank, 2009, retrieved from: http://siteresources.worldbank.org/EXTAFRSUMAFTPS/Resources/chapter4.pdf.

become one of the most important responsibilities of the function of any state to ensure that adequate security is put in place in order to safe guard the lives and property of the people. Unfortunately, decades after the decolonization of Africa, the many countries are battling with internal security issues arising from political, ethnic and religious conflicts. Therefore, one of the most important challenges inhibiting African countries to benefit from its relationship with China is the precarious security situation as not many investors will like to risk their lives and property in foreign countries.

5. Corruption

It is a global known fact that many African countries are characterized by problems of corruption as such when it comes to doing business the major challenge is that of corruption. According to Larossi, corruption remains a major problem for entrepreneurs on the continent. [1] Hence, African managers place corruption among the most important constraints of doing business. For example, the concept of giving or building 10% for corrupt public officials has become an institutionalized syndrome in many African countries. A World Bank sponsored study by Larossi Benchmarking Africa's Costs and Competitiveness showed that the pattern of corruption across countries in Africa is pretty much the same across landlocked and coastal countries. [2]

China-Africa Industrial Cooperation: the Way Forward

As an important strategy to move forward swiftly in the China-Africa cooperation program, the authors recommended the following strategies to be adopted by all African countries pursuing serious industrial cooperation with China.

---

[1] Giuseppe Iarossi, p. 84.
[2] Ibid. p. 95.

(1) A proper plan and target should be laid down and agreed with the Chinese counterpart on the milestone to be achieved and the timeline involved.

(2) The relationships must address the Investment Disparity particularly the need for a shift from the Mining and extraction to actual industrial and manufacturing activities.

(3) The relationship and objectives must be shifted from commodities to trading to strengthen the African industrialization program through China-Africa industrial cooperation.

(4) More Chinese investment in infrastructural development, especially in transport and energy sectors, would be needed to become a strong foundation and as catalyst for building African industrial sector.

(5) The relationship must seriously look at the Trade Balance as an important consideration in the programs so that the medium and long term benefit could be accrued from the cooperation.

(6) A serious program of industrial costs reduction should be initiated by setting up an Institute of Quality and Productivity Development to address the inefficiency in industries operation.

(7) A program of local employment opportunities must be initiated to channel and spread down the benefit from the industrial cooperation to the mass public in Africa.

(8) A program on Vendors development need to be initiated to create opportunities to local SME and Micro-businesses to be involved in the industrial cooperation program.

(9) A serious program to curtail corrupt practices should be initiated by emphasising on promoting Corporate Governance and Ethical practices in Africa by setting up credible Anti-Corruption institutions in Africa to reduce the cost and administrative bottlenecks faced by potential investors in doing business.

(10) Communication and promotional program should be eleviated to inform the public — in the most transparent way on the development and benefit derived from the Africa-China Industrial Cooperation programs to gains total support of the citizen for more positive effect.

Conclusion and Recommendations

The foregoing suggest that, despite the fact that China-Africa industrial capacity cooperation has yielded some progress in recent period there is a need to address some issues in order to achieve the desired objectives of the relationship. In particular, it is the opinion of the authors that to attain its main objectives, China being the major economic partner in Africa now needs to redirect its investments to the manufacturing and Services sector in order to boost the industrial capacity of the continent. This is because investments within the industrial sector will provide potential for promoting growth and economic transformation via the creation of jobs and skills transfer at both managerial and technical levels.

"一带一路"倡议背景下江苏与非洲的产能合作与教育交流

甘振军

内容摘要： 江苏与非洲的关系源远流长，不仅体现在古代陆路和海上丝绸之路的交往上，中华人民共和国成立以来特别是改革开放以来，江苏企业就已经进军非洲大陆，勤劳智慧的江苏人民就已远赴非洲创业，为双边友好关系奠定了基础。"一带一路"倡议提出以后，一大批具有相当实力的江苏企业在非洲取得成功。究其原因，不仅仅是客观上由于江苏和非洲具有较大的合作潜力和发展空间，企业自身也根据市场变化善于调整方向，加强内部管理，注重经济效益，也归功于江苏省各级政府及业务主管部门积极应对，主动为江苏企业走出去提供配套政策和优质服务。在这个过程中江苏人在非洲创业积累了几十年的经验，形成了较强的以业缘为基础的华商群体和以地缘为基础的同乡社会网络。江苏与非洲进行产能合作具有相当的配套优势，如包括职业教育在内全方位教育交流合作，积极开展"留学江苏"项目，江苏高校积极做好非洲问题的教研，各类文化艺术团体赴非演出交流，还广泛开展财经、科技、文化和卫生等领域的人力资源培训。通过梳理江苏与非洲产能合作和教育交流的历史过程和近几年的实践，笔者认为，江苏企业应当继续改变陈旧观念，尊重当地文化，带动当地基础设施建设和社会进步。特别是政府要高度重视江苏民间力量和非政府组织,对民间参与对非经济交流要鼓励、支持、引导,同时做好企业发展所需要的各类人力资源培训和教育合作等配套工程和软件服务,也要充分认识和利用文化艺术在人文交流领域的润滑作用,准确定位江苏在"一带一路"背景下与非洲进行产能合作和教育交流的优势,从而优化布局非洲的江苏企业。

关 键 词:一带一路;江苏;非洲;产能合作;教育交流
作者简介:甘振军,天津职业技术师范大学非盟研究中心助理研究员,博士

自中国政府提出传承"丝绸之路"精神、倡导共建"丝绸之路经济带"和"21世纪海上丝绸之路"(以下简称"一带一路")的倡议以来,国际社会高度关注并积极响应。产能合作正是国家"一带一路"倡议的重要内容,也是中非全面战略合作伙伴关系的支柱之一,这有助于中非双方实现互利共赢、共同发展。中非产能合作潜力巨大,但也面临多方面的挑战。

2013年3月,国务院授权三部委发布的《推动共建丝绸之路经济带和21世纪海上丝绸之路的愿景与行动》中,明确将非洲作为"一带一路"的实施区域之一。中国企业选择"走出去"发展战略,不仅拓展自身发展空间的内在驱动力,从根本上也符合国家对外战略的需要。推进"一带一路"建设不仅有利于中国继续深化对外开放、实现产业转型升级,也同"一带一路"沿线国家、特别是非洲国家自身的工业化和现代化的发展目标相契合,这也是双方互利合作的基础。

江苏与非洲的关系历史悠久。江苏历史上是连接陆上丝绸之路和海上丝绸之路的关键地。江苏生产的丝绸、漆器远销各地,特别是700年前明朝的南京是海上丝绸之路的主要策源地、起终点和物资人员的汇合地。从江苏太仓港出发的郑和船队,曾远航非洲东海岸。这些友好交往的历史,不仅体现在古籍文献中,也得到了考古实物的证实。

在这样的背景下,习近平总书记在访问江苏期间要求江苏主动参与"一带一路"建设,放大向东开放优势,做好向西开放文章,拓展对内对外开放新

空间。非洲正是江苏对外投资创业的热土和方向,对江苏实施"走出去"发展战略和江苏经济的可持续发展具有重大意义。江苏和非洲的产能合作面临广阔的前景。

一、江苏大型企业走进非洲的成功实践案例

(一)江苏其元集团创建埃塞俄比亚东方工业园区

江苏其元集团走出国门,在埃塞俄比亚首都亚的斯亚贝巴建立了东方工业园区。这是目前中国在埃塞俄比亚唯一的一家国家级境外经贸合作区。集团董事长卢其元经过考察之后了解到钢材在埃塞会有不错的销路,于是决定投资建立工业园区并在商务部境外经贸合作区招投标中成功中标。东方工业园区如今是"全国县级市第一个、苏州市唯一的国家级境外经贸合作区",2015年4月被财政部和商务部确认为境外经贸合作区。埃塞政府将工业园作为国家"持续性发展及脱贫计划(SDPRP)"的一部分,列为工业发展计划中重要的优先项目。截至2015年8月,园区已建成2.33平方千米,入园企业20余家,包括联合利华等大型企业,投资额16 855万美元,入园企业总产值达36 642万美元。①

(二)江苏海企集团创办"中坦现代农业产业园"

坦桑尼亚农业资源丰富。资源丰富,成本低,是吸引江苏企业投资非洲的主要因素。2013年,在双方高层的支持下,江苏海企集团同坦桑尼亚新阳嘎省合作建立现代农业产业园区。江苏省也将这一项目列为"一带一路"重点工作。新阳嘎省离首都900千米,是坦桑尼亚著名的棉花产区。2015年,达到设计产能,年产1.1万吨棉纱。生产出来的棉纱全部运回江苏。江苏海企集团的发展方向是从目前园区现阶段主要经营棉纱厂,逐步实现向上种植

---

① 《江苏企业与非洲发展》,《国际商报》2015年8月25日。

棉花、向下建配套的棉纱包装、仓库、物流、榨油等产业链条。

(三) 江苏杰龙科技集团在坦桑尼亚设立杰龙控股(坦桑尼亚)有限公司

杰龙集团是盐城市射阳县一家全资民营企业，主营油脂加工。此前因国内农业结构调整，棉籽加工原料不足，棉籽油产能严重过剩，杰龙的发展一度停滞且有下滑趋势。坦桑尼亚棉花等油料资源丰富，但油脂加工工艺、产能相对滞后。在国家鼓励农业加工企业加快"走出去"，转移国内过剩油脂产能政策的引导下，杰龙集团于2012年7月在坦桑尼亚西部的新阳嘎省出资成立控股有限公司，建设油脂加工项目，总投资3 000万美元。2014年元月正式投产，投产两年就实现销售5 000万美元、利税600多万美元的效益。企业产销两旺，雇用当地工人420余人，占企业总人数93%。[1] 整个园区集葵花子、棉花种植、纺织、油脂、饲料加工、物流、包装服务多种经营为一体，这将带动更多国内民营企业走出去，实现抱团发展。这也促进了非洲农业的发展和就业水平，提高当地农民收入。

(四) 江苏农垦集团走进非洲

江苏农垦集团早在20世纪90年代就涉足非洲农业开发，在赞比亚成立了中赞友谊农场，拥有2 000公顷土地的永久性产权。据报道，现有的3个农场年年营利。截至2018年，农场累计形成利润超过250万美元，向投资主体上缴利润50万美元，每年用于再发展的投入不少于15万美元。据估价，3个农场市场价值已达400万美元，是原投资额的4.5倍。[2]

江苏农垦集团以赞比亚为中心，还在周边的坦桑尼亚、津巴布韦、南非和博茨瓦纳建立起海外企业群。由于江苏农垦集团在赞比亚的出色表现，塞拉利昂、赤道几内亚等国都主动请求合作开发当地农业。

---

[1] http://www.sheyang.gov.cn/zgsy/xwzx/20160605/002002_1daa43a7-33da-4a02-81cc-f29922acb761.htm.

[2] 卞洪登：《江苏农垦在非洲"坐收渔利"》，http://www.worldmr.net/MBBS/MBBSList/Info/2018-01-03/221576.shtml.

二、江苏企业成功走进非洲的原因

江苏企业在非洲实现成功创业,取得了突出的成绩,总结起来,有如下原因:

(一)企业发展困境和海外创业实践促使企业谋求新的发展方向

无论江苏杰龙集团还是农垦集团的发展历史和经验表明,企业内在的发展困境和瓶颈促使企业领导层及时进行改革,不断根据客观形势的变化为企业的发展调整方向。如杰龙集团是因为产能富余,生产和销售停滞不前。而江苏农垦集团海外创业起步于计划经济向市场经济的转型期,动力来自自身面临的压力。企业人多地少,土地资源缺乏,30万职工连家属,却只有200万亩可用耕地;再加上价格双轨制等原因,农资价格偏高,而农产品价格不断走低。在这种情况下,江苏企业较早就考虑到了利用国外土地资源、外出创业的思路。江苏农垦就曾先后在美、加、欧、澳、中东等国家和地区创办了近10家境外企业,然而由于各种原因都相继失败。出现这种情况的根本原因就在于没有发挥自己的优势,技术和管理、产品和服务在当地市场缺乏竞争力,没有及时调整企业的发展方向。

(二)非洲和江苏优势互补,合作共赢的空间较大

非洲大陆的土地资源得天独厚,且价格便宜,一些国家对外国人购买土地使用权和使用期限目前没有太多的限制,这无疑也是我们经济外向发展和对外投资的黄金时机。以赞比亚和江苏对比为例,赞比亚仅仅以7倍于江苏的土地,却只承担相当于江苏1/7的人口。目前,该国可耕地面积还不到1/10,农业合作和开发的空间很大。如果能够继续调整优化目前的种养结构和经营方式,用足土地资源,发展连锁经营,深化农畜产品加工,以农业带动工业和服务业的发展,最终彻底解决非洲国家的粮食问题,这将会为非洲农业的发展和实现工业化带来新的机遇,切切实实为非洲人民带来切身利益。

非洲经济的发展也能够给江苏带来利好。如协鑫能源集团响应"一带一路"倡议,联合保利集团布局在东非的液化天然气开采项目,还实施"点亮非洲"的计划。埃塞俄比亚的欧加登盆地油气资源就很丰富。2018年,液化天然气将通过吉布提港口运至江苏,未来五年将会达到1 000万—1 500万吨的投产规模,江苏人民会用上非洲的天然气。这对苏南地区的煤改气也是极大的推动。①

(三) 江苏企业在非洲投资兴业中坚持效益优先,注重加强内部管理

与非洲国家相比,江苏农业生产企业的优势比较突出,这表现在组织化程度较高,农业支持服务体系较强,技术上先进,人才队伍素质较高等方面。

我国企业的早期海外经营中,常常因为管理机制不健全出现两种弊端:一是激励不够,经营者不能尽心尽力,国家的投入达不到预期收益;二是约束不够,经营者谋取大量私利,国有资产流失严重。江苏农业企业建立了良好的自我积累、约束和发展的健康机制。一靠约束,二靠激励。早在1993年,江苏农垦友谊农场的经营者就签订了"非洲版"的"承包经营责任制":确定利润基数,确定逐年利润递增比例,确定超基数部分的分配比例。同时,责任制对不同职级的人员逐个明确岗位分配系数。

正在筹建中的第四个农场具有4个鲜明的特点:一是成立股份制公司,投资主体变为4个,既有江苏农垦及其子公司,也有外行企业,还包括自然人;二是经营者被要求入股25%;三是在规定的5年期限内,要保证国有资本的回收;四是5年后如果经营者按规定完成经营任务,国有资本将无偿转赠27%的股份给经营者,让经营者在股份公司中处于控股地位。总之,约束是为了最大限度地保障国有资本的收益,包括上交指标和再投入的指标;激励是为了最大限度地调动农场工作人员的积极性。江苏农垦通过一系列管理改革,实现良好的经济社会效益。

---

① 参阅王伟健:《协鑫能源项目向非洲延伸》,《人民日报》2017年12月4日。

(四)江苏人在非洲创业积累了近20年的经验,形成了较强的以业缘为基础的华商群体和以地缘为基础的同乡社会网络

据南通市侨办统计,目前在世界各地打拼的南通人已突破10万,其中约有6万多侨胞分布在全非洲50多个国家和地区,约占江苏在外创业人数的80%。

南通具有以纺织为代表的优势产业基础。20世纪90年代中后期,一批批南通人怀揣梦想,从经营家纺用品起步,到涉足采矿、建筑、物流、连锁超市等领域,逐渐在非洲新大陆打开了商业局面,甚至还进军媒体业创办《非洲时报》等报纸。无论是在南非、纳米比亚、尼日利亚,还是非洲腹地的乌干达、津巴布韦,还是位于天涯海角的西非国家冈比亚、佛得角,在非洲当地土著居民身上都不难看到来自南通的家纺或者衣裙、披肩和鞋帽等服装。在建筑业,以南通为代表的江苏人也非常活跃。南通作为有名的"建筑之乡",30多家对外承包工程企业90%在非洲开展业务,南通四建还承担了安哥拉首都最大的购物中心建设项目。

南部非洲江苏同乡会是南通32个境外商会的缩影,也是商会成员最多、会务最活跃、影响最深远的南通海外商会。2009年成立的南通世界通商总会是江苏首个海外侨胞联合体,更是打造南通"新侨之乡"的有效载体。世界通商总会已经在全球32个国家和地区成立了分会,这在全国地级市中是绝无仅有的。[1]

(五)江苏省各级政府及业务主管部门积极应对,主动为江苏企业走出去提供配套政策和优质服务

江苏省从省到各地市县乃至乡镇,各级地方政府积极为民间企业和个人赴非创业提供各种配套支持。江苏省对外友好交流促进会、江苏省侨办、江苏省贸易促进会、江苏省教育厅、江苏省档案馆等部门,包括连云港、徐州、南京、

---

[1] 《江苏南通赴海外创业人数突破10万,6万人在非洲》,http://www.gqb.gov.cn/news/2014/1125/34504.shtml。

无锡、苏州、南通地方相应业务主管部门都做了大量工作，出台政策和优惠条件，积极联络民间企业力量和地方团体，从外贸、侨务和教育文化等多角度全方位提供支持，形成了浓郁的干事创业的文化，积极服务"走出去"的战略。江苏作为东部沿海发达和率先实现现代化的省份，较好地发挥了对非合作排头兵的作用。南通市外侨办就积极筹划帮助建立海外同乡组织和商会组织，逐步形成了通商"互联、互帮、互通"的全球性网络。前文提到的江苏杰龙集团就是盐城市射阳县一家全资民营企业，在发展过程中得到了地方的大力支持。地方行政职能服务的意识为企业的发展带来了实惠。海港城市连云港地理位置优越，市委书记李强带经贸代表团赴南非，推动连云港港口集团分别与中钢集团南非公司、新加坡丰益集团脂肪酸甲脂等项目的合作，这将加快连云港建设现代化国际海港中心城市步伐，发挥港口优势，推动连云港与非洲的合作。[①]

正因为这些，江苏对非企业投资取得了极大的增长。肯尼亚、埃塞俄比亚、坦桑尼亚是非洲经济发展相对不错的国家，也是中非产能合作先行先试的试点国家。据统计，截至 2015 年 6 月，江苏在这 3 个国家的投资项目已达65 个，投资金额 8.47 亿美元。到 2016 年，江苏与整个非洲进出口贸易额连续两年超过 100 亿美元。江苏累计在非洲投资项目达到 355 个，中方协议投资 32 亿美元，有效扩大了创业和税收。[②]

三、江苏与非洲产能合作实践过程中的重要配套举措

（一）加强包括职业教育在内全方位教育交流合作

第一，和非洲职业院校合作办学。2016 年 9 月，南通职业大学与纳米比

[①] 《李强一行非洲访问考察　与南非举行项目签约》，http://js.people.com.cn/html/2013/04/22/222556.html。

[②] 《南共体 14 国期盼江苏企业走进非洲》，http://news.163.com/16/0524/07/BNQK0SAJ00014AEE.html。

亚科技大学签署了备忘录,南部非洲南通职业大学职业教育中心在纳米比亚揭牌成立。两校合作共建本科职业人才,围绕南部非洲工业化进程急需培养的技术应用人才需求,就课程体系与国际通用资格证书对接,通过双方优势互补共同为中非产能过程中所需要的人才提供职业教育。该中心的成立,不仅拓宽了双方合作办学渠道,也服务了南通"走出去"战略,为海外通商培养适用性人才,有利于为深化双方产能合作奠定人才基础。

第二,江苏省教育厅开展"留学江苏"计划,还专门设立了"茉莉花留学江苏政府奖学金",为包括非洲在内的留学生提供充分的在华学习费用。《留学江苏行动计划》显示,外国留学生来江苏学习每年可获得5万至9万元政府资助。到2020年,江苏计划成为外籍人士来华学习的主要目标省份,每年各类外国留学生达到5万人。2006年中非合作论坛北京峰会以来,非洲各国留学生到江苏学习水利、气象、中医等专业,他们学成回国,大都成为所在国的技术骨干或者部门领导。以河海大学为例,其水利工程领域具有鲜明特色和专业优势,已有坦桑尼亚、刚果、埃塞俄比亚和赞比亚等近30个非洲国家选派学生到该校学习水利,乃至攻读研究生进行深造,培养的非洲学生也有好几百人。教师也经常派出进行专业授课和技术指导。此外,南京信息工程大学的气象学专业具有很强的专业优势,世界气象组织在该校设立了区域气象培训中心。多年来,该校为非洲培养了大批气象学专业人才,成效显著。这些举措进一步增强了江苏在教育方面的海外吸引力。

第三,江苏高校积极做好非洲问题的教学研究,认真做好"中非高校20+20合作计划"。该计划是根据2009年11月在埃及的沙姆沙伊赫举行的中非论坛第四次部长级会议的制订的"沙姆沙伊赫行动计划",中非在教育领域的合作计划。中方高校与非洲高校展开一对一的校际合作,整合中国政府和社会的资源,向非洲提供人力资源培训、共同开展学术研究、中国政府奖学金和汉语培训、中国政府奖学金和汉语培训等,共同推动教育援外工作。江苏有三所高校进入该计划名单,分别是苏州大学、扬州大学和南京农业大学。

值得一提的是,扬州大学对口苏丹的喀土穆大学,还专门成立了苏丹研究中心并积极承办2017年的中国非洲史研究会年会,这是全国唯一一家苏丹研究机构。此外,南京大学非洲研究所和江苏师范大学亚非研究所专门从事非洲问题的教研,在学界具有较大的影响力。江苏作为教育资源大省,在教育国际化水平和对非教育援助方面大有作为。

(二)通过包括官方渠道在内的各种文化艺术演出交流,打出江苏品牌

江苏作为中国沿海开放省份和文化资源大省,能够在中非合作中发挥更多作用。2016年5月,为庆祝非盟使团成立一周年,文化部精心组织了"精彩江苏·走进非洲"系列活动,江苏艺术团通过二胡、古筝、扬琴和竹笛等器乐演奏了《喜洋洋》、《茉莉花》、《二泉映月》、《春江花月夜》等优美的传统江苏音乐曲目,展示了中国传统音乐和中国艺术的独特魅力。非盟各国政要、使馆人员、中资机构和华侨华人近500人欣赏了民乐。借助非盟的平台,本次活动对非文化公共外交活动取得圆满成功。2016年,南通华侨艺术团还对南部非洲江苏同乡会进行慰侨演出。此外,以南京小红花艺术团为代表的江苏艺术团也多次赴非进行文化演出,开展"欢乐春节"和"中非艺术家交流互访"等一系列文化交流活动。

(三)广泛开展财经、科技、文化和卫生等领域的全方位人力资源培训

江苏积极参与审计署多次开展中非业务交流活动。2011年,来自南非、苏丹等17个非洲国家的审计官员30余人,应邀参加在南京审计学院举行的第四届非洲英语国家高级审计研讨班并到南通参观世界上唯一以国家审计为主要内容的专题博物馆。博物馆内展示了我国不同历史时期的审计制度、审计管理及其所体现出的审计文化。通过审计领域多年来的人力资源培训,用实实在在的财务数据让非洲国家感受到中国对非援助和中非产能合作的诚意。

江苏和非洲在农业科技方面合作空间巨大,职业院校积极开展短期业务培训。2012年,江苏畜牧兽医职业技术学院为来自苏丹和津巴布韦的留学

生开展为期三个月的专业培训,培训内容涉及动物科技、兽医。2014年,来自纳米比亚、南苏丹和肯尼亚等国家的非洲国家农业经济发展研修班学员专门对江苏农林职业技术学院进行访问学习,还参观考察了江苏农博园和江苏茶博园,对食用菌培育、园林花卉栽培、茶叶种植等技术表示浓厚的兴趣。2016年,非洲英语、法语国家区域航空合作研修班的近50名学员再次考察该校的茶文化和农业种植技术,取得了不错的示范效应。

江苏和非洲在以化妆品、服装类为代表的企业人力资源培训方面成果丰硕。2017年,"非洲法语国家进出口商品质量检验和安全监管员研修班"的31名学员,到江苏常熟考察调研。江苏检验检疫部门在隆力奇集团和中国常熟服装城分别设立国际合作交流教学基地,以非洲商务和质量官员为纽带,加强双方贸易衔接度,帮助非洲官员了解优秀的中国制造企业和中国检验检疫工作,促进中非经贸往来和多边质检合作。10余年来,江苏检验检疫质量研究中心承办发展中国家质检援外培训项目近百期,共计培训135个发展中国家和国际组织的2 000多名质检官员及专业技术人员,遍布"一带一路"沿线国家。对非培训活动使非洲专业技术人员切身感受到"江苏品牌"和"江苏制造"的品质信誉,有利于中国产品产销国际化和走出去。

医疗卫生领域的人力资源培训方面,江苏与非洲的交流合作也具有良好的基础。中华人民共和国成立后,江苏派出了第一支医疗队,并连续几十年一直向非洲国家派出医疗队。2016年,世界卫生组织批准江苏省血吸虫病防治研究所为"世界卫生组织消除疟疾研究与培训合作中心"。这是我国唯一一个、全球第二个明确以消除疟疾为核心工作职责的世界卫生组织合作中心。江苏省在抗击疟疾方面具有丰富的成功经验和先进的医疗条件。从2002年至今,省血防所已为56个发展中国家培训了966名专业防治技术人员和官员,并赴35个非洲国家进行了现场培训指导。曾受过培训的非洲卫生官员和抗疟专家中,接受过省血防所培训的占一半以上,可谓名副其实的培养抗疟疾人才的"黄埔军校"。① 2017年,来自坦桑尼亚的抗疟专家专门到昆山江苏省寄生虫病防治研究所考察江苏消除疟疾的成功经验和具体做法。江苏的成果经验得到世卫组织官员和非洲同行高度,非方期望加强合作,借鉴推广经验,促进非洲地区控制和消除疟疾进程。

特别值得一提的是,2017年江苏省公安厅国际合作局组建包括3名全国摔跤、拳击、散打冠军在内的江苏公安教官团,还有来自省公安厅、南京市公安局和江苏警官学院、南京森林警察学院的7名骨干及资深教练,赴安哥拉对该国刚组建的警察快速反应部队进行集中培训,快速补齐当地警察近身格斗"短板"。笔者以为,从长远来说,此类短期培训也有助于中资企业的安保工作,为中非合作做好人力资源支持,如果多年积累下来也会有长期的效果。

四、余论

江苏与非洲的关系源远流长,当前的"一带一路"倡议又为中非合作带来新的历史发展机遇。江苏与非洲的产能合作与教育交流既有一定的历史基础,取得了丰富的实践经验,又为新时代江苏与非洲关系的发展注入了新的内涵和血液。笔者在梳理双方关系史料的过程中,形成了初步的思考。

(一)江苏企业走进非洲应该改变自身不合时宜的陈旧观念,尊重当地文化

中国政府非洲事务特别代表钟建华在做"如何看待中非企业"的报告时也指出,中国取得的经济建设成就举世瞩目,非洲人从中也看到了自身发展的希望。无论是个人还是企业,到非洲投资经营要改变两种观念,一是对其自然环境、人种的不当偏见。事实上,赞比亚首都卢萨卡就是有名的花园城市。大多非洲人善良而温顺。二是认为非洲不发达,市场需求小。其实市场

---

① 《世界卫生组织消除疟疾合作中心落户无锡》,http://js.people.com.cn/n2/2016/1124/c360306-29363960.html。

的大小是一个相对概念,只要市场需求大于供给,就会有商机。对于民营企业,要注意改变观念,敢于吃苦,抓住机遇。对于江苏大型国有企业,更要继续树立榜样。[①]

江苏企业在对非投资的过程中要十分注意尊重当地的文化,避免不必要的文化上观念上的不理解乃至冲突,对于海企、徐工等这样大型的江苏企业,对非投资要有耐心。从长远看,现在投资非洲,无论从单纯的援助还是双方产能合作,将来必会惠及中国。

(二) 加强卫生医疗援助,为产能合作和教育交流做好后勤配套工程

江苏在对非医疗援助具有丰富的经验,应当继续加强人道援助和慈善救助。作为文化大省和经济大省,江苏在援非医疗卫生事业上继续有所创新,可以尝试将派出医生和在当地建立医院和卫生站结合起来,江苏人建立起来的医院和卫生站可以由江苏人来进行前期的维护管理,防止出现中国人建立了医院等基础设施,却由外国医生施展对非医疗服务,从而被当地人称为医生所在国医院的尴尬情况。在这个过程中,江苏对非医疗援助应该创新管理模式,形成"江苏品牌"。

(三) 重视企业的社会责任

江苏企业在走进非洲的过程中要注意同时改善当地人民群众的生活,带动当地的基础设施建设和社会进步发展,真正为当地普通民众谋福祉,而不是仅仅为了短期的经济效益和为"政治正确"而做的面子工程。如2016年非洲各地面临严重的旱灾和水灾,民众缺食少水,光是埃塞俄比亚就有1 000多万人面临紧急救助,徐工集团成立专项基金,帮助建立50多口水窖以及其他小型水利基础设施,还帮助奥罗莫州等地的小学改善日常饮水条件。这些取得了良好的实用价值和示范效应。企业在注重经济效益的同时,做到了改善民生和扶贫救助,这为中国企业的海外社会公益事业树立了榜样。这当然也

---

① 参阅赵晨曦:《一带一路上的江苏国企人,远行非洲的中国骆驼》,http://www.fmprc.gov.cn/zflt/chn/zxxx/t1524587.htm。

是企业的"公共外交"。

（四）加强文化艺术领域的人文交流是双方理解合作的润滑剂

各级政府文化事业主管部门应当在做好各类对非人力资源培训，注重培训效果，在加强非洲所急需的职业技能类的实用培训之外，应当多重视文化交流和合作。江苏省文化厅和各地文化主管部门、艺术团体、事业单位应当完善省部合作机制，积极配合做好文化部主办的"欢乐春节"、"艺术家互访"等项目，做好文化领域的交流，为艺术团体争取更多的机会赴非演出，展示江苏艺术的风采。这不仅是政府不可回避的重要职能，也是文化事业团体承担社会责任的具体体现。比如2017年12月，埃及国家文明博物馆和江苏省博物馆以及相关地市档案局联合举办了以《江苏与"一带一路"走进非洲》为主题的展览，双方档案和文博领域的学者专家进行了密切交流，参观民众也受益匪浅。笔者也对江苏和非洲悠久的文化交往历史所深深吸引。通过档案主题展览，以档案史料讲述中非人民友好交往的历史和动人故事，这非常有利于弘扬中国传统文化，讲好"江苏故事"，对促进民心相亲具有润滑作用。今后继续加强此类交流是政府事业部门和艺术团体的职责所在，不能仅仅依靠企业做过多的与企业生产和营利无关的事情。特别值得一提的是，连云港的非洲艺术博物馆作为民间艺术机构，在普及非洲艺术方面做得有声有色。

（五）高度重视江苏民间企业力量、非政府组织和个人，对民间参与对非经济交流要鼓励、支持、引导，积极打出"江苏品牌"

前文述及，江苏人地域归属感强，在非洲创业积累了近20年的经验，形成了较强的以业缘为基础的华商群体和以地缘为基础的同乡社会网络。对以南通人为代表的江苏华商资源和侨务资源应当因势利导，增强其积极为江苏对外开放和中非产能合作和教育交流服务的积极性和主动性。近年来，江苏企业表现突出，无锡的民企还投资莫桑比克的矿产资源，据估值超过2 000亿元。[①] 连

---

① 《无锡民企买下非洲400平方公里矿山》，http://js.people.com.cn/n/2015/0420/c360301-24564842.html。

江苏洋河白酒品牌也走进了以南非、肯尼亚为代表的非洲国家,这不仅有利于中非企业合作,也成为传播中国饮食文化一张新的名片。① 特别指出的是目前有一批大学生辞职创业回老家开展非洲艺术品的制作生产和销售,这种文化产业的集聚带动作用明显,取得了不错的生产效益和社会影响。② 对于大学生这种形式的创业,也应当出台政策鼓励支持。

(六)准确把握江苏在"一带一路"倡议中的优势和定位,为江苏企业布局非洲做好通盘准备

可以加大对非直接投资,将"边际产业"企业转移到非洲;拓宽贸易渠道,提升江苏产品知名度;积极促进企业—智库—政府互动,为江苏企业在非洲的发展提供支持。③ 在这个布局的过程中,笔者认为,还要妥善安排大型国有企业和民间企业资本的关系和比重,既要注重涉及非洲基础民生的农业和轻工业,也要开展大型矿业的开发合作;既要重视各级政府的职能工作和各种配套,也要充分调动民间乃至个人的积极性创造性;既要企业加强管理,提高经济效益,也要高度重视各类华侨华人组织、商会等非政府组织的情感纽带和社会网络;既要加强经贸合作,也要高度重视教育交流,开展人力资源培训,加强人文社会文化医疗等领域的交流。这是不可分割的整体。此外,既要处理好不同行业的关系,也要注意江苏企业在非洲的利益协调,避免不必要的恶性竞争。对非洲不同国家和地区,由于国情民风习俗不同,更要注意总体布局,加强针对性,扬长避短,规避企业在海外的风险,从而真正达到文化上民心相通,经济上互利共赢的目的。

注:本文是安徽省哲学社会科学规划项目"安徽对非洲援助与合作的问题与对策研究"(AHSKY2014D61)阶段性研究成果。

---

① 《"一带一路"往前走,非洲也喝洋河酒》,http://www.sohu.com/a/209901571_658712。
② 《宿豫大学生返乡创业把生意做到非洲》,http://wm.jschina.com.cn/9665/201801/t20180109_5007132.shtml。
③ 参阅张振克:《"一带一路"战略中的非洲机遇》,《新华日报》2015年5月20日。

Challenges and Prospects of Industrialization and Educational Development in Africa: Lessons and Experiences from China

Gambo Babandi Gumel

Abstract: Industrialization and education plays a major role in the development of any country, especially developing countries and other nations in Africa. The study analyses the challenges and prospects of Industrialization and Education in Africa, using China experience as lessons for African countries. The objective of this paper is set to unleash the hidden treasures in Africa in terms of education and industrialization for economic development. The focus of the paper is to boost productivity and the associated emphasis on rapid and large investments in human and physical capital to consistently drive toward long-term achievement. The study reviewed secondary sources of data, such as journals, books, and research reports. The results reveal that education, industrialization are confronted with enormous challenges in Africa. The paper recommends that it is important to develop the educational sector to provide the needed support to the industrial and services sectors to meet up with the demand of human resource. Such a strategy can be expected to encourage the development and economic growth of Africa, especially for a developing country like Nigeria.

Keywords: Industrialization; Education; Africa

Author: Gambo Babandi Gumel, Head of the Department of Economics and Development Studies, mFaculty of Arts and Social Sciences, Federal University Dutse, Jigawa State, Nigeria

Introduction

The importance of industrialization and educational development to the economic development of any country cannot be overemphasized. In fact, the relationship between the two variables is a direct one. Thus, almost all economically developed countries are highly educated and leading to industrialization. That is, industrialization have more to do with the knowledge base of the educated elite than the typical employee. The structure of the African economy is typical of an underdevelopment. The primary sector, in particular, the agriculture and oil & gas sector, dominate the gross domestic product accounting for over 95 per cent of export earnings and about 85 per cent of government revenue between 2011 and 2012.[1]

The depressing state of affairs in Africa creates a cycle of continuous dependency, leaving African countries dependent on the selling overseas of raw products and easily open to the elements to exogenous shocks, such as falling European demand.[2] Without strong industries in Africa to add value to raw materials, foreign buyers can dictate and manipulate the prices of

---

[1] L. N. Chete, J. O. Adeoti, F. M. Adeyinka, and O. Ogundele, "Industrial development and growth in Nigeria: Lessons and challenges", Learning to Compete Working Paper No. 8, Nigerian Institute of Social and Economic Research, retrieved from https://www.brookings.edu/wp-content/uploads/2016/07/L2C_WP8_Chete-et-al-1.pdf on 9th October, 2017.

[2] Lawrence Mbae, "Industrialization in Africa: Can the continent make it?" 4 March 2014, Retrieved from http://www.allvoices.com/contributed-news/16646879-industrialization-in-africa on 9th October, 2017.

these materials to the great disadvantage of Africa's economies and people.

At this moment, Africa's steady growth in real GDP — averaging 5% per year over the past decade, was possible, thanks to strong underlying fundamentals in terms of inflation, fiscal deficits and financial sustainability.① It resulted from factor accumulation as investments in extractives and other commodities helped to grow the labour force. As positive as such growth is, in fact, it equates to 2.1% per capita real growth, and it has not been accompanied by an increase in productivity levels, and has been further limited by high rates of population growth. The bottom line is that African economies must address the challenges of productivity, especially in both education and industrialization in order to achieve sustained, shared growth and reduce overall poverty within the continent.

Nevertheless, a significant amount of China's productivity growth has been driven by the high level of education and industrialization reforms. While African nations enacted major reforms throughout the 1980s, 1990s, and 2000s, the increases in productivity were not at the levels that were hoped for. The question is what is Africa misses out to meet up with the improvements of China?

There has been resurgence in the debate over the factors and prerequisites to structural transformation in Africa. Overall, economic transformation characterized by a reallocation of resources from low-productivity activities in modern, high-productivity sectors such as education and industry has been lacking from Africa's boom. This has fueled a debate on whether sustainable growth in fact requires a shift in favor of the duo (as advocated by McMillan, Rodrik, Verduzco-Gallo); or moving up the quality ladder in sectors where countries can exploit and build on their

---

① Makhtar Diop, "Lessons for Africa from China's Growth", retrieved from http://www.worldbank.org/en/news/speech/2015/01/13/lessons-for-africa-from-chinas-growth on 9th October, 2017.

current patterns of comparative advantage and sustain growth (as promoted by Hausmann and Hidalgo). As another example, India's growth pattern suggests that a shift into high-productivity services, bypassing education and industry, represents yet another path to sustainable growth (as noted by Ghani, Goswami and Kharas). Although there is clearly no "one size fits all" approach, cross-country analysis points to a set of "horizontalist" (i. e., neutral across sectors) factors which have contributed to the growth and development of the continent: Improving infrastructure and trade networks; investing in human capital, etc.

1. Objective of the Paper

This paper is set to unleash the hidden treasures in Africa in terms of education and industrialization for economic development. The focus of the paper is to boost productivity and the associated emphasis on rapid and large investments in human and physical capital to consistently drive toward long-term achievement. I believe that African countries can draw important lessons from the ways in which China achieved this steady course of growth. This paper aims to change that. It provides a broad overview of how China's education system is organized and operates, and how reforms, both past and current, have reshaped education in China over time. The paper then examines in greater detail education in the four economies within China that participated in PISA 2015. It provides the context in which China's participation in PISA — and its results in PISA — should be interpreted.

2. Challenges of Education and Industrialization in Africa

The educational system in Africa apart from being in a poor state lacks quality, proper orientation and quantity, which affects the industrialization of the continent to its optimal levels. Most of the nations in the continent have a poor education system which is incapable of creating well trained and knowledgeable graduates who can successfully compete in the global job market. The truth is African education is presently facing a number of challenges like political, social and economic challenges, terrorism, poverty, illiteracy and inadequate infrastructure in schools among others. While some specific noticeable challenges include:

(1) Access to early childhood education, primary and post primary education, including vocational education and training, remains a key challenge for the continent. For example, of the 61 million children of primary school going age who are still out of school, 31 million of them (more than 50%) are found in Sub-Saharan Africa. Most of these are girls and children from poor and remote rural areas and those affected by conflict and discrimination. Continuing use of child labour has exacerbated the problem and denied children their basic right to learn.

(2) Educational quality remains a serious challenge in Africa. Many countries continue to experience shortages of basic facilities, infrastructure, equipment and teaching and learning materials. For example, children continue to learn under trees, exposed to harsh weather conditions and to struggle to learn without sufficient textbooks and reading materials. The unavailability of electricity, clean water and sanitation facilities, including toilets for both girls and boys remain a challenge, particularly in rural schools. For example, UIS reports that at least 60 percent of schools have no toilets in Chad, Côte D'Ivoire, Equatorial Guinea, Madagascar and Niger.

(3) The shortage of qualified teachers is a serious challenge affecting the continent. UIS projections show that Sub-Saharan Africa would need to recruit more than 1.1 million additional primary school teachers between 2009 and 2015 to ensure that every child has access to primary education. Many countries have resorted to hiring unqualified or contract teachers, most often, without adequate academic qualifications and with no professional qualifications at all. This has had a serious negative impact on the

quality of education.

(4) Financing remains another challenge affecting education in most African countries. The inadequacy of investment in education and of international development aid has impeded access, quality and the achievement of international targets for education.

However, despite all these efforts by the government to revamp the economy. And place it on the part of development, Africa remains largely under developed and industrialized. To this end, we shall look at the following factors militating against industrialization in Africa:

(1) Lack of credit/access to credit: This remains the major hindrance to industrialization in Africa. This problem is caused by the industrialists themselves, the government and financial institutions. Most industrialists in Africa are unwilling to share the ownership and control of their establishments with other investors so as to accumulate enough finance to run their business. This leaves them most companies with little capital to run the business. Hence, limiting their growth. Also, the stiff requirements and interest on loan of most lending houses in Africa coupled with government negligence discourage industrialists from borrowing. And stifles industrialization on the continent.

(2) Over dependence on foreign machines: Most of the technology and the machines used by local manufacturers in Africa are imported from other countries. And these machines are usually very expensive. This hinders potential industrialists from venturing into production.

(3) Inadequate raw material: Due to the poor state of our agricultural sector. The amount of raw materials produced by the sector for the manufacturing sector is not enough to support massive industrial production. Thus, the manufacturers depend largely on foreign raw materials for production. This hinders industrialization in the

continent.
(4) Production of sub-standard goods: Most of the products made in Africa are usually substandard. This has decreased the reliance of the masses on locally made goods. Hence, dependence on foreign goods for their satisfaction.
(5) Illiteracy/inadequate skilled manpower: The illiteracy rate in the continent is very high. This problem is worsened by the lack of adequate technical education in our secondary schools and universities. Thus, skilled manpower required for high industrial growth is grossly inadequate in Africa.
(6) Lack of basic infrastructures: This has always been the major obstacle to development. And industrialization in Africa. The continent lack facilities like good roads, water and rail transport facilities, communication facilities. And most importantly electricity supply. This hinders the progress of the industrial sector. And discourage potential industrialists.
(7) Political instability and militancy: Frequent changes in government policies and incessant insurgencies have been a bane of industrialization and development in Africa. The Niger delta militants and of recent the Boko Haram group have continuously hindered economic activities in the countries of Africa. And even discouraged local and foreign investors from investing in Africa.

"Industrialization cannot be considered a luxury, but a necessity for the continent's development," said South Africa's Nkosazana Dlamini-Zuma shortly after she became chair of the African Union in 2013. This economic transformation can happen by addressing certain priority areas across the continent. First, African governments, individually and collectively, must develop supportive policy and investment guidelines. Clearly-defined rules and regulations in the legal and tax domains, contract transparency, sound communication, predictable policy environments, and currency and macroeconomic stability are essential to attract long-term investors in terms of industrialization. Moreover, incentives — such as tax rebates to multinational companies that provide skills training alongside their commercial investments will help local economies grow and diversify. In addition, each industrial policy should be tailored to maximize a country's comparative sector-specific advantages.

Mauritius, one of Africa's most prosperous and stable countries, provides important lessons for other African countries. In 1961 this Indian Ocean island nation was reliant on a single crop, sugar, which was subject to weather and price fluctuations. Few job opportunities and yawning income inequality divided the nation. This led to conflict between the Creole and Indian communities, which clashed often at election time, when the rising fortunes of the latter became most apparent. Then from 1979 on the Mauritian government took practical steps to invest in its people. Realizing that it was not blessed with a diversity of natural resources, it prioritized education. Schooling became the critical factor in raising skills and smoothing the lingering religious, ethnic and political fractures remaining since independence from Britain in 1968. Stronger governance, a sound legal system, low levels of bureaucracy and regulation, and investor-friendly policies reinforced the country's institutions.[1] Under a series of coalition governments, the nation moved from agriculture to manufacturing. It implemented trade policies that boosted exports. When outside shocks hit such as loss of trade preferences in 2005, and overwhelming competition from Chinese textiles in the last 15 years, it was able to adapt to business-friendly policies. From being a mono-economy reliant on sugar, the island nation is now diversified through tourism, textiles, financial services and high-end technology, averaging growth rates in excess of 5% per year for more than three decades. Its per capita income also rose from USD 1,920 to

---

[1] Lawrence Mbae (2014).

USD 6,496 between 1976 and 2012, according to the World Bank.

Historically, countries have succeeded by focusing on education in science and technology and promoting research. For example, in the 1960s and 1970s South Koreans, like Singapore, Taiwan and Hong Kong reformed its education system and made elementary and high school compulsory. From an adult literacy rate of less than 30 percent in the late 1930s, South Korea now boasts a literacy rate of nearly 100% and has one of the highest levels of education anywhere in the world, according to UNESCO, the UN's education agency. Its highly-skilled population has helped South Korea to become one of the world's foremost exporters of high-tech goods.[1]

Africa, the world's youngest continent, is currently undergoing a powerful demographic transition. Its working-age population, which is currently 54 percent of the continent's total, will climb to 62 percent by 2050. In contrast, Europe's 15 - 64 year olds will shrink from 63 percent in 2010 to 58 percent. During this time, Africa's labour force will surpass China's and will potentially play a huge role in global consumption and production. Unlike other regions, Africa will neither face a shortage in domestic labour nor worry about the economic burden of an increasingly ageing population for most of the 21st century.[2] This "demographic dividend" can be cashed in to stimulate industrial production. An influx of new workers from rural areas into the cities, if harnessed correctly and complemented with the appropriate educational and institutional structures and reforms, could lead to a major productivity boom. This would then increase savings and investment rates, spike per capita GDP, and prompt skills transfers. Reduced dependency levels would then free up resources for economic development and investment. Without effective policies, however, African countries risk, high youth unemployment, which may spark rising crime rates, riots and political instability. Rather than stimulating a

---

[1] Lawrence Mbae (2014).
[2] Ibid.

virtuous cycle of growth, the continent could remain trapped in a vicious circle of violence and poverty. The continent's youth represents a huge potential comparative advantage and a chance to enjoy sustained catch-up growth. Or they could remain shackled in joblessness and become a major liability. [1]

Utilization of Education and Industrialization for Development of China

The Chinese government assigns a high value to education. It holds the belief that education is the basis of national development and modernization. In China, there are many laws and regulations in education. They are regarded as effective ways of steering and monitoring implementation across a large and complex system. The government uses laws and regulations to protect access to education, and to guarantee high-quality education. The Ministry of Education often drafts these laws, and submits them for approval by the National People's Congress. Once approved, the State Council enacts the law. Finally, the National People's Congress formalizes local policies and implementation measures at the respective levels. [2]

The Law on Compulsory Education enacted, in 1986, was a milestone for China. According to this law, all school-age children with Chinese nationality have the right to receive compulsory education; and parents are responsible for enrolling their children in school and making sure they finish nine years of compulsory schooling. This law established a comprehensive system, and described the rules for schools, teachers, teaching and learning, as well as education financing and the legal responsibilities of social sectors. The law was revised in 2006, and it now stipulates that all

---

[1] Lawrence Mbae (2014).
[2] "OECD economic surveys: China", OECD Publishing: Paris retrieved from http://dx.doi.org/10.1787/eco_surveys-chn-2015-en. on 9th October, 2017.

students in compulsory education are exempted from tuition and miscellaneous fees. The 2015 version of the law stipulates that textbooks can be priced only at a marginal profit.①

China's education system has undergone continuous reforms since the early 1980s. From expansion of access to promotion of quality education as a core value, the government regularly adjusts and advances education policy to make the system compatible with the country's social and economic development, as well as new education needs and trends. Within the Ministry of Education, the Department of Development and Planning is responsible for national educational development. In 2010, the department proposed the National Long Term Education Reform and Development Plan (2010 - 2020). This document is a strategic plan for reform and development of education at all levels in China during these years. It has become the most important guidance document in Chinese education. It delineates national strategies, tasks and system reforms.②

China has the largest education system in the world. With almost 260 million students and over 15 million teachers in about 514,000 schools③, excluding graduate education institutions, the China's education system is not only immense but diverse. Education is state-run, with little involvement of private providers in the school sector, and increasingly decentralized. Country-level governments have primary responsibility of the governing and delivery of school education. For the most part, provincial authorities administer higher education institutions. In recent years, the Ministry of Education has shifted from direct control to macro-level monitoring of the education system. It steers education reform via laws,

---

① "OECD economic surveys: China", OECD Publishing: Paris retrieved from http://dx.doi.org/10.1787/eco_surveys-chn-2015-en. on 9th October, 2017.
② Ibid.
③ National Bureau of Statistics of China, *China statistical yearbook 2014*, retrieved from www.stats.gov.cn/tjsj/ndsj/2014/indexeh.htm on 9th October, 2017.

plans, budget allocation, information services, policy guidance and administrative means.①

In China, students must complete nine years of compulsory education. Most students spend six years in primary school, though a few school systems use a five year cycle for primary school. Primary education starts at age six for most children. This is followed by three to four years of junior secondary education. Before the 1990s, secondary schools recruited students on the basis of an entrance examination. To emphasize the compulsory nature of junior secondary schools, and as a part of the effort to orient education away from examination performance and towards a more holistic approach to learning, the government has replaced the entrance examination with a policy of mandatory enrolment based on area of residence.② The gross enrolment ratio in primary education in 2014 was 103% compared with 104% in 2006, while for secondary education gross enrolment ratio was 94% compared with 64% in 2006.③

After finishing compulsory education, students can choose whether to continue with senior secondary education. Senior secondary education takes three years. There are five types of senior secondary schools in China: general senior secondary, technical or specialised secondary, adult secondary, vocational secondary and crafts schools. The last four are referred to as secondary vocational schools. Students undergo a public examination called *Zhongkao* before entering senior secondary schools, and admission depends on one's score on this examination. The government uses

---

① National Centre for Education Development Research, "National report on mid-term assessment of education for all in China", Beijing, China, retrieved from http://planipolis.iiep.unesco.org/upload/China/China_EFA_MDA.pdf on 9th October, 2017.
② Yuan Zhenguo, "China: Promoting Equity as a Basic Education Policy", in Yan Wang (ed.), *Education Policy Reform Trends in G20 Members*, Springer: Verlag, Berlin/Heidelberg, 2014, pp. 359-375.
③ UNESCO-UIS Education database, retrieved from www.uis.unesco.org/Education/Pages/default.aspx.

examination results from *Zhongkao* to assign students to different senior secondary schools. China has made significant efforts to expand participation in secondary vocational schools in recent years in order to meet the country's fast-evolving economic and manpower needs. In 2014, secondary vocational schools accounted for a little less than 22% of total senior secondary school enrolment in China.① Although senior secondary education is not part of compulsory education in China, in 2014, 95% of junior secondary graduates continued their studies in senior secondary schools.② This figure is notable because in 2005 only around 40% of junior secondary graduates attended senior secondary schools.③

Tertiary education in China experienced a huge expansion in the first decade of the 21st century. The gross enrolment ratio of tertiary education throughout China increased from 21% in 2006 to 39% in 2014. During this period, various institutions and programmes were established and international mobility and cooperation were promoted dramatically. As a result, the tertiary education system became more diverse. In China, undergraduate degrees require four years of study. Associate degrees take three years to complete, and students spend two to three years completing a master's degree. A doctoral degree requires five years of study after a bachelor's degree, and three years after a master's. In addition to these tertiary education programmes, Chinese students can also be enrolled in professional higher education programmes, which normally take three years.

In the 1960s, about 60% of the Chinese Labour Force were employed in agriculture. The figure remained more or less constant throughout the early

---

① UNESCO-UIS Education database, retrieved from www.uis.unesco.org/Education/Pages/default.aspx.
② National Bureau of Statistics of China, *China statistical yearbook 2015*, retrieved from http://www.stats.gov.cn/tjsj/ndsj/2015/indexeh.htm.
③ National Bureau of Statistics of China, *China statistical yearbook 2005*, retrieved from http://www.stats.gov.cn/tjsj/ndsj/2005/indexch.htm.

phase of industrialization between the 1960s and 1990s, but in view of the rapid population growth this amounted to a rapid growth of the industrial sector in absolute terms, of up to 8% per year during the 1970s.[1] However, China possesses the largest population in the world and Chinese education has made a great achievement in the past decades. The average educations of Chinese residents are among the highest in the 9 developing countries with big populations. In 1949, the percentage of the illiterates is above 80%. Since then, the illiterates have been reduced by 230 million. In 2000, the total illiterate rate has dropped to 6.72% below, and the people at the age of 15 – 50 dropped to 4.8% below.[2]

Growth in China has been sustained at a high level, averaging 9.7% over the last two decades, contributing 1.45% of the world's total; growth of 5.2%.[3] Measured by PPP GDP, China has grown 21 fold in the last 25 years, and her contribution to global output is much higher than that of India by almost three times, hence India has had a smaller impact on Africa. There is need to understand the drivers behind the remarkable growth of China and the reforms they undertook. The rapid growth in this Asian giant has been brought about by rapid industrialization and liberalization in China since. Reforms in China began in 1978, in most cases taking a gradual approach, permitting the authorities to pick and choose successful reforms.

Furthermore, Mwega noted that success with market oriented reforms,

---

[1] Wikipedia, "China Industrialization", retrieved from https://en.wikipedia.org/wiki/Chinese_industrialization on 9th October, 2017.

[2] UK Department of International Development (DFID) and the World Bank (WBG) Study, "The Education and Training of China's Rural Migrants", retrieved from http://siteresources.worldbank.org/EDUCATION/Resources/278200 – 1126210664195/1636971 – 1126210694253/English_Education_Training.pdf.

[3] F. M. Mwega, "China, India and Africa: Prospects and Challenges", A paper prepared for the AERC – AFDB International Conference on accelerating Africa's development five years into the Twenty-First century, November 22 – 24, Tunis, Tunisia, p. 12, retrieved from https://www.researchgate.net/publication/267218599_CHINA_INDIA_AND_AFRICA_PROSPECTS_AND_CHALLENGES.

especially with respect to agriculture, which led the authorities to proceed with liberalization of industrial and service sectors in the 1980s, generally through delegating more authority to enterprise and service sectors in the 1980s, allowing them to retain a large share of the generated profits.① This was implemented through an industrialization plan, which allowed a gradual liberalization of the product pricing as well as setting up a system that rewarded local government development. Key industrial reforms included reform of state-owned enterprises (SOEs); deregulation of product prices; labour reforms to introduce greater mobility and flexibility in terms of hiring and firing as well as allowing job-seekers to choose and find work in SOEs, collectives or the private sector; reform of SMEs resulting in them playing an important role as a growth driver of industrial output.

Lessons for African Countries

Using China's success in industrialization and educational development achievement as a background, this paper identified a range of relevant lessons for Africa's to learn in order to experience economic development, drawing heavily on the Africans themselves. The key lessons for African states to share include:

(1) Beyond reforms increase productivity, China had taken care of a population with high levels of human capital. The average years of schooling for Chinese adults (ages 15 and up) rose from 1.5% in 1950 to more than 7.5% in 2010, a fivefold increase. Obviously, human capital development has been one among many enabling factors in China's impressive development. When we look at human capital in Africa by the simple metric of years of schooling during the same period, average years of schooling rose from 1.3%

---

① F. M. Mwega, p.14.

to 5.2%, a fourfold increase. The really stark differences arise, however, when we examine the quality of schooling. While there are no direct comparisons of learning outcomes in various regions of China versus individual countries in Africa, there is a very real disparity between learning outcomes with profound related impacts in Africa and China.

(2) Africa needs a skilled labour force in order to experience growth like China's. After decades of limited engagement in post-secondary education, the World Bank Group and other partners are directing a long-overdue focus on higher education and, most importantly, on the content of university studies and the skills students need to enter the job market and contribute to Africa's growth and development, notably in science and technology for industrial development. However, skilled graduates are crucial for Africa to move up the value chain and achieve critical productivity increases in key industries by learning also from China, where more than 40% of all tertiary degrees are awarded in science, technology, engineering, and mathematics. In contrast, the number of African university graduates students in science, technology, engineering, and mathematics fields is just closer to 22%. Hence, Africa needs scientists and engineers to improve the productivity of its crops and to build the infrastructure required by Africa's booming cities.

(3) Prospects are for Africa to grow by 4.6% in 2015, and reach a growth level of 5.1% in 2017, lifted by infrastructure investment, increased agricultural output, and an expanding services sector. On the external front, African growth has been closely linked to the commodities boom — growth in China and the emergence of China as one of Africa's main trade and investment partners — as well as the surge in cross-border financial flows.

(4) One central idea behind China's trajectory and geometrical growth is its focus on boosting productivity — and the associated emphasis on rapid and large investments in human and physical capital, high savings rates, and an overarching ability to consistently drive toward long-term objectives.

Conclusions

Africa is ripe for high level of education and industrialization. A strong and positive growth path, rapid urbanization, stable and improving economic and political environments have opened a window opportunity for Africa to achieve economic transformation, by leaning on the lessons of what China has done in the past years to experience growth and development.

While, I end this discussion with an emphasis on higher education, secondary (and even basic, quality primary) education remains essential to boosting productivity, particularly in the informal sector. Poor learning outcomes in turn impact the industrial sector, in terms of shortages in qualified labour to meet the needs of the growing sector, and to increase productivity in services sectors as well.

Recommendations

(1) Another critical area of African human capital development is technical and vocational education and training. China's success in developing the skills needed to adopt technology has created the conditions to attract investment in manufacturing. Here again, Africa has much to learn from China's experience in order to adopt new technologies and thereby create jobs.

(2) There is a need for development approaches that are entirely driven

by Africa's own qualities, views, intellects and interest. This would mean focusing on internally established strategies and processes that could certainly have a higher payoff that externally borrowed ideas.

(3) The infrastructures of governance in Africa need to be strengthened. This would give room for improvement in Africa's human development index score.

(4) African nations should pursue favourable policies that would encourage industrialization; tax holidays, excise duty reduction and tariff protection.

(5) Improved Educational System and Manpower Development. There is a need to introduce technical courses in both the secondary and university curricula. More emphasis should be placed on practical rather than theory. Thus, Africa can emulate the strategy adopted by China of sending identified talented students to study in technologically advanced countries.

(6) Political stability should be maintained. Inconsistency in policies due to changes in political administration has negatively affected the growth of Africa.

(7) Promoting trade and crafts association for mutual support and capacity building would positively impact on our level of industrialization.

(8) Promoting and supporting research, development and trainings in tertiary institutions.

中非国际产能合作背景下职业教育的交流与合作
——以中国与埃塞俄比亚为例

李炜婷

内容摘要："国际产能合作"是近年来国家领导人根据国内外经济发展的新常态而提出的国际合作战略。在非洲众多产能合作的国家之中，埃塞俄比亚以其稳定的政治环境、本国大力发展其工业化进程的决心，成为中非产能合作的"样板国家"。中国已与埃塞俄比亚在众多领域达成了效果颇丰的产能合作项目，双方通过此举互利共赢，贸易联系越发紧密。但由此带来的一个必然问题就是，在中埃产能合作如火如荼地进行之中，必将涉及埃塞俄比亚对大量职业技能人才的需求。中国在其自身发展职业教育的基础上，也与埃塞俄比亚开展了职业教育领域的合作与交流，已经形成了一定的品牌效应和社会影响力，但仍旧存在一定的挑战。

关 键 词：中非产能合作；职业教育；埃塞俄比亚

作者简介：李炜婷，天津职业技术师范大学非盟研究中心实习研究员

一、背景

国际产能合作是党和国家领导人根据现阶段我国经济

发展的新常态而提出的区域发展与国际合作战略,这对于我国与国际上的合作国家来说,都是具有划时代意义的举措与战略思想。当前,面对新的经济形势,传统贸易方式和工业生产结构已经难以担当推动经济可持续发展的重任,全球产业结构加速调整,基础设施建设方兴未艾,正逢发展中国家大力推进工业化、城镇化进程,为推进国际产能和装备制造合作提供了重要机遇。[①]如何创造性利用国际国内两种资源、两个市场,推动我国优质产能走出去,进而有效优化整合、发挥合作国家间的各自优势已经成为新时期的重大课题。

非洲是我国开展对外产能合作的重要伙伴之一,双方不仅在历史发展进程和国家大政方针上具有很强的相似性,更在经济结构与规划层面具有很强的互补性。自2000年的中非合作论坛成立以来,中国与众多非洲国家建立了全天候战略合作伙伴关系,在政治、经济、文化、教育等众多方面开展务实合作。非洲拥有丰富的自然资源和人力资源,市场潜力巨大,非洲国家也普遍谋求加快工业化进程,急需资金、技术以及基础设施。中国正在实施经济结构调整和产业升级,有资金、技术、高性价比的装备和水泥、钢铁、光伏等优质产能。因此,产能合作是符合双方发展需求的共赢战略。埃塞俄比亚,作为非洲其中一个具有高度国家统治力与政治自主权的国家,拥有丰富的自然资源与人力资源,但不可否认的是,作为发展中国家,埃塞俄比亚现行经济仍然以农副业产品、原材料及低加工商品为主,工业化水平不足。中国与埃塞俄比亚自建交以来,双方始终保持互信友好的外交关系,两国政治上的互信友好与外交上的稳定和谐,奠定了两国大力深化产能合作与发展各领域交流合作的坚实基础。中国在工业化进程上摸索的经验与道路,以及中国经济社会转型的优质产能转移,与埃塞俄比亚的国家发展需求切实吻合,两国合作潜力巨大。因此,两国产能合作的蓬勃深入发展,势必会在非洲产生大量的产业技术人才需求,同时,高素质的技术型人才也是社会财富的直接创造者,

---

① 国务院(国发〔2015〕30号):《国务院关于推进国际产能和装备制造合作的指导意见》,http://www.gov.cn/zhengce/content/2015-05/16/content_9771.htm。

在经济社会的总体运转中,也将为经济发展产生最直接也最积极的作用。

中国的职业教育经历了150多年的发展,已经形成了具有中国特色的职业教育体系,不仅在理论知识层面具有系统化的架构,而且在实践操作方面也行成了完善的配套体系。相较于埃塞俄比亚,自1994年以来,虽取得了显著发展,但是仍旧存在教学资源不足、教学质量不高、与劳动力市场需求不匹配等问题。因此,中国与埃塞俄比亚的职业教育合作不仅将服务于埃塞俄比亚的国内技术型人才增长需要与经济发展需求,更将进一步加快中埃两国的产能合作。本文在中国与埃塞俄比亚在产能合作的背景下,探讨两国的职业教育交流与合作的现状与挑战,以期为两国的产能合作与各自的国家经济发展建言献策。

二、中国与埃塞俄比亚的产能合作

李克强总理指出,埃塞俄比亚是中国开展对非产能合作的优先伙伴。中方将以产能合作的形式助力埃塞俄比亚自主工业化进程和可持续发展,打造中非友好互利共赢合作全面升级的样板。[①] 得益于地理区位、资源优势以及人口红利等优越条件,埃塞俄比亚现已成为中国开展对非产能合作的"先试先行国家"与"样板国家"。在众多西方媒体以及非洲本地媒体的相关报道中,也将埃塞俄比亚喻为"非洲的下一个中国",中国与埃塞俄比亚的合作之深入以及发展道路之相似可见一斑。埃塞俄比亚驻华大使伯哈内·加布雷-克里斯托斯(Berhane Gebre-Christos)也曾表示,中埃关系是最佳的两国关系模式,为非洲和世界其他地区的国家树立了互利共赢的良好典范。就基本前景而言,中国和埃塞俄比亚持有相同观点,特别是在发展方面,这使得两国

---

① 李克强:《埃塞俄比亚是中国开展对非产能合作优先伙伴》,http://finance.ifeng.com/a/20150904/13954654_0.shtml。

之间的经验交流变得更加容易。①

（一）中国与埃塞俄比亚产能合作成果丰硕

自2001年《非洲发展新伙伴计划》(The New Partnership for Africa's Development, NEPAD)中提出的以基础设施建设和人力资源开发为主要方向的消除贫困以及实现非洲大陆可持续性发展的长期战略以来，中非双方的政策沟通和战略对接呈现及时性、对应性和布局性的良性态势。2013年，非盟出台了《非洲2063愿景》，而后中国与非盟签署的"三网一化"建设的备忘录与2015年中非合作论坛约翰内斯堡峰会上的"五大支柱"、"十大合作计划"，都为中国与非洲各国的产能合作指明了方向，确立了坚实的基础，深化了中非命运共同体的伙伴关系。在中非的国家方针政策与高效合作机制的大框架支撑下，中埃产能合作效果显著，成绩斐然，涉及众多领域，多方位服务埃塞俄比亚的国家发展需求。

世界经济论坛发布了《2017非洲竞争力报告》，认为基础设施仍是非洲发展的主要瓶颈。因此，中方瞄准埃塞俄比亚发展的命脉需求，开展了领域广泛的援建、承包工程以及劳务合作项目。从交通运输方面援建了埃塞俄比亚的第一条环城高速公路(亚的斯—阿达玛高速公路)、东非第一条现代化轻轨(亚的斯亚贝巴城市轻轨)、非洲第一条中国二级电气化标准铁路(亚吉铁路)，②打通了埃塞境内各个主要的运输通道，尤其是亚吉铁路的建成，将亚的斯亚贝巴至吉布提的运输时间从目前公路运输的3天减少至10小时，成为埃塞重要的出海运输通道。高速公路和轻轨的建成，不仅改善了当地的民生，更加拉动了相应的经济增长与相关岗位就业。除交通运输外，中国还致力于提升能源供给能力，包括水电站、热电站、输变电和配电网、地热钻井工

---

① 《中埃关系是非洲其他国家的典范——埃塞俄比亚驻中国大使专访》，http://www.mfa.gov.cn/zflt/chn/zxxx/t1538220.htm。
② 姚桂梅：《"一带一路"建设下的中非产能合作》，http://www.fmprc.gov.cn/zflt/chn/zxxx/t1478626.htm。

程等。同时注重建设高质量稳定的通信系统,使得基础设施援建形成一套"车轮"模式,加速扶持埃塞俄比亚经济良性且可持续性的转动。

除此之外,基于双方在产业转移承接方面的优越匹配性,以及广阔的合作空间,通过"政府搭建,企业合作"的方式,中方在埃塞俄比亚已中标或投入使用阿瓦萨工业园、孔博查工业园、德雷达瓦工业园、埃塞-阿达马工业园、东方工业园等工业发展园区,对于加快埃塞当地工业化进程、带动当地劳动力就业与鼓励埃塞进出口贸易等都起到了积极的促进作用。

据统计,中埃之间开展的合作承包工程以及劳务合作,在双方紧密频繁的互动下呈极速增长趋势,如图1、2所示:

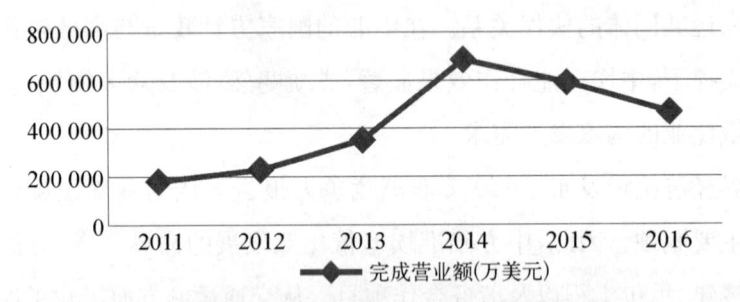

图1 中国与埃塞俄比亚间承包工程完成营业额量

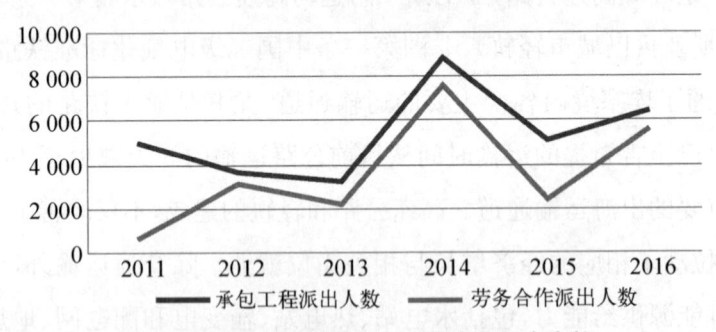

图2 中国与埃塞俄比亚间劳务合作派出人数

数据来源:中华人民共和国国家统计局《中国统计年鉴》。

据《中国与非洲的经贸合作(2013)白皮书》所示,目前中国已成为非洲最大贸易伙伴国,非洲成为中国重要的进口来源地、第二大海外工程承包市场和第四大投资目的地。由此数据可见,中国与埃塞俄比亚之间各种工程合作趋势自2011年起基本保持上升趋势,尤其是2014年显著增长。随着各项工程大量展开,后续的2015—2016年呈平缓趋势。本着服务非洲,解决非洲人民切实需求的原则,各项工程、工业园区的发展与基础设施建设,必将导致大量的高素质专业性技能人才的需求。

(二)中国与埃塞俄比亚产能合作潜力

中国与埃塞俄比亚的产能合作关系已经进入了蓬勃发展的阶段,各方面成果丰硕,涉及领域广阔,不仅涵盖了各项基础设施建设,而且带动了中埃两国相关领域的人才双向流动。据《产业蓝皮书:中国产业竞争力报告(2016)No.6》称,中非产能合作潜力巨大,尤其在"一带一路"倡议构想支撑下,中埃两国的产能合作互补性与结合度都很密切。[①] 本文将从中国与埃塞俄比亚的贸易互补性[②]为切入点,以2012—2016五年期间的数据为基准,分析两国的产能合作潜力。若两国双边贸易互补性强,则证明两国间产能流向更加符合本国和双边发展需求。

贸易结合度是一个比较综合性的指标,用来衡量两国在贸易方面的相互依存度。贸易结合度是指一国对某一贸易伙伴国的出口占该国出口总额的比重,与该贸易伙伴国进口总额占世界进口总额的比重之比。其数值越大,表明两国在贸易方面的联系越紧密。贸易结合度的计算公式如下:

$$TCD_{ab} = \frac{X_{ab}/X_a}{M_b/M_w}$$

此公式中,TCD_{ab} 表示 a 国对 b 国的贸易结合度,X_{ab} 表示 a 国对 b 国的出口额,X_a 表示 a 国出口总额;M_b 表示 b 国进口总额;M_w 表示世界进口

---

① 基于由中国社会科学院工业经济研究所"中国产业竞争力研究课题组"与社会科学文献出版社共同主办的"2016《产业蓝皮书》发布暨中国产业竞争力"研讨会上的成果。
② "贸易结合度指数"(Trade Intensity Index, TII)是由经济学家布朗(A. J. Brown,1947)提出,后经过小岛清(1958)等人的研究得到了完善。

总额。如果 $TCD_{ab}>1$，表明 a、b 两国在贸易方面的联系紧密，如果 $TCD_{ab}<1$，表明 a、b 两国在贸易方面的联系松散。

经计算，具体结果如图 3 所示：

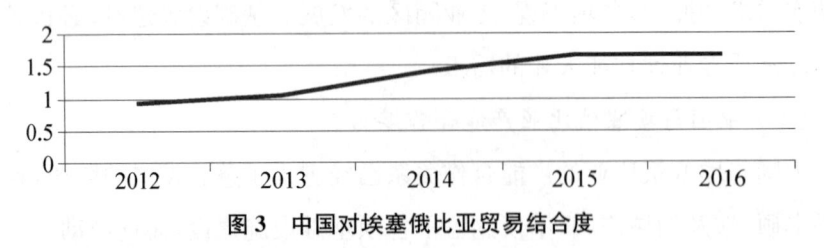

图 3　中国对埃塞俄比亚贸易结合度

数据来源：UNSTATS 与 World Integrated Trade Solution。

图表中数据清晰表明，在 2012 年至 2016 年 5 年期间，中国对埃塞俄比亚的结合度呈现稳步增长的势头，2012—2015 年极速增长，关系更加紧密。中国现已在非洲成为主要的市场国、金融国、投资国、承包国、建设国以及援助国。[①] 因此，在未来中埃两国的合作中，两国关系将更加紧密，合作将进一步深入开展，由此，如何保持双方在互利共赢、相互尊重的原则上进一步务实合作，建立健全人才资源与配套设施体系，以实现两国间的可持续性发展是目前亟须正视的一个问题。

三、中国与埃塞俄比亚的职业教育交流与合作

职业教育是指为使受教育者获得某种职业技能或职业知识、形成良好的职业道德，从而满足从事一定社会生产劳动的需要而开展的一种教育活动。在我国的工业化进程中，职业教育发挥了至关重要的作用。据估计，从 1978 年到 2011 年的 30 多年中，我国职业教育为国家累计输送了 2 亿

[①] J. Y. Wang, & A. Bio-Tchane, "Africa's Burgeoning Ties with China," *Finance and Development*, A quarterly magazine of IMF, Vol. 45, No. 1, 2008.

多高素质的劳动者和技能型人才,为我国的工业化,尤其是制造业的发展提供了扎实的人才保障。开展对非职业教育合作是中国建设性介入非洲专业技术人才培养进程的有效路径,应该作为重要配套举措纳入中非产能合作框架之中。

目前,我国富余产能主要集中在工程承包、钢铁、水泥、平板玻璃、服装制造、煤化工、风电设备、光伏等需要大量中、低层次技术工人的产业。中国与非洲在相关产业的产能合作必然会在非洲产生大量的产业技术人才需求。"三网一化"等相关配套基础设施建设项目的开展也必然产生大量的高速铁路、公路、航空设备维护方面的技能型人才需求。此外,中非产能合作的深入开展也必然产生对非洲汉语高级技术、技能型人才和管理人才的需求。这三大领域的人才供应情况将很大程度上影响甚至决定中非产能合作战略可持续性发展的效果。

(一)中国与埃塞俄比亚的职业教育交流与合作的战略支撑作用

目前,我国与非洲国家在职业教育的合作已经对中非各领域的合作产生良性的推动作用,中国职业教育的发展与特色,加之埃塞俄比亚国家对于大力发展职业教育的政策倾斜,由"政府搭台,高校唱戏"为模式的中埃职业教育合作项目已经进入了较为成熟的阶段。作为非洲约有1亿人口的人口大国,埃塞俄比亚也成为非洲少数真正能利用起人口红利,发展劳动密集型产业的国家之一。早在1994年的《教育和培训战略》的政策性文件,就意识到要大力发展职业教育。此后的一系列文件的出台以及举措的实施,比如2008年的《国家职业技术教育和培训战略》(*National Technical and Vocational Education and Training Strategy*)、2010年的《教育发展五年规划》(*Education Sector Development Program IV*)等都为埃塞俄比亚的职业教育发展提纲挈领,也反映了埃塞俄比亚对职业教育的重视以及对技能型人才的渴求。中国政府各相关部门也积极地从多方位开展了与埃塞俄比亚的职业教育合作,以中国政府在埃塞俄比亚援建的职业技术教育与培训学院

(Technical and Vocational Education and Training Institute)为例,该学院不仅是中国政府在非洲援建的第一个高等职业教育学校,也开创了中国高校直接参与学校管理与教学的"硬件+软件"式深层次教育援助模式,开设专业主要有机械技术、汽车应用技术、电气自动化技术、电子技术、现代纺织技术、计算机应用技术等,为当地经济发展培养急需人才。此外,2009年埃塞俄比亚第一所孔子学院在该学院落成后,该学院开始借助孔子学院的汉语教育资源探索职业教育与汉语培训相结合的教学特色。成立以来,该学校不仅为埃塞俄比亚培养了大量的职业教育师资,也直接为中兴、华为、华坚集团、中地海外等中资企业培养和培训了大量汉语和技术人才,在很大程度上缓解了这些企业的高素质技术人才和汉语人才缺口问题,也一定程度上为埃塞当地劳动适龄人口解决了就业问题。

另外,中非论坛第四次部长级会议制定的"沙姆沙伊赫行动计划"中的中非高校"20+20"项目中决定,中方高校将与非洲高校展开一对一的校际合作,整合中国政府和社会的资源,向非洲提供人力资源培训、共同开展学术研究、中国政府奖学金和汉语培训、中国政府奖学金和汉语培训等。在此大框架的行动指导下,中国许多院校瞄准了职业教育领域,秉承中国职业教育"校企合作"的丰富经验和优良传统,推动了中国职业教育在埃塞俄比亚落地开花。例如重庆工业职业技术学院与埃塞俄比亚最知名的应用技术学院——中埃理工学院在师资培训、学生交换等方面达成了框架协议,与力帆汽车集团成立"中埃人才培养基地",旨在对力帆汽车埃塞俄比亚市场提供技术支持,包括当地员工的技术培训、汽车维修技术和汽车配件物流管理指导和员工来华培训等项目。[①] 重庆城市管理职业学院与埃塞俄比亚将军温格特职业技术学院在鲁班工坊共建、留学生联合培养等方面达成了合作意向,并与

[①] 《重庆工业职业技术学院在埃塞俄比亚成立"中埃人才培养基地"》,http://www.gx211.com/news/20170413/n14920703171420.html。

三圣实业股份有限公司(埃塞)和当地的埃塞俄比亚东方工业园明确了三方在学生培养、技能培训与人才需求方面的合作意向。①

中埃间的职业教育合作不仅服务于中国的产业转型、埃塞俄比亚本国的工业化进程,也惠及当地民生,改善人民的生活水平,这从根本上遵循了中埃产能合作的基本原则与发展策略。本文对在埃塞俄比亚当地的中资企业中有过实习经历或成为固定员工的人员进行了问卷调查与面对面访谈。②受访者均是参加过来华培训,在华学习毕业回国就业的学历生,或者是在校学习的孔子学院学生。在所收集的问卷中显示,96.3%的人认为,中国与埃塞俄比亚的职业教育合作项目对两国未来的产能合作有着积极的推动作用;72.8%的人认为,通过参与相关的培训项目或者在华学习的经历,自己的就业竞争力有了一定程度的提升;特别是系统学习过汉语,并且持有 HSK 语言水平测试证书的准就业者来说,97.2%的认为自己的就业表现有了很大的改善,符合招聘方对技术型人才的要求。其中一位受访者表示,自己曾在职业技术教育与培训学院孔子学院进行汉语的学习之后,以奖学金生的身份前往中国进行专业的学历学习,通过系统的专业知识学习,以及过硬的汉语水平,在学习结束后回国,成为中资企业眼中急需的"高素质技术人才",月工薪收入较其他同学相比,高出 3 000—4 000 元的水平。

(二)中国与埃塞俄比亚的职业教育交流与合作的挑战

全球范围内,非洲的劳动适龄人口数将在 2035 年达到 4.5 亿人口或全非洲人口数的 70%,这是在世界上任何其他国家或地区都不会发生的现象。若维持此增长速率,那么未来将只有 1 亿的人能维持稳定的工作。在职业技能培训方面,非洲国家平均参与率从 6.5%上升至 8.5%,但仍然只有东南亚

---

① 重庆城市管理职业学院:《我校与埃塞俄比亚开拓新的合作领域》,http://www.cswu.cn/2017/1121/c42a29461/page.htm。
② 本文作者曾于 2017 年 6—7 月前往埃塞俄比亚对此研究课题进行实地调研。

国家的1/3左右。① 由此可见，虽然职业教育发展对于非洲的工业化进程起到了支撑和促进作用，但长远来说，非洲若要发展自身较薄弱的职业教育，将会是缓慢且艰巨的任务。虽然在上一部分中提及，埃塞俄比亚政策性上重视本国职业教育的发展与同中国的职业教育交流与合作，但总体趋势还是需要力争突破非洲的客观大环境，致力于发展本国社会经济水平与推动其工业化进程。

除此之外，中埃职业教育交流合作还需要进行进一步调整的是中国的基础教育的普及化与职业教育在国际上的通用化情况。有74.5%的受访者认为，前往中国进行专业上的中、长期培训，所带来的效果影响显著，但是前期教育基础和毕业所取得的证书，在国家间的通用性较低。换言之，很多学生在接受职业教育或培训的初期感觉有些吃力，因为中国的基础教育与职业教育基础比埃塞俄比亚当地的教育发展水平要稍高一些，在采访中，一些援外的教师也表示，学员的水平参差不齐，有些学生对于"安培"和"伏特"等非常基础的定义还存在混淆现象等。而中国职业教育的系统机制与其他国家无法有效接轨，导致有的受训者在寻求进一步发展的同时受到一定的局限性。作为已经形成自己一套职业教育发展系统的中国来说，应该有条理地梳理本国职业教育发展的特殊性和可复制性，积极与其他合作国家从政策、施行、课程设置等方面全方位开展因地制宜的合作项目。就援非项目而言，应该切实将受教育者之前的受教育程度和水平纳入整体的系统机制中来，包括前期调研与课程设置等。同时，与其他国家积极统一协调相关的专业水平评估条件与机制，在形成伙伴关系的基础之上，开发多方达成协议的资格证书标准和课程标准，相互沟通与交流两国职业教育制度，增进相互了解，为进一步的合作与交流获得政策保障，继而鼓励人才的多方向流动。

---

① Akinwumi Adesina, Jim Yong Kim and Klaus Schwab, "The Africa Competitiveness Report 2017: Addressing Africa's Demographic Dividend", World Bank, 2017, https://www.afdb.org/fileadmin/uploads/afdb/Documents/Publications/Africa_Competitiveness_Report_2017.pdf.

其次,中埃职业教育合作还需要进一步落实"理论＋实践"与"校企融合"的模式。在接受采访的一位职教学院的院长提出,目前,他认为职业教育发展的瓶颈就在于动手实践这一方面。其原因,一是由于设备落后、不足,无法满足大量、频繁的动手实践需求;二是指导实践的教师数量不足,一线教师资源相对集中或有限,不同岗位和企业的同一工种,可能具体操作的仪器标准和程序不尽相同,经验不足的指导教师无法满足学生的这一需要;三是可提供上岗实习的中资企业不多,学生毕业以后除了要熟悉操作实践本身,更加需要熟悉工作环境与在岗机制,现虽然有很多在埃的中资企业,但可提供的实习岗位与每年毕业的职教学生的比例存在失衡现象。就此问题,本文也采访了中国电建集团国际工程有限公司的市场经理,他表示,从公司的角度出发,对埃塞当地的技术人才会有倾向性地提供就业和实习机会,不论是从两国合作的基本原则,还是从公司在当地的形象塑造上来说,都是互利共赢之举。但是同时,公司作为营利性组织,更倾向于最大化获得利润,以及利润产生的效率性。而埃塞俄比亚当地的就业人员普遍表现出基础知识薄弱,以及语言交流不畅等问题,因此会影响生产效率,校企合作等形式更加适合企业性质较弱的机构。就这一问题,应在加强语言能力培养与实践能力结合的基础上,着力将学生培养、职工培训、技能鉴定融为一体,形成教育资源的利用最大化和效应集团化,形成跨部门、跨领域、跨专业协作的良性运行机制。

四、结语

产能合作背景下,加强中埃职业教育合作的战略导向性的重要意义。当前,中国面临经济结构转型升级的艰巨挑战,大量产能需要转移。埃塞俄比亚是非洲具有强大人口红利的大国,也是非洲经济发展最快的国家,其政治与安全形势较为稳定,执政党也具有承接中国富余产能的强烈意愿。加之两国彼此间贸易与工业互补性强,因此,中埃两国开展产能合作的潜力巨大。

但中埃产能合作战略的实施很可能面临严峻的技术人才供应问题,发展职业教育是解决技术人才供应不足的根本途径。目前,中埃两国在职业教育合作方面已经初有成效,不仅有政府层面的交流,也有高校间的对口合作,促进了中埃两国产能合作的同时,也惠及民生,为埃塞俄比亚当地适龄劳动力与就业人员改善了生活水平。但长远来看,随着两国间产能合作的逐步推进与涉及领域的增多,埃塞俄比亚职业教育发展因经验较少或受其他因素制约,很可能无法满足中埃产能合作的技术人才的培养需求。为保障产能合作战略的顺利实施,中国有必要在相关领域加强与埃塞俄比亚的职业教育合作,推动埃塞俄比亚技术人才的培养。目前,中埃两国的职业教育需要更进一步因地制宜,在全面统筹健全机制之前,做好中国与埃塞俄比亚当地的基础教育与技能背景间的衔接,中国在职业教育领域取得的经验与成就,不能一味地照搬到埃塞俄比亚,尤其是"理论+实践"与"校企合作"的模式,在埃塞俄比亚本地推行,需要更精细化,不能流于表面,而是更加注重就业人员与相关企业、机构间的互动性与适用性。中非产能合作是一个宏大的战略构想,需要在政策、金融、基础设施、智力支持、人文交流、人力资源等多领域打造一个"立体化"配套支撑体系。

职业教育服务"一带一路"倡议：进展、问题与对策*

王 静

内容摘要：自2013年习近平主席提出"一带一路"倡议构想以来，我国职业教育就开始走上了为"一带一路"倡议服务之路。三年多来，在服务"一带一路"倡议上，职业教育取得了重要进展，主要包括：政策层面，国家出台一系列政策，支持职业教育服务"一带一路"倡议；实践层面，服务"一带一路"倡议的职业教育取得一定进展。但是，随着"一带一路"倡议的深入发展，职业教育发展存在的问题也逐渐显现，主要有：对沿线国家国情不够了解；既具有高素质专业又具有高语言水平的人才短缺；合作内容深度不够，合作对象不够广泛等突出问题。为了更好地推动"一带一路"倡议的实施，职业院校应做好对沿线合作国家进行深入细致调研考察；大力培养高素质综合人才；深化合作内容，拓宽合作对象。

关 键 词：一带一路；职业教育；国际化

作者简介：王静，天津职业技术师范大学在读研究生

---

* 本文发表在《职业教育研究》(2018年第1期)，编入本书时有改动。

2013年,中国国家主席习近平提出了"共建丝绸之路经济带"和"21世纪海上丝绸之路"两个重要合作倡议,简称"一带一路"。在"一带一路"倡议的实施过程中,职业教育发挥着培养技术技能人才的重要作用。[1] 三年多来,职业教育在服务"一带一路"倡议上取得了重要进展,有力地促进了"一带一路"建设。但从"一带一路"倡议进一步深入推进的角度来看,职业教育发展还存在诸多不足,急需改进。[2]

一、我国职业教育在服务"一带一路"建设中取得新进展

(一)政策层面:国家出台一系列政策,支持职业教育服务"一带一路"倡议

2013年以来,国家出台了多份政策性文件,支持职业教育的国际合作与交流,为职业教育服务"一带一路"奠定了重要基础。2014年,《国务院关于加快发展现代职业教育的决定》(以下简称《决定》)明确提出要加强职业教育国际交流与合作,实施中外职业院校合作办学项目,探索和规范职业院校到国(境)外办学。[3] 同年6月,国务院颁布了《现代职业教育体系建设规划(2014—2020年)》。其中,第十二条明确指出要建设开放型职业教育体系,鼓励职业院校系统学习国外先进办学模式,并拓展职业教育合作领域,如加强同联合国教科文组织、世界银行等国际组织的合作和交流。加快骨干职业院校走出去的步伐从而更好地服务于国家开放战略,加强同沿线国家合作的力度,使一批职业院校具备自身特色的核心竞争力,在国际竞争舞台上脱颖

---

[1] 《习近平出席"一带一路"国际合作高峰论坛》,2017年5月14日,http://www.beltandroadforum.org/。

[2] 刘延东:《加快推进职业教育现代化,开创我国现代职业教育新局面——在推进职业教育现代化座谈会上的讲话》,《中国教育报》2017年1月24日。

[3] 《国务院关于加快发展现代职业教育的决定》(国发〔2014〕19号),《职业技术教育》2014年第18期,第45—49页。

而出。使职业教育培养的专业技术人才与我国"走出去"战略的内在要求相匹配。① 2015年,国务院颁布了《关于推进国际产能和装备制造合作的指导意见》,要求加快职业教育"走出去"步伐,支持"一带一路"倡议的软实力发展。② 同年12月25日,教育部办公厅印发了《关于同意在有色金属行业开展职业教育"走出去"试点的函》(教职成厅函〔2015〕55号)明确了以中国有色集团作为试点企业在赞比亚开展职业教育"走出去"试点工作,从而迈出了我国职业教育"走出去"的第一步。③

2016年7月,为了推动教育服务"一带一路"倡议,教育部印发了《推进"一带一路"教育行动》,设立了"丝绸之路"中国政府奖学金,每年资助1万名沿线国家的新生来中国学习或研修。同时,"以'一带一路'万名师生交流计划为主线,推动实施'鲁班学堂''中非20+20''丝路1+1''友好使者'等特色项目"。还实施了"丝绸之路"合作办学推进计划,鼓励我国优质职业教育配合中国特色基础行业企业走出去与沿线国家开展多种合作办学形式,合作设立职业院校、技能实训中心,合作开发教学资源,开展多层次宽领域职业教育和技能培训活动,培养当地急需的各类"一带一路"建设者。④

这一系列顶层设计的政策文件为职业教育服务"一带一路"倡议指明了方向,也表明了职业教育的发展得到了国家层面的重视。在和平与发展仍然是当今世界的主题的大背景下,这些政策的出台,有助于发挥了职业教育在

---

① 《教育部等六部门关于印发〈现代职业教育体系建设规划(2014—2020年)〉的通知》(教发〔2014〕6号),《职业技术教育》2014年第18期第50—59页。
② 《关于推进国际产能和装备制造合作的指导意见》(国发〔2015〕30号),中华人民共和国政府,2015年5月16日,http://www.gov.cn/;刘威:《与"一带一路"沿线国加强文化互动》,《经济日报》2016年5月16日。
③ 《关于同意在有色金属行业开展职业教育"走出去"试点的函》(教职成厅函〔2015〕55号),教育部官网,2015年12月25日,http://www.moe.edu.cn;刘威:《与"一带一路"沿线国加强文化互动》,《经济日报》2016年5月16日。
④ 《推进共建"一带一路"教育行动》(教外〔2016〕46号),教育部官网,2016年7月15日,http://www.moe.edu.cn/srcsite。

推动"一带一路"倡议在加强同沿线国家合作这一大方向上的作用。在贯彻落实"一带一路"倡议在受益国的实践活动中,职业教育扮演着源源不断地培养人力资源,输送合格的技术人才的角色。顶层设计政策文件的出台,为加强这一角色的作用提供了诸多方便,比如政府各部门的支持和社会重视层度也会随之提高。

(二)实践层面:服务"一带一路"倡议的职业教育取得一定进展

1. 职业院校面向"一带一路"国家开展职业教育合作取得一定成效

2007年起,宁波职业技术学院就开始承办中国政府人力资源援外培训项目,10余年来该校与诸多"一带一路"沿线国家建立了联系,为北非、西亚等"一带一路"沿线国家和地区培训了千名产业界、教育界官员和院校教师,并已在贝宁建立中非(贝宁)职业技术教育培训学院,开创了浙江高职院校海外办学的先河。[1] 云南国土资源职业学院依托云南省"桥头堡"战略,充分依靠"中国面向东南亚、南亚矿产资源人才培养基地"的优势,凭借学校在职业教育中地质、国土资源勘查的特色,与柬埔寨工业和矿产能源部、老挝工业手工业部地质矿山局签订联合培养矿产资源人才协议,与此同时,还与老挝理工学院共建联合培训中心对该校学生进行职业技能培训。海南经贸职业技术学院充分利用海南岛丰富的旅游资源和在"一带一路"中的地理优势,与沿线国家的多所大学建立合作办学通道,其中,就包括俄罗斯、哈萨克斯坦、巴基斯坦、白俄罗斯等国家。南宁职业技术学院为了能够全面推进与中南、西南以及东南亚地区国家进行职业教育课程培训、技能竞赛、资格认证和国际交流合作,特建设了贵港现代职业教育发展中心,充分利用地理位置优势积极推动国内产业转移的同时,服务于"一带一路"在东盟地区"走出去"战略。[2]

---

[1] 董洪亮:《打造一带一路职业教育共同体》,《人民日报》2017年6月15日。
[2] 刘红:《"一带一路"战略背景下我国职业教育发展机遇、挑战与路径——"一带一路"产教协同峰会会议综述》,《中国职业技术教育》2017年第4期,第20—23页。

2. 行业企业与学校合作推动职业教育服务于"一带一路"倡议

在"一带一路"教育开放发展政策的指引下,2015年年底经教育部批准,中国有色金属行业率先开展职业教育"走出去"试点工作,并将中国有色矿业集团作为试点企业。为了能更好地服务"一带一路"倡议,中国有色金属工业协会和有色金属工业人才中心最终确定了8家试点院校,并由此形成了政府、企业与学校多方努力,多元合作、多种形式的办学模式。[①] 其中,北京工业职业技术学院承担了中国有色集团在赞比亚合作的三个主要任务:一是选派北京工业职业技术学院教师赴赞比亚培训当地企业员工,进行技术培训和学历教育;二是在当地的培训学校建立北京工业职业技术学院分院;三是接收赞比亚留学生来华进行技能培训或者学历教育。[②] 广西经贸职业技术学院配合希尔顿酒店集团在泰国和马来西亚开展"伊尹学堂"项目,共建中华美食文化研究传承基地,传授中华民族烹饪技艺技法的同时,也惠及当地旅游业的发展,使中国传统文化在"走出去"战略背景下得以广泛传播。使"一带一路"倡议不仅在经济领域也在文化领域上发挥了积极的带动效应。[③] 柳州城市职业学院与上汽通用五菱股份有限公司、印尼西爪哇省共建汽车学院,满足了区域经济发展需求,也加速了职业教育走出去的步伐。

此外,不仅政府、行业企业在积极推动职业教育服务于"一带一路"倡议,学界也在理论支持上作出了努力。中国—东盟职业教育研究中心设立在广西,更好地推动中国与东盟在职业教育领域的深入合作,加速了中国—东盟区域职业教育改革发展和政策研究,同时也为中国和东盟国家职业教育交流

[①] 《关于公布有色金属行业职业教育"走出去"首批试点项目学校的通知》(教职成厅函〔2016〕42号),教育部官网,2016年10月25日,http://www.moe.edu.cn/srcsite。
[②] 《中国有色金属矿业集团来我校洽谈"职业教育走出去"试点项目》,北京工业职业技术学院官网,2016年9月8日,http://www.bgy.org.cn/web/news/4416。
[③] 董洪亮:《打造"一带一路"职业教育共同体》,《人民日报》,2017年6月15日;李欢:《中马两国职业院校以美食为媒推动国际职教合作》,中国新闻网,2017年4月20日,http://www.chinanews.com/sh/2017/04—20/8204387.shtml。

合作提供决策咨询、推广和宣传等服务,为职业教育更好地服务"一带一路"倡议不断地提供新思路。

二、职业教育服务"一带一路"倡议存在的问题

(一)对沿线国家的国情不够了解

职业教育在服务"一带一路"倡议建设的过程中,虽然已经取得了一些成功,但还依然存在着一系列问题。其主要问题是对沿线国家的国情还没有透彻了解。2015年9月28日,"五矿秘鲁事件"即秘鲁Apurimac区域发生矿业抗议活动,当地人要求中国五矿集团下属的五矿资源公司(MMG)修改环保计划:将距离三个矿口3千米处的铜钼处理平台进行改造。[1] 因为印第安人对很多自然山川存在着宗教信仰的崇拜,通常喜好安逸的生活。而事件中的企业项目投资虽然极大地改善了当地白人、政府官员等少部分利益群体的生活条件,但没能够了解到印第安农民的生活习惯、宗教信仰,投资对他们来说非但没有从中受益,还要承担生态环境被破坏,安逸生活被打破的结果。根据CCG统计,2015年,我国职业教育在与沿线国家合作中,由于对合作方的法律法规不够了解导致合作项目终止或失利的案件约占16%,其中,1/3是因为职业教育领域派出去的工作人员不了解当地的劳工法所致。[2] 又如2016年5月,新加坡国立大学东亚研究所某高级研究员表示,"一带一路"教师群体自身缺乏对国际通行的职教标准、教学方法、课程模式等进行深刻的思考和理解,过分依赖于自己的经验,在与外国师生进行交流、开展教学互动或是接受国外专业培训时容易出现一些理念上的冲突,导致实效性降低。[3]

---

[1] 姚丽瑾:《首钢秘鲁矿业"一带一路"如何避免地雷?》,钢联资讯,2017年10月20日,http://info.glinfo.com/15/1023/10/49A5D13AABFBE0F8.html。

[2] 中国与全球化智库:《中国企业"走出去"困难与解决建议》,中国与全球化智库官网,2016年12月1日,http://www.ccg.org.cn/Research/View.aspx?Id=5332。

[3] 刘威:《与"一带一路"沿线国加强文化互动》,《经济日报》2016年5月16日。

总之,职业教育在服务"一带一路"倡议顺利进行过程中,还严重缺乏对沿线国家政治、经济、文化、宗教、法律、思想、习俗观念上的了解,这给我国企业"走出去"带来很多不必要的影响。

(二) 缺乏高素质的师资队伍

在服务"一带一路"倡议过程中,职业院校教师是一支重要力量。职业教育要想服务好"一带一路"倡议,不仅要求教师具有较高的专业素养,同时还需要具备较高的语言水平。2017年10月12日上午,国家信息中心发布的2017年度《"一带一路"大数据报告》中指出,"一带一路"沿线国家众多、语言种类丰富,语言人才需求迫切。[①] 然而,我国职业教育领域内的职教教师这两方面的素养出现了严重脱节现象。一是拥有较高的专业技术水平的教师普遍缺乏运用外语进行教学和交流的能力。目前,我国职业教育行业拥有高技术水平的教师大多是年纪较长的一代人,受时代限制,没有接受过良好的、系统的外语学习机会。二是外语水平相对较高的职教教师又非职业教育相关专业毕业的。他们虽拥有能与沿线国家师生、工人进行顺畅交流的能力,但又对所在专业领域的专业性缺乏深入了解。合作过程中,会在理解、翻译方面出现很大的纰漏,使得合作很难顺利进行。三是我国职业教育课程体系中缺乏对职教教师外语能力的培养,大多数职业院校外语课程中仅开设英语课程,其他语种课程几乎没有。在开设的英语课程中,也只是完成国家要求的基础层次的学习,专业类英语开设时期很短,而且课时很少,教学质量很低,达不到与国外无语言障碍交流、教学的水平。[②]

总之,职教教师普遍缺乏运用外语进行教学和交流的能力,加之"一带一路"沿线国家语种众多,国内教师在与这些国家师生、工人进行交流互动的时

[①] 苏向东:《"一带一路"大数据报告:国家急需这方面的人才》,中国新闻网,2017年10月12日,http://www.chinanews.com/gn/2017/10-12/8351227.shtml。

[②] 武琪:《"一带一路"案例:职业教育走出去主动培养"一带一路"建设者》,中宏网,2017年10月28日,https://www.sohu.com/a/164164788_808891。

候就更容易产生一些问题和困惑,不能将我国职业教育办学特色、办学模式、人文政策等很好地传递给当地人民,对交流造成不利影响。从而影响职业教育对"一带一路"倡议的服务功能。

（三）合作内容不够深入,合作对象不够广泛

我国职业教育在与"一带一路"国家合作过程中还存在着合作对象和合作内容两个方面问题。其一,在合作对象上。首先,在中外合作办学的过程中,很多职业院校缺乏与国外职业院校、企业、培训机构交流学习的资源和渠道,往往使得中方所选择的合作对象多为学校。其次,我国仅重视学生交流和合作办学,而在教师交流、课程、研究的合作进展甚微。相比较而言,学生交流是一个显性现象,容易被人用来掩盖其他要素的合作。而教师交流、课程与研究的合作则更需要政府和职业院校主动对外开放的意识与行动。再次,我国职业教育缺乏与沿线国家中的一些大型知名企业、劳工组织等组织机构开展职业教育领域的合作和交流。比如澳大利亚有 TAFE 指导联盟,通过这个机构和全球其他国家推进合作,而我们很多职业学校还处于单打独斗的阶段,国外是多个职业学校形成一个教育集团与我们一个学校进行合作,同一个产品可能会与我国多个职业学校重复合作,我们经常是被动接受。[1] 这也是我们在对外合作过程中面临的很大问题。其二,在内容上。首先,目前,我国职业教育与沿线国家合作的种类在不断丰富,但在合作的深度上不够,比如教学方面,我们只是大致的学习到合作的办学模式、课程管理体系,没能够深度学习它们被实施的背景,或对象的层次,一旦运用到我们自己国家的职业院校中时,往往出现各种不协调状况,适得其反。其次,在企业项目上,缺乏与沿线国家共同推进国际骨干通道建设、港口合作建设、跨境电力和输电管道建设,缺少保护生态环境、维护生物多样性和应对气候变化等绿

---

[1] 李晓喻:《中国提出"一带一路"五大合作重点》,人民网,2015 年 3 月 28 日,http://www.chinanews.com/gn/2015/03－28/7166616.shtml。

色生态合作项目。① 再次,在与沿线国家合作中具有民族特色的产品、工艺、文化等方面的项目寥寥无几,是目前存在的另外一个问题。

三、职业教育更有效服务"一带一路"的建议

(一)对沿线国家进行深入细致的调研考察

面对合作双方国情的不同,职业教育在服务"一带一路"倡议,与沿线国家开展合作交流的同时,应对合作伙伴所在国进行深入调研,为双方合作交流架设桥梁。② 例如,中国有色集团在赞比亚境内进行深入调研,对赞比亚的职业教育现状、企业员工需求和卢安夏技工学校的实际情况有了一定的了解,形成了详细的调研报告,并提出了在赞比亚建设学院的基本设想。③ 调研工作不仅要对合作方的职业教育制度、政策文件、法律法规进行深入调研,也应对当地民众的生活习惯、宗教信仰进行调研考察。因为,合作的项目能否成功的要素之一就是当地民众的心声——是否支持合作项目在本地开展。但是,这样的案例在职业教育服务"一带一路"倡议中少之又少。为了更好地推动我国与"一带一路"沿线国家职业教育领域的合作,我们有必要在合作之时,对合作方所在国家的政治、经济、文化、宗教、科技和职业教育的基本情况进行深入研究,为合作的顺利开展打下坚实基础。另一方面,任何一项合作活动最终都由人去落实。因此,职业教育在服务"一带一路"倡议过程中,需要形成行之有效的对相关人员特别是派出人员进行培训的课程与教育机制,并能实质性地为对外交流的各类人员进行针对性培训。对于派驻"一带一

---

① 纪洪江、徐绍华、王颖:《"一带一路"战略下的教育国际交流与合作研究述评》,《昆明理工大学学报》2017年第1期,第10—17页。
② 李梦卿、姜维:《"一带一路"我国内陆节点城市职业教育国际化发展研究》,《职教论坛》2017年第1期,第16—21页。
③ 许树森:《"走出去",职教应与企业同行》,《光明日报》2017年2月16日。

路"沿线国家的工作人员尤其如此。政府可以选择一些有基础的职业院校,设立跨文化沟通的培训基地。

(二) 多措并举,破除语言障碍

为了能更好地服务"一带一路"倡议的推进,国家应多措并举,破除语言障碍。首先,对于专业技术水平高的但缺乏外语交流能力的教师,国家及职业学校应提供给他们继续深造学习的机会;开展教师专业外语课程,职业教师定期使用外语做汇报;提高对派出工作人员外语等级水平的要求,尤其是口语交际能力。其次,对于职业教师中外语水平高但专业素养缺乏的教师,国家及职业学校应提供给他们学习专业知识的机会,加强对这部分教师的专业素养的培训,鼓励他们对与职业教育相关的企业、产品、经营模式等专业知识进行深入了解。当与沿线国家进行合作交流的时候,职业教师能很精准、顺畅地将我国职业教育办学特色、办学模式、人文政策等很好地传递给当地人民,从而促进合作的开展。另外,职业院校应重视从学生时代就开始培养学生们的外语交际能力,为服务"一带一路"培养人才打好坚实的基础。实施一系列有助于提高职业学校师生外语能力的措施,例如,丰富外语课程种类、延长外语学习周期,招聘高质量的外语教师、互派留学生等。当然,沿线国家语种众多,单靠我国职业教育一方的努力破除语言障碍远远是不够的。职业教育走出去的过程中,可以鼓励沿线国家职业教育师生、工作人员来华学习汉语,或通过当地开设的孔子学院学习汉语。例如,中国有色集团将携手中南大学在赞比亚开办孔子学院,将职业汉语作为基础课程,提升中国有色集团在当地的雇员的汉语沟通水平。[1] 这有助于中国有色集团在赞比亚合作项目的顺利进行。总之,语言是心灵沟通的桥梁,合作双方语言互通了,才能将各自的想法、观点告知对方,才能推进合作的深入开展。职业教育才能更好地服务"一带一路"倡议的实施。

---

[1] 刘海、荣国丞:《"一带一路"战略下职业教育的机遇与挑战——中国职业技术教育学会"一带一路"战略与职业教育研讨会综述》,《职业教育技术》2015年第30期,第18—21页。

（三）深化合作内容，拓宽合作对象

从目前职业教育在沿线国家合作内容、对象上来看，还是显得比较浅显、单一。职业教育为更好地服务"一带一路"倡议的建设，应积极地深化与沿线国家合作的内容，拓宽合作的对象。首先，在课程体系上，职业院校应加强与沿线国家在跨文化交流相关的公共课、先进的应用技术课程方面的合作。推进职业教育与沿线国家在技术设备、教材、课程课件、教学项目、教师海外授课、教学管理、专业标准、课程体系、教学方案与评估体系等方面的深层次交流，而不仅仅是停留在基础层面的学习和了解，应根据实际情况，取其精华，去其糟粕，形成最优最先进的职业教育课程管理体系。其次，在绿色低碳化建设和运营管理理念的基础上，共同推进跨境通信干线网络建设，畅通信息丝绸之路；共同推进国际骨干通道建设、港口合作建设；共同推进民航全面合作的平台和机制建设，逐步形成连接沿线国家的基础设施网络。[1] 再次，加强职业教育与沿线国家在新兴产业领域的深入合作，如新一代信息技术、生物、新能源、新材料等。[2] 另外，在中外合作办学的过程中，中方所选择的外方合作伙伴多为学校。[3] 产学融合、产能合作是职业院校合作办学的倡导途径。今后，应该大力拓展合作面，努力拓宽与沿线国家合作对象的数量与类型，职业院校在进行校校合作、校企合作的同时，也应该着眼于沿线国家中的一些大型知名企业、劳工组织等组织机构开展职业教育领域的合作和交流。

---

[1] 《白春礼：科技合作在"一带一路"建设中发挥不可替代作用》，中科院科技支撑"一带一路"建设成果情况举行发布会，2017年5月9日，http://www.cas.cn/zt/sszt/roadbelt_cas/yw/201705/t20170509_4600119.shtml。

[2] 李晓喻：《中国提出"一带一路"五大合作重点》，人民网，2015年3月28日，http://www.chinanews.com/gn/2015/03-28/7166616.shtml。

[3] 《白春礼：科技合作在"一带一路"建设中发挥不可替代作用》，中科院科技支撑"一带一路"建设成果情况举行发布会，2017年5月9日，http://www.cas.cn/zt/sszt/roadbelt_cas/yw/201705/t20170509_4600119.shtml。

图书在版编目(CIP)数据

中非教育交流与产能合作的现状和前景:"中非教育交流与产能合作国际研讨会"论文集 / 潘良等主编. —上海:上海社会科学院出版社,2018
ISBN 978-7-5520-2374-9

Ⅰ.①中… Ⅱ.①潘… Ⅲ.①教育-国际交流-中国、非洲-国际学术会议-文集 Ⅳ.①G523.3-53

中国版本图书馆 CIP 数据核字(2018)第 151332 号

中非教育交流与产能合作的现状和前景
——"中非教育交流与产能合作国际研讨会"论文集

主　　编:	潘　良　甘振军
副 主 编:	翟风杰　王玉华　李炜婷
责任编辑:	路征远
封面设计:	梁业礼
出版发行:	上海社会科学院出版社
	上海顺昌路 622 号　邮编 200025
	电话总机 021-63315900　销售热线 021-53063735
	http://www.sassp.org.cn　E-mail:sassp@sass.org.cn
排　　版:	南京展望文化发展有限公司
印　　刷:	上海龙腾印务有限公司
开　　本:	710×1010 毫米　1/16 开
印　　张:	17
插　　页:	10
字　　数:	223 千字
版　　次:	2018 年 8 月第 1 版　2018 年 8 月第 1 次印刷

ISBN 978-7-5520-2374-9/G·758　　　定价: 98.00 元

版权所有　翻印必究